The International Libel Handbook

The International Libel Handbook

A practical guide for journalists

Edited by *Nick Braithwaite*
Clifford Chance

Butterworth-Heinemann
Linacre House, Jordan Hill, Oxford OX2 8DP
A division of Reed Educational and Professional Publising Ltd

⬅ A member of the Reed Elsevier plc group

OXFORD BOSTON JOHANNESBURG
MELBOURNE NEW DELHI SINGAPORE

First published 1995
Reprinted 1996

British Library Cataloguing in Publication Data
International Libel Handbook: Practical Guide for Journalists
  I. Braithwaite, Nick II. Chance, Clifford
  342.5256

ISBN 0 7506 2488 4

Typeset by David Gregson Associates, Beccles, Suffolk
Printed and bound in Great Britain by Clays Ltd, St Ives plc

Contents

Foreword

For the British newspaper editor, scarcely a day goes by without a thought of libel. Most titles employ a lawyer to sit alongside the night news editor to scrutinize copy, hoping to search out and destroy the unintended allegation, the dangerously waspish aside or the outright bungle. Any of these can so easily land a newspaper in court, although most terminate in costly settlements before the matter comes to trial. Every day, editors talk to lawyers about contentious stories and conclude their conversations with the view that a particular item is, or is not, 'a fair business risk'.

To American journalists, nourished on the First Amendment to the US Constitution, with its wide-ranging commitment to freedom of speech, all of this seems, as it is, an antique affair. And yet as journalism becomes irreversibly more international, journalists are doomed to confront the laws of countries other than their own. A book, magazine or article may be safely sold in one country, but published only at great risk in another. Not only the laws of libel arise here, of course; laws of official secrecy, contempt of court, issues of taste and decency also erect legal fences across the international information superhighway. Thus, bizarrely, citizens of one country may travel to a country where a book or magazine is available and, in some cases, bring it back into their home country with impunity, even though it would be legally impossible to publish the work in that same home country.

Today, even the most resolutely parochial British newspaper will circulate in small quantities across Europe. At the newsgathering end, business and finance, the source of many of journalism's necessarily riskier investigations, is global. Titles like the *Wall Street Journal*, the *Financial Times*, the *International Herald Tribune* and many magazines print and circulate in a variety of countries. Television, only ten years ago a series of national and highly regulated industries, has been transformed by satellite into a complex, international grid of pictures and words. As broadcasting collides with telecommunications, as the Internet threads together millions of individuals across continents, who can predict where this international media explosion will end? Who can predict where and when someone will pick up the 'phone to his or her libel lawyer, immortalized in much-sued satirical magazine *Private Eye* as Messrs Sue, Grabbit and Run?

This book is therefore warmly to be welcomed. Journalists have a love–hate relationship with their lawyers. The official story is that journalists always want to publish and that lawyers always want to restrain them. The reality is that a first-class lawyer will often contribute to the construction of a better story.

In any event, with six-figure libel payments no longer extraordinary in Britain, hard-pressed publishing companies are scarcely in the business of casually increasing the risks they take. Here is a book which will need to be within reaching distance of the journalist's electronic work-station.

Ian Hargreaves, Editor, *The Independent*,
formerly Deputy Editor, The *Financial Times*, and
Director, News and Current Affairs, for the BBC.

Preface

The aims of this book are threefold. First, to set out a rough libel benchmark for international publishing. Second, to provide information on the restrictions that apply in different countries, both for journalists working there and for others who may be interested. Finally, to offer some practical guidelines to help in managing risk.

Freedom of expression, the first of the four great freedoms set forth by Franklin D. Roosevelt, is still far from universally accepted. Some barriers are blatant – witness the ban in Iran in early 1995 on television satellite dishes to stem Western encroachment. More insidious, though, than overt governmental restrictions, a panoply of disjointed libel laws still disrupts access to information around the globe. News flows past backwaters where repressive defamation laws thrive. In 1994, for example, the American magazine *Business Ethics* refrained from distributing copies of an article critical of Body Shop International plc in any Commonwealth country, for fear of the oppressive laws in those countries.[1]

The tide may now be turning. The 'strict liability' libel laws that persist in many Commonwealth countries – 'strict' because it requires defendants to prove truth – has been the main constraint upon media freedom. That law has now undergone its most significant reverse since the decision of the United States Supreme Court in *New York Times* v *Sullivan* in 1964. *Sullivan*, a landmark case which introduced a 'public official' defence in US libel law for the first time, embodied 'a profound national commitment to the principle that debate on public issues should be uninhibited, robust and wide-open'.

Over a period of thirty years, that principle, encapsulating the First Amendment ideal of freedom of expression, seems to have lost little of its force. Recent judgments of the Indian Supreme Court and the Australian High Court, handed down within a few days of each other late in 1994,[2] have articulated a *Sullivan* public official-type defence based on abstract principles of free speech, breaking with the old common law traditions. Has the First Amendment now been exported?

One of the main rationales for the *Sullivan* defence has been that, because public figures can defend their reputation through access to the media, they do not require protection through 'strict liability' libel laws. If the momentum of the gathering communications revolution lasts, victims of defamatory attack may one day be able to state their side of the story direct to the public – perhaps via the Internet or its successors. Personal access to the media will have ever greater importance for libel plaintiffs.

For the foreseeable future at least, though, the mass media will retain a unique capacity, reach and authority to inflict damage upon individual reputation. That being so, libel laws may retain a place in journalistic demonology for some time yet.

It is not my intention in choosing only eight countries to offend other countries which, in the interests of space and simplicity, have had to be omitted. Had more been included, the treatment of each might have been unacceptably thin.

Finally, a word of caution. Libel is a highly technical area. This book is intended primarily as a diagnostic tool to identify potential legal problems and to help in writing around them. It cannot be definitive, and it is important always to seek legal advice where a significant risk appears.

This book attempts to state the law as at 1 January 1995.

1 *Financial Times*, 28 August 1994.
2 *Theophanous* v *Herald and Weekly Times Ltd* (1994) 124 ALR 1 and *R. Rajgopal* v *State of Tamil Nadu* (1994) 8 SCC 632.

Acknowledgements

I owe thanks first and foremost to those who have contributed chapters to this book in the midst of hectic professional commitments, but also to my colleagues in the Media, Computer and Communications Group at Clifford Chance, and especially Michael Smyth, for all their encouragement and support. The staff of Butterworth-Heinemann have been tremendously patient and helpful throughout. I am also grateful to many others who have given generously of their time and expertise, especially David Kohler of Turner Broadcasting, Alastair Brett and Pat Burge of Times Newspapers, and Eliot Simpson and Deborah Rawlings for their helpful comments on the manuscript.

Finally, the book is dedicated to Hilary and my daughters Isobel and Phoebe, for giving me every incentive to finish it.

The United States of America

R. Bruce Rich of Weil, Gotshal and Manges, (New York) and Susan L. Amster of Weiss, Dawid, Fross, Zelnick & Lehrman, P.C. (New York)

The roots of press freedom in the United States run deep. The First Amendment to the US Constitution, in words of spartan simplicity, protects from governmental intrusion the rights of the citizenry to free speech and a free press. The embodiment in the Bill of Rights of the mandate that the government 'shall make no law ... abridging the freedom of speech, or of the press' reflects a profound belief, dating back to the Founders, that unrestrained speech and an unrestrained press are fundamental rights which have an exalted place in our society and our legal system.

Underlying these First Amendment guarantees is the belief that the key to effective government is an informed citizenry, one that is not told by the government what is right, but instead makes those determinations itself, through its own education. Armed with the knowledge provided to them in a free 'marketplace of ideas', these citizens elect officials who, with the citizens' informed consent, steer the government on its proper course.

This marketplace of ideas can be, indeed, is expected to be, rough and tumble. On the theory that no one, authoritarian voice possesses all wisdom, or the 'truth', it has been our perspective that the truth can only emerge through the clash of conflicting ideas. The result of this process can be very strong and passionate debate. Unpleasant, harsh and unpopular statements can be published, critical of the status quo and of current government officials and policy. Such a policy of rejecting one voice in favour of many, of making room for the minority point of view alongside the majority, of not merely tolerating, but actively encouraging, criticism of government, is the basis of the US system of free speech and press. As one of our distinguished judges, Learned Hand, wrote of this policy some years ago: 'To many this is, and always will be, folly; but we have staked upon it our all.' [1]

It is against this backdrop that modern US libel jurisprudence has developed. The courts have encouraged the press to provide society with critical commentary about issues and people that affect our lives, while at the same time providing some measure of protection to the reputations of individuals against false speech that causes injury.

The structure under which US libel laws operate today was established in the landmark Supreme Court case of *New York Times* v *Sullivan*[2], decided in 1964. In his memorable opinion for the Court, Justice William Brennan referred to our 'background of a profound national commitment to the principle that debate on public issues should be uninhibited, robust, and wide-open, and that it may well include vehement, caustic, and sometimes unpleasantly sharp attacks on government and public officials'.[3] Not only is it fundamental to our societal well-being that the press be free to criticize those elected to govern, but it is also inevitable, in the process of performing that role, that honest error will occur. Accordingly, the court declared, 'neither factual error nor defamatory content suffices to remove the constitutional shield from criticism of official conduct'.[4]

The court in *New York Times* laid down the rule that press critics of official conduct cannot be punished for false speech alone, no matter what its impact on individual reputation. Instead, it must be shown that the publisher acted with 'actual malice'. That term was defined by the court to denote statements of fact which either were known to be false when made or were made with reckless disregard as to their probable falsity.[5]

This standard of liability is not the 'objective', or 'reasonable man', test that operates in other areas of tort law, whereby the press' conduct would be judged by what a jury would determine a 'reasonable' person to have known or understood in the circumstances. Instead, the test calls for an examination of the *subjective* state of mind of the publisher. As the Supreme Court explained in *St Amant* v *Thompson*,

> reckless disregard is not measured by whether a reasonably prudent man would have published, or would have investigated before publishing. There must be sufficient evidence to permit the conclusion that the defendant in fact entertained serious doubts as to the truth of his publication.[6]

From this judicial cornerstone of constitutional protection for libellous utterances has developed a considerable body of doctrine endeavouring to define further the boundary lines drawn by the Federal Constitution on the right of an individual (or, for that matter, a corporation) to recover for supposedly libellous utterances by the press. Notable milestones along the path of constitutional libel law, discussed below in greater detail, have included: the expansion of the 'actual malice' rule to embrace so-called public figures in addition to public officials; the requirement that the libel plaintiff prove the falsity of the statement(s) at issue, rather than the media defendant being required to prove its truth; the conclusion that 'there is no such thing as a false idea' – to wit, that words claimed to inflict injury be factual in nature, not merely an expression of opinion; the requirement that, for any matter of public interest, even one involving the libelling of private figures, there be a showing of some fault on the part of the press in publishing the statement (e.g. negligence); and the determination that awards of punitive damages are constitutional only if 'actual malice' has been proven.

It is important to note, at the outset, that any overview of US libel law is necessarily that – an overview. While federal constitutional doctrine sets minimum requirements binding on all fifty states, each state is free to provide the press with even greater protection, and important centres of publishing activity such as New York have done so. Because the precise laws that govern the disposition of libel claims vary from state to state, it would be impossible, in this limited space, to conduct a comprehensive analysis of US media libel law. What follow are the broad federal constitutional parameters with examples of these principles in application, taken from states such as New York and California where media litigation has been particularly prevalent.[7]

The libel claim

Distinction between libel and slander

In the United States, defamation is actually made up of two separate torts: libel and slander. At the most basic level, libel is defamation by written, printed or some other non-transitory form of expression, and slander is defamation by spoken word or gesture. The difference between the two is often difficult to apply, especially in modern times, where distinctions between 'written' and 'oral' statements inadequately cover the communications terrain. Consider, for example, the case of radio, television and other electronic forms of media. A number of jurisdictions have taken the position that offending radio and television broadcasts should be treated as libel. Others choose to consider such communications as slander. Some courts have held that statements read on the air from a script are libel, while statements made extemporaneously are slander. Some states have enacted statutes in an attempt to resolve this lack of clarity in the law. The statutes, however, much like the case law, offer no harmonious approach.

For the purposes of this broad overview, libel will be defined to embrace any form of communication that has the potentially harmful qualities characteristic of written or printed words; hence, will be treated as embracing broadcast and other electronic media. Moreover, for simplicity's sake, the terms 'libel' and 'defamation' will be used interchangeably.[8]

The elements of a libel claim

In order to sustain a cause of action for libel, a plaintiff must establish the following elements:

- the existence of a *false* statement of *fact*;
- that is *defamatory*;
- that is *of or concerning* the plaintiff (i.e. the statement identifies the plaintiff to a reasonable reader or viewer);
- that was published by the defendant with the *requisite degree of fault* – either actual malice, gross negligence or negligence depending on the identity of the plaintiff; and
- that causes *damage to the reputation* of the plaintiff.

Each of these elements – as well as certain of the defences that may be asserted by defendants in response to them – are discussed below.

The requirement that there be a false statement of fact

Falsity

In the United States truth is an absolute defence to a libel action. Under common law rules, the burden of proving truth fell on the defendant. In the absence of an affirmative showing by the defendant that the published defamatory statements were true in every respect, the falsity of those statements was presumed, even if no proof of falsity was offered by the plaintiff.

The constitutionalization of US libel law brought about a reversal of this burden. The 1964 US Supreme Court decision in *New York Times* v *Sullivan*, in addition to establishing the 'actual malice' standard to govern media liability arising out of publications dealing with public officials (and subsequently public figures), also established that proof of truth is no longer a burden to be carried by a defendant in such cases.[9] Instead, the burden was expressly shifted to the public official or public figure plaintiff to establish falsity by specific evidence. As the New York Court of Appeals observed in the case of *Rinaldi* v *Holt, Rinehart & Winston, Inc.*

> The burden is now on the libel plaintiff to establish falsity of a libel … this requirement follows naturally from the actual malice standard. Before knowing falsity or reckless disregard for truth can be established, the plaintiff must establish that the statement was, in fact, false.[10]

The public official or public figure plaintiff must, moreover, demonstrate falsity by 'clear and convincing evidence'; put another way, falsity must be shown with 'convincing clarity.'

The burden of proof as to truth or falsity in situations involving private plaintiffs was not settled in *New York Times* v *Sullivan*. It was not until twenty-two years later, in *Philadelphia Newspapers, Inc.* v *Hepps*,[11] that the Supreme Court explicitly extended the constitutional requirement that the plaintiff bear the burden of showing falsity to cases involving private figure plaintiffs. As the Court of Appeals for the Sixth Circuit subsequently summarized in *Wilson* v *Scripps-Howard Broadcasting Co.*:

> The Supreme Court has said that the First Amendment requires that the plaintiff prove fault. Falsity is an element of fault under the First Amendment that should be proved and not presumed.... As a matter of federal First Amendment law, the burden must be placed on the plaintiff to show falsity.[12]

Factual statements versus hyperbolic speech and opinion

Hyperbolic speech, including insults, name-calling, obscenities and other verbal abuse, no matter how vulgar or offensive, will generally not give rise to a defamation cause of action, on the grounds that such colourful speech is not normally intended to be understood literally. To be sure, the issue of whether a particular statement is merely an insulting hyperbole or a defamatory statement of fact is an often litigated one, in which the setting in which the challenged statement is made may be crucial. For example, to call an expensive merchant a 'crook', though highly insulting, likely will not give rise to a defamation claim. In contrast, to call someone a 'crook' in the context of making charges about his or her involvement in a tax evasion or securities fraud scheme will be likely to be construed as a defamatory statement of fact that would give rise to a defamation claim.[13]

Much case law has developed around the elusive distinction between statements of fact and statements of opinion. Building on a broad pronouncement in the Supreme Court's 1974 opinion in *Gertz* v *Robert Welch*[14] that, 'under the First Amendment there is no such thing as a false idea', ensuing court opinions strove to articulate a bright line distinction between legally actionable statements of fact and legally protected statements of opinion. The degree of their success in doing so is debatable.

In its 1991 opinion in *Milkovich* v *Lorain Journal Co.*,[15] the US Supreme Court complicated the analysis by indicating that labelling a statement as opinion does not automatically end the legal inquiry in favour of the defendant. The court instructed that what must be determined is whether the opinion states or implies the existence of undisclosed defamatory facts. If so, it is actionable; if not, it is not.

The facts of *Milkovich* entailed a lawsuit brought by Michael Milkovich, wrestling coach for Maple High School, against Ted Diadum, a sports columnist, and the columnist's newspaper. The wrestling team had been suspended from competition after a fight with another team during a match in which several people were injured. In two separate hearings, the coach testified to the innocence of his team. Diadum reported in his column (entitled 'TD says') under the headline 'Maple beat the law with the 'big lie', that' anyone who attended the meet, whether he be from Maple Heights, Mentor, or impartial observer, knows in his heart that Milkovich … lied at the hearing after … having given his solemn oath to tell the truth.' The Supreme Court reversed a lower court's finding that the foregoing statements were protected expressions of opinion, instead concluding that the article could be construed as implying an assertion of objective fact, namely, that the coach had perjured himself. The court thus remitted the case to a jury for determination of possible liability.

The lower courts have begun to grapple with the *Milkovich* ruling, which some observers have predicted will increase the number of libel cases submitted to juries. Some courts, including in New York, have read *Milkovich* as not intending to upset the jurisprudence protective of the publication of opinions. New York's highest state court has even resorted to state constitutional protections in aid of giving expressions of opinion wide constitutional berth.[16] Other jurisdictions, such as California, have read *Milkovich* more favourably to the libel plaintiff [17] – sending equivocal statements to juries for determinations as to whether they imply undisclosed defamatory facts.

An important recent case is *Moldea v New York Times Co.*,[18] involving a book author's defamation claim against the *New York Times* arising out of an unfavourable book review. A principal charge of the review was that the book was marred by 'sloppy journalism', supported by examples supplied by the reviewer. The Court of Appeals reversed the trial court's dismissal of the suit on the grounds that some of the criticisms levelled in the book review were actionable as they were verifiable and susceptible of being proven true or false. In an extraordinary move, following a request for reconsideration, the appellate court subsequently reversed itself, finding that no cause of action existed after all. The revised opinion indicated that the court's earlier decision had failed to take into account the context of the offending article, a book review, 'a genre in which readers expect to find spirited critiques of literary works that they understand to be the reviewer's description'. So long as statements made in a book review were supportable by reference to the book, they would be treated as non-actionable.

Libel by implication

It is often contended that reputational injury has resulted not from what was actually said, but what was implied by a particular statement. Courts have generally held that in cases involving public figures (a category of plaintiff discussed below), a false implication, without more, is not sufficient to satisfy the constitutional actual malice standard and thus is not actionable. To prevail on a theory of 'libel by implication', a public figure plaintiff would have to prove that the defendant was aware of the implication of its statements and harboured substantial doubts as to its truth. This is a difficult burden for a libel plaintiff to meet. For example, in the New York case of *Pierce* v *Capital Cities Communications, Inc.*,[19] the plaintiff, a former mayor and Port Authority Commissioner, alleged that a television broadcast created 'the false impression that he had misused his public position in seeking private pecuniary gain'.[20] The broadcast had accurately reported that the plaintiff had (1) voted not to seek new bids on a steel contract for the construction of a bridge and (2) owned land near the site where the bridge was to be built that increased in value as a result of the vote. The plaintiff charged the defendants with raising the incorrect implication that he had cast his vote in order to expedite construction and resell his land near the bridge. The court held that the defendants had not acted with the requisite degree of fault in publishing the accurate facts despite the possible inferences that might derive from such facts.

With respect to private plaintiffs, a 'false fact' is more likely to be found in cases in which the only alleged falsity is implied. In one case, a Tennessee court determined a routine police story to be defamatory because it failed to mention several facts and, thus, created the false implication that the plaintiff and a suspect's husband were having an affair. Although every fact included in the report was accurate, the false implication that resulted from the omission of certain facts was said to have injured the plaintiff's reputation.[21]

The requirement that the challenged statement be defamatory

Before a plaintiff can recover in a libel action, the plaintiff must plead and prove that the challenged statement is 'defamatory'. Each state has its own definition of what constitutes a defamatory statement. New York, for example, has declared a defamatory statement to involve "words which tend to expose one to public hatred, shame, obloquy, contumely, odium, contempt, ridicule, aversion, ostracism, degradation, or disgrace, or to induce an evil opinion of one in the minds of right-thinking persons, and to deprive one of their confidence and friendly intercourse [in] society'.[22] As a general matter, a defamatory statement is considered to be a false statement of fact printed or broadcast about a person which tends to injure that person's reputation.

In most jurisdictions, it is up to the judge to decide whether the statements at issue are reasonably susceptible of a defamatory connotation, that is, whether the statements, as a matter of law, are capable of defamatory meaning. Once the judge concludes that the statements are, in fact, capable of defamatory meaning, it becomes the job of the jury to decide whether the statements were likely to be understood as defamatory by the ordinary or average reader or listener. In determining whether statements are capable of defamatory meaning, courts will examine the offending language in the context of the entire broadcast or publication, paying attention to the circumstances surrounding their publication.

In this regard, the issue has arisen as to whether defamation may result, in the print media context, from an inaccurate headline. Jurisdictions differ with respect to the issue of whether a defendant can be liable for a headline alone or whether the headline must be read in the context of the entire article. Some states, such as California, have held that a headline must be considered in connection with the accompanying article to determine whether the headline is supported by the content in the article.[23] Other states, such as Nevada, have concluded that a defamatory headline is actionable by itself even if the body of a story is accurate and non-defamatory, since readers often only have the time or the interest to read a headline and not the entire story which accompanies it.[24]

The 'of and concerning' requirement

Because the harm being addressed in an action for libel is injury to reputation, practically any individual or entity capable of having a reputation – as well as the capacity to sue – may assert a cause of action for libel. Thus, corporations may maintain actions for defamation. Although corporations do not have personal reputations capable of being injured, they have other reputational interests, such as their business integrity and credit standing, that can be damaged as a result of false statements made about them to the public.

Before a defamation action can proceed, however, the plaintiff, be it an individual, corporation, partnership or association, must plead and prove that the allegedly defamatory statements refer directly to this plaintiff. The publication or broadcast need not specifically name the plaintiff, as long as at least some readers or viewers could reasonably conclude that the statements being made are about the plaintiff. A number of courts have delegated this issue to the jury; others have considered the issue of whether a libellous statement is 'of and concerning' the plaintiff to be one for the judge to determine. In either case, the focus of such a determination is not on who is meant, but who is hit: it is the impact of the challenged statement on the reader, not the intent of the author, that is generally relevant.[25]

As a general rule, no action for defamation lies on behalf of an individual who is a member of a group or organization as the result of a general statement made about the group or organization as a whole. Thus, for example, in a recent New York case, individual members of the Church of Scientology were determined to be unable to maintain a libel action against a newspaper based on statements made about the organization generally.[26] This result is based on the notion that such statements are too diffuse to be construed as 'of and concerning' individual members of the group or class. Where, however, the size of the group is small or the individual has been specifically named or referred to in some way, individual members of groups can successfully maintain actions for defamation. In the United States only a living person is capable of being defamed. There can be no liability for defamation of the dead, whether the claim be made by the estate of the deceased or by the deceased's friends or relatives. Whether or not an action for the defamation of a living person survives his or her death depends on the survival statutes of each state. While, at common law, defamation actions were considered to be strictly personal and thus did not survive death, several states have enacted statutes which permit the survival of defamation actions.

The requisite degree of fault: classifying the plaintiff

In the United States, libel plaintiffs are classified into two broad categories: public officials/public figures, and private figures. Determining into which category a given plaintiff falls is extremely important because it will determine, as a condition of recovery, the degree of fault that a plaintiff will be required to show that the defendant exhibited in publishing or broadcasting an allegedly defamatory statement (see discussion on page 11). As discussed below, proper categorization of public versus private figures can be an elusive task.

Public officials

Public officials are those elected or appointed individuals who are charged with the responsibility of controlling or overseeing governmental and public affairs. The definition of public officials is not limited to those individuals who hold policy-making positions at the top of governmental organizations. Generally, unless an employee has had only a peripheral or transient connection to governmental activity, he or she will be deemed a public official. Examples of public officials include elected officials, judicial and administrative personnel (both elected and appointed), law enforcement personnel, officers in the military, and public school and state university officials. An individual remains a public official for libel law purposes even after he or she leaves office with respect to articles or stories that refer to that person while he or she was in office.[27]

> The Supreme Court has indicated that the scope of commentary about public officials that receives treatment under the 'actual malice' test (as described below) is extremely broad: generally, it covers anything that might touch on an official's fitness for office. For example, a charge of criminal conduct, no matter how remote in time and place, has been held by the Supreme Court to be relevant to a public official's fitness for office.[28] Statements concerning a public official's business activities, regardless of whether or not they fall within the period during which he or she held office, are generally treated under the 'actual malice' standard as well.

Public figures

The Supreme Court has defined 'public figures' as those individuals who 'have assumed roles of special prominence in the affairs of society'.[29] The essential element underlying inclusion in this category is that the individual has, in some way or another, attracted the attention of the public. In general, the category of public figures can be further divided into two sub-categories:

- *All-purpose public figures* are those individuals who occupy positions of such pervasive power and influence that they are deemed public figures for all purposes. Examples of all-purpose public figures include political candidates, prominent entertainers and sports figures, business and community leaders, prominent writers and other social commentators, and religious leaders. Major corporations generally will fall into this category as well.
- *Limited-purpose public figures* are otherwise private figures who have either voluntarily injected themselves into a public controversy or have otherwise been drawn into a public controversy and achieved 'pervasive notoriety' as a result. To qualify the plaintiff as a voluntary, limited-purpose public figure, a defendant typically must show that the plaintiff has:
1 prior to the statements complained of, successfully invited public attention to his or her views in an effort to persuade others;
2 voluntarily injected him or herself into the controversy to which the litigation is connected;
3 assumed a position of prominence in the controversy;
4 maintained regular and continuous access to the media.[30]

To qualify as an involuntary public figure it is generally not sufficient that the plaintiff was drawn into a single public exchange. For example, courts in various jurisdictions have found individuals who appear in courtrooms to answer single, albeit controversial, charges of criminal conduct not to be public figures. According to the reasoning of these courts, to be deemed involuntary public figures, such individuals must have been involved in courses or patterns of particularly notorious or heinous criminal conduct that invite pervasive public attention and comment.[31]

> Illustrating the sometimes curious application of these principles is *Time, Inc.* v *Firestone*,[32] a case emanating out of a *Time* magazine article reporting on a divorce order ending the marriage of a prominent Florida socialite. *Time* reported that the divorce was granted on the grounds that Mrs Firestone, the plaintiff, was guilty of adultery and extreme cruelty. In Mrs Firestone's defamation suit, the Supreme Court rejected the argument that Mrs Firestone was a public figure, either generally or for the limited purpose of the case, despite the notoriety of the Firestone family and the fact that she had convened several press conferences during the seventeen months of the divorce trial. The Court reasoned that (1) Mrs Firestone did not occupy a role of special prominence in the affairs of society, and (2) her public exposure did not result in her becoming a limited public figure for the conflict since her involvement in the case was not voluntary, but a result of having to use the court system to 'obtain legal release from the bonds of matrimony'.

Standards of fault governing a libel plaintiff's right to recover

The classification of the plaintiff as either a public figure (public official, all-purpose public figure, limited-purpose public figure) or a private individual will determine how the defendant's conduct in researching, writing, printing or broadcasting the allegedly defamatory statements is to be assessed, since even if a publication is determined to contain false and defamatory statements of fact made 'of and concerning' the plaintiff, the plaintiff may not recover unless he or she can demonstrate that the defendant exhibited a degree of culpability in making the challenged statements that meets constitutional requirements. This constitutionally-mandated standard of care varies according to the status of the plaintiff.

The actual malice standard applicable to public official and public figure plaintiffs

Public official and public figure plaintiffs, both all-purpose and limited-purpose, face the most formidable standard-of-care burdens. In its 1964 opinion in *New York Times* v *Sullivan*, the US Supreme Court declared that, to prevail, public official libel plaintiffs must demonstrate that the defendant published a false or defamatory statement either with knowledge of its falsity or in reckless disregard of its truth or falsity – a state of mind labelled by the court as 'actual malice'.[33]

> The facts of *Sullivan* are noteworthy. The plaintiff was the Commissioner of Public Affairs for the City of Montgomery, Alabama. Included in his duties was supervision of the Police Department. He sued the *New York Times* for libel arising out of its publication of a paid advertisement by a group supporting the civil rights movement in the South which contained allegations that Montgomery had facilitated the commission of acts, such as the expulsion of several black students, the padlocking of their dining hall 'to starve them into submission', and the harassment of Dr Martin Luther King through inadequate protection and wrongful arrest. Sullivan claimed that as Commissioner of the Montgomery Police Department he was libelled by the allegations, many of which proved to be factually incorrect. Citing the compelling First Amendment policy arguments favouring harsh criticism of public officials, even if those criticisms may prove factually false, the US Supreme Court reversed a jury damage award of US $500 000, and concluded that recovery against the *Times* was barred in the absence of the constitutionally required proof that the *Times* had published with 'actual malice'.

A series of subsequent Supreme Court opinions expanded the group of libel plaintiffs subject to the actual malice test to include all manner of so-called public figures.[34]

Malice in the constitutional libel context is very different from the common law concept of malice, the latter of which is generally defined as evil intent, hatred or ill-will. Statements are considered to have been made with constitutional malice where the defendant had a 'high degree of awareness of … probable falsity' or 'entertained serious doubts as to the truth of his publication'.[35] Given the confusion over the term 'actual malice', the US Supreme Court, in the recent case of *Masson* v *New Yorker Magazine, Inc.*, suggested, '[i]n place of the term actual malice, it is better practice that the jury instructions refer to publication of a statement with knowledge of falsity or reckless disregard as to truth or falsity'.[36]

Actual malice is a subjective standard, and must be proven by the plaintiff by 'clear and convincing evidence'. The plaintiff must show that, at the time the statement was made, the defendant knew the statement to be false or entertained serious doubts about its veracity. The test is not what the defendant should have known or should have foreseen, but what the defendant subjectively knew or believed at the time the statement was made.

From the perspective of the press, one of the unfortunate consequences of the otherwise protective 'actual malice' fault standard developed in *New York Times* is the licence that standard provides to the plaintiff to engage in intrusive pre-trial discovery. Since the actual malice test involves the subjective state of mind of the publisher, the Supreme Court has ruled that it is permissible for a libel plaintiff to examine virtually the entire editorial process underlying the publication. Drafts, notes, out-takes, editorial conferences and the like are all fair game in discovery; the accompanying depositions (i.e. pre-trial examinations of the defendants) accordingly can be arduous, intrusive and disruptive of the day-to-day operations of the press – not to mention extremely expensive.

Because of the difficulty of adducing direct proof of actual malice, the libel plaintiff is entitled to prove actual malice by circumstantial evidence. The following are some types of circumstantial evidence that courts have found probative of actual malice:

Purposeful avoidance of the truth

A good example of this type of circumstantial evidence is found in the 1989 Supreme Court case of *Harte-Hanks Communications* v *Connaughton*.[37] In *Harte-Hanks*, two sisters had informed a candidate for a judgeship of an instance of bribery in the court administration of the incumbent. Based on this information, the candidate instigated a grand jury investigation of several members of the incumbent's staff. One of the sisters then contacted a newspaper, known in the community to support the incumbent, and informed the newspaper that the candidate had promised the sisters various 'quid pro quos' in exchange for the information they had provided to him. The newspaper ran a front-page article quoting the sister as stating that the candidate had used 'dirty tricks' in conducting the investigation and had offered her and her sister jobs and a trip to Florida 'in appreciation' for their help in the investigation.

Before publishing the article, the newspaper contacted the candidate, who denied the sister's charges. No one at the newspaper ever contacted the other sister to confirm the allegations. Neither did anyone at the newspaper listen to several tapes of discussions between the candidate and the sisters that had been given to the newspaper by the candidate. In addition, the five people that the newspaper did contact had denied the allegations made by the sister.

The Supreme Court determined that there was sufficient evidence to support a finding of actual malice. In the words of the court: 'Although failure to investigate will not alone support a finding of actual malice, the purposeful avoidance of the truth is in a different category.'[38]

Known unreliability or bias of a source

Evidence that a defendant had obvious reasons to doubt the veracity or integrity of a source on which it places primary reliance, while perhaps not sufficient by itself to establish actual malice, is probative of the issue. Similarly, reliance on anonymous sources without further verification or confirmation may, in appropriate circumstances, give rise to a finding of actual malice.

Purposeful distortion of facts or adherence to a preconceived storyline

It is entirely appropriate for a publication or broadcast to have an editorial point of view. Libel claims predicated on asserted lack of balance, or selective choice of facts, in publishing or broadcasting a story do not, by themselves, give rise to an actual malice finding. Courts have, however, found evidence of actual malice in situations where facts were so mischaracterized or were edited in such a way so as to create the possibility that a defendant acted with knowing or reckless disregard for the truth. Similarly problematic would be evidence that a publisher conceived a storyline prior to beginning an investigation and then consciously set out to make the 'information' gathered conform to the preconceived facts.

> An interesting recent case is *Prozeralik* v *Capital Cities Communications, Inc.*,[39] a lawsuit brought against a local television station for inaccurately reporting that the plaintiff was the victim of an abduction and beating by organized crime figures (with whom, by inference, he was associated). The station identified the plaintiff based on a reporter's hunch that, since the victim reportedly was a local restaurateur, it might have been the plaintiff (a prominent local restaurateur). To make matters worse, the station claimed that it had had the plaintiff's identity confirmed by the FBI, a claim flatly denied by the reported FBI source. The station's effort at a retraction was to report that the plaintiff had been wrongly identified notwithstanding prior confirmation by the FBI.

Although the multi-million dollar jury award in the case was overturned due to faulty jury instructions, the New York Court of Appeals found that 'the plaintiff met his *prima facie* evidentiary burden of establishing actual malice sufficient to allow the jury (had it been instructed correctly) to find that the defendant acted with a high degree of awareness of "probable falsity" or entertained "serious doubts" as to the truth of the broadcasts'. The court found that it was a question of fact for the jury whether the station lied about the FBI confirmation and whether it reported the plaintiff's name solely on the basis that he was the most famous restaurateur in the area.

The standard applicable to private figure plaintiffs

In another leading Supreme Court case, *Gertz* v *Robert Welch, Inc.*, the court determined that individual states need not impose the actual malice burden of proof on private, as opposed to public, figure libel plaintiffs. The court held that 'so long as they do not impose liability without fault, the States may define for themselves the appropriate standard of liability for a publisher or broadcaster of defamatory falsehood injurious to a private individual'[40] involved in a matter of public concern.

In the subsequent case of *Dun & Bradstreet* v *Greenmoss*[41], the Supreme Court appeared to loosen the constitutional reins further in situations involving private plaintiffs not involved in matters of public concern. Whereas *Gertz* prohibits liability without fault in attacks upon statements involving matters of public concern, *Dun & Bradstreet* appears to dispense with this restriction in situations involving individual plaintiffs not involved in matters of public concern.

The states have variously addressed the issue of the governing standard of care in libel actions involving private plaintiffs. Some states – Alaska, Colorado, Indiana, New Jersey – have retained the 'actual malice' standard, and at least one state – New York – as discussed below, has developed a 'gross irresponsibility' standard of care to govern situations involving private plaintiffs involved in matters of legitimate public concern. A majority of states have, however, selected the negligence or reasonable care standard.[42] In these states, a private plaintiff, in order to prevail, must demonstrate that the defendant acted 'unreasonably' in failing to ascertain the falsity or defamatory nature of the published statements. The Supreme Court of the State of Washington, in the case of *Taskett* v *King Broadcasting Co.*, viewed the relevant inquiry as involving whether, 'in publishing the statement, the defendant knew or, in the exercise of reasonable care, should have known that the statement was false, or would create a false impression in some material respect'.[43]

One important state – New York – has opted to apply neither the negligence nor the actual malice standard of care to defendants in private figure plaintiff cases. Instead, in the case of *Chapadeau* v *Utica Observer-Dispatch Inc.* it was made clear that a private figure plaintiff involved in a matter of 'legitimate public concern' has the burden of proving, by a preponderance of evidence, that 'the publisher acted in a grossly irresponsible manner without due consideration for the standards of information gathering and dissemination ordinarily followed by responsible parties'.[44]

The focus of the gross irresponsibility inquiry is on the objective aspects of the defendant's behaviour and not on the defendant's state of mind. Courts will generally examine a wide variety of factors, including: (1) whether sound journalistic practices were followed, (2) whether normal editorial procedures were adhered to, and (3) whether there existed any apparent reason to doubt the veracity or accuracy of the sources relied upon. As a practical matter, the gross irresponsibility test has proven to be quite protective of publishers and broadcasters. The New York courts have construed the standard as intended to provide considerable leeway for honest error, with due recognition of the realities that mistakes of fact are inevitable, and that many types of publishers, e.g. of books, simply lack the wherewithal to fact-check every item submitted for publication.

> Several cases illustrate application of the *Chapadeau* standard. In *Weiner* v *Doubleday & Co.*,[45] a psychiatrist claimed that he was defamed by the defendant's book, *Nutcracker*, a non-fictional account of a family murder. The plaintiff claimed that the book implied that he was sleeping with his patient, who was subsequently convicted of planning the murder and dispatching her son to carry it out. The account, which reported other family members' suspicions that the plaintiff was guilty of this violation of his professional ethics, was found by the court not to be actionable. As the plaintiff had to prove that the publisher acted in a 'grossly irresponsible' manner, the court found that he could not meet this burden where the publisher relied on a distinguished author ('whose experience and reputation are unquestioned'). The author, in turn, was held to have fulfilled her burden by conducting several interviews with multiple parties that supported the family's suspicions regarding the relationship between the plaintiff and his patient.

> In *Naantaanbuu* v *Abernathy*,[46] the Reverend Ralph Abernathy's autobiography contained an account of the evening before Dr Martin Luther King, Jr's assassination which implied that Dr King slept with the hostess of the dinner party he attended that evening. Although not mentioned by name, the plaintiff sued for defamation, claiming that it was well known that Dr King and Rev. Abernathy spent that evening at her house. The court found for the author and publisher defendants, concluding that the publisher permissibly relied on the author's account and had not departed from its normal editorial practice with respect to vetting its manuscripts for libel. As for the author, the plaintiff 'has produced no evidence … that Abernathy told anyone else a different account of that night, or published this account of events with the realization that his recollection was faulty. Such evidence is required when the applicable standard, gross irresponsibility, calls for a showing of fault'.

Standards of care: practical considerations

Regardless of the standard of care employed in a particular case, certain core questions will be of interest to the court. These include:

- Did the defendant undertake as thorough an investigation as was reasonable under the circumstances? If doubts as to the veracity of a statement became apparent prior to publication, did the defendant attempt to dispel them?
- What types of sources did the defendant rely on? Did the publisher have reason to find them reliable? Did any of the sources demonstrate a bias that should have raised a red flag for the defendant? Were attempts made to

verify or confirm the information received from potentially biased sources?

As a general proposition, US courts are particularly troubled by evidence of sloppy journalism and sloppy editorial 'fact-checking'. For the most part, the cases that have resulted in massive jury verdicts that have withstood appellate review reflect seriously deficient journalism and/or an editorial process that broke down. While such lapses might not, under appropriate interpretation of the governing constitutional standards, in all cases give rise to a right to libel recovery, perhaps the best lesson to learn from what has transpired in court-rooms across the United States to date is that careful journalism, and diligent editorial supervision, ultimately are the best antidotes to potentially debilitating libel lawsuits.

Defences

Beyond the constitutional protections afforded the press in defending against libel claims, a number of common law and statutory privileges – both absolute and qualified – also serve to limit such claims.

Fair and true reports

United States common law has long recognized a privilege for fair and accurate reports of judicial, legislative and executive proceedings. Jurisdictions vary on precisely what types of proceedings are covered by this privilege. They also differ on whether the privilege is absolute or qualified.

In New York, for example, the common law privilege for fair and accurate reports of governmental proceedings has been codified as NY Civil Rights Law Section 74, which provides:

> A civil action cannot be maintained against any person, firm or corporation, for publication of a fair and true report of any judicial proceeding, legislative proceeding or other official proceeding, or for any heading of the report which is a fair and true headnote of the statement published.[47]

The New York Court of Appeals, in *Holy Spirit Association for the Unification of World Christianity* v *New York Times Co.*,[48] has held that a report is 'fair and true' within the meaning of the statute when the report is 'substantially accurate'. The court noted that the concept of fairness and accuracy allows for a 'degree of liberality'.[49]

New York Civil Rights Law Section 74 has been held to cover a wide range of official proceedings and documents, including intelligence reports released by legislative committees, newspaper headlines read aloud in the course of legislative debate, and findings made and reports generated by executive bodies. Moreover, Civil Rights Law Section 74 is absolute on its face, providing defendants with an absolute privilege with respect to publishing fair and accurate reports of governmental proceedings and, thus, an absolute defence to libel actions brought based on their publication.

Republication

At common law, in the absence of the availability of some other privilege, it is no defence that a publisher has merely republished, accurately and with attribution, another's defamatory utterance. Subject to the protections afforded by the constitutionally mandated standards of fault, such republication may subject the publisher to liability.

Neutral reportage

Some jurisdictions nevertheless recognize a 'neutral reportage' privilege, which protects accurate reports of newsworthy charges against public figures made by responsible and prominent non-governmental sources. This neutral reportage privilege is often described as an extension of the fair and true report privilege, as discussed above.

Even those jurisdictions which have adopted a neutral report privilege have tended to construe the privilege fairly narrowly in terms of what constitutes 'newsworthy charges'. In the leading New York case of *Edwards* v *National Audubon Society, Inc.*,[50] the *New York Times* accurately reported statements made by the National Audubon Society, in the midst of a long-standing public dispute, that several scientists were 'paid to lie' about the size and variety of bird populations by misuse of the Society's Bird Count data. The *New York Times* requested that the Society identify the scientists that it referred to in its statements, and the Society provided a list of scientists whom it believed to have persistently misused the Bird Count data. The *New York Times* then reported the Society's accusations, along with responses by three of the five named scientists. The Court of Appeals for the Second Circuit held that such a report was privileged under the First Amendment:

> When a responsible, prominent organization like the National Audubon Society makes serious charges against a public figure, the First Amendment protects the accurate and disinterested reporting of those charges, regardless of the reporter's private views regarding their validity.... What is newsworthy about such accusations is that they were made. We do not believe that the press may be required

under the First Amendment to suppress newsworthy statements merely because it has serious doubts regarding their truth.... The public interest in being fully informed about controversies that often rage around sensitive issues demands that the press be afforded the freedom to report such charges without assuming responsibility for them.[51]

This leading case notwithstanding, New York courts, as well as courts in many other jurisdictions, have wavered as to the general availability of this privilege as a defence to a charge of libel. For example, in the subsequent New York case of *Cianci* v *New York Times Publishing Co.*,[52] involving an article which recapped the accusations of a woman who had allegedly been raped by the mayor, the court found the neutral reportage doctrine not to apply to the statements published by the defendant. As at least a partial rationale for its holding, the court found that the defendant did not simply report the charges but espoused or concurred in them'.[53]

Republications generally

Apart from reliance on the 'neutral reportage' privilege, courts in most states have recognized that it is both reasonable and necessary for news organizations to rely on articles and reports published by other prominent news organizations – daily newspapers of record such as the *New York Times* and *Wall Street Journal*, and wire services such as AP and Reuters. In the absence of a showing by a plaintiff that a republisher of a news story or article had, or should have had, substantial reason to question the accuracy of the original publication, a republisher from such sources can generally successfully defend against a libel claim based on its reliance upon the bona fides of the original publisher.

Circumstances can sometimes lead a potential republisher to conclude that reliance on other published reports may not, by itself, be reasonable. The following are some practical considerations that a news organization should keep in mind when deciding whether or not to republish defamatory allegations from an article, report or book chapter:

- Consider the status of the individual(s) who are the subject of the article. The degree of fault that a public figure plaintiff will have to show will be greater than that required of a private figure – especially a private figure not involved in an issue of public importance.
- Consider the immediacy of the need to get the news out. In the absence of deadline pressure, independent efforts to confirm a story represent good journalism and mitigate legal exposure.
- Consider the source. If a newspaper, reporter, or author is known to be

reputable, and there seems to be no substantial reason to doubt the accuracy of its, his or her story, a republisher will rarely be judicially second-guessed as to the reasonableness of relying on that source. If, on the other hand, a source is not known to be particularly reliable, a court may well question whether the republisher acted reasonably or potentially in reckless disregard of the truth or falsity of the original publication.

Libel law and the new technology

US courts have begun to grapple with the application of libel law to defamatory speech occurring on-line, for example, in the context of chat forums sponsored by computer bulletin board operators. In the one decided case to date, a federal district court declined to hold the on-line service provider responsible for allegedly defamatory statements transmitted to its subscribers via a forum the operation of which was, by contract, the responsibility of a third party. On these facts, the court likened the on-line service provider to an electronic, for-profit library, with no more editorial control over a publication's contents than a public library, book store, or newsstand. Absent actual knowledge or reason to know of the statements in issue, such on-line providers, the court reasoned, will not be held liable for libellous speech they disseminate.[54]

Remedies

Damages generally

As with other critical aspects of US libel law, the damages recoverable by successful libel plaintiffs have been circumscribed by constitutional limitations. Nevertheless, juries still enjoy a great degree of latitude in awarding actual and punitive damages, to the extent that media defendants are on occasion stung by staggering damage awards, and are regularly chastened by the prospect of being victimized by such an award. Reviewing courts frequently reverse or reduce awards of damages found to be excessive, but the prospect of awaiting such relief from an appellate tribunal is a costly one, fraught with risk for the libel defendant.

Presumed damages

At common law, a libel plaintiff who had established that he or she was the subject of a defamatory statement was presumed, without specific proof, to have been damaged. No proof of actual injury was required. The Supreme Court has sharply cut back the availability of such damages as a matter of constitutional law. Presumed damages are prohibited unless the plaintiff has demonstrated that the defendant acted with actual malice, i.e. published the defamatory statement with knowledge of falsity or in reckless disregard of its truth or falsity.[55]

Actual damages

Proof of 'actual injury' is required by the Constitution in all cases which involve matters of public concern and in which actual malice has not been established. Such damages can take the form of evidence of impairment of the plaintiff's reputation and standing in the community; personal humiliation; mental anguish; and emotional distress.

Special damages

Special damages are awarded to compensate a plaintiff for actual – 'out-of-pocket' – pecuniary loss. They are generally quite difficult to prove. In certain circumstances, e.g. where the publisher has complied with a state retraction statute (discussed in the section on retraction, page 23) by promptly publishing a correction, the plaintiff will be limited to recovering special damages if successful on his libel claim.

Punitive damages

Punitive damages are not aimed at compensation but at punishment and deterrence. In *Gertz* v *Robert Welch, Inc.*, the US Supreme Court determined that punitive damages could not be recovered without a showing of actual malice.[56]

In that punitive damages have historically been considered to be an extreme remedy reserved for cases involving especially egregious conduct, many states, including New York, California, Delaware, Pennsylvania and Vermont, require a showing by the plaintiff of something more than constitutional 'actual malice'. These states require in addition that the defendant has published or broadcast the defamatory statement with 'common law malice' – that is, ill-will, hatred, spite or vengeance.

Recent trends in damage awards

The Libel Defense Resource Center, a non-profit organization which as one of its activities monitors trends in libel litigation, has compiled statistics revealing the outcomes of jury trials in libel cases. These statistics reveal that three out of four such trials result in verdicts for the plaintiff. In thirty-five libel cases tried before a jury over the 1990–1991 period, the average award was over US $9 million (median award US $1.5 million); three-fifths of all awards exceeded US $1 million. Three out of every four awards included punitive damages which averaged US $8 million (median award US $2.5 million).

During this period, various newspapers were stung with damage awards as high as US $13, US $16 and US $34 million, while various local television stations sustained damage awards as high as US $15, US $29 and US $58 million.

To be sure, not every libel case – indeed, only a minority – actually reach a jury. Many are successfully terminated at a pre-trial stage by the award of 'summary judgment' in the media defendant's favour. (It is also the case that an unquantifiable (but very likely increasing) percentage of cases are terminated by settlements.)

Also lending some comfort is the fact that appellate courts have tended to reverse jury verdicts in favour of libel plaintiffs and/or severely curtail the damages awarded. Many media defendants stung by disastrous trial outcomes will stay the course, hoping for such relief. Others, however, sufficiently traumatized and economically taxed by the experience through trial, reach settlements with the plaintiff – generally for undisclosed sums of money.

The successful plaintiffs in the most notable recent cases have not been household names. They have instead either been public officials at state or local levels or private citizens who have become involved in matters of public concern. A few examples illustrate the types of cases that have generated mega-verdicts:

- Eleven-part investigative series by a local television station, critical of performance of a district attorney under federal investigation for bribery and racketeering. Result: US $58 million jury verdict (US $17 million in actual, and US $41 million in punitive, damages) against broadcaster.[57]
- Newspaper series examining Pennsylvania Supreme Court, and charging nepotism, apparent conflicts of interest and appearance of impropriety. Result: US $6 million libel judgment (US $3 million actual, and US $3 million punitive, damages) in favour of one Justice of that court.[58]
- Newspaper articles linking assistant district attorney to an apparent cover-up in a murder investigation. Result: US $34 million verdict (US $2.5 million actual, and US $31.5 million punitive, damages).[59]

- Local television station broadcast mis-identifying plaintiff as victim of abduction and noting a possible link between the victim and organized crime. Result: US $15.5 million verdict (US $5.5 million compensatory, US $10 million punitive, damages).[60]
- Series of local-station broadcasts detailing plaintiff heart surgeon's mishandling of several cases, and revocation of hospital privileges. Result: US $31.5 million verdict (including US $17.5 million in punitive damages).[61]

Retraction

A retraction is a withdrawal of a defamatory statement. At common law the issuance of a retraction was not a complete defence to a charge of libel based on the view that the renunciation might not be read or heard by the same people who had read or heard the original defamation. Thus, a retraction was admissible solely for the purpose of mitigating damages.

Today, over half of the states have retraction statutes,[62] the majority of which apply to media defendants only. Some of the statutes differentiate between types of media outlets, applying only to 'libel in a newspaper' or 'slander by radio broadcast'. The typical retraction statute requires that the defamed person give the publisher or broadcaster written notice of the alleged defamation and an opportunity to retract. Notice is usually required to be given within a specified time period after the defamed person learns of the defamation. Some of these statutes require notice and demand for a retraction as a prerequisite to the filing of a lawsuit. Many of these statutes condition the award of certain types of damages, such as punitive, on compliance with the statute. The most common effect of a proper retraction is a limitation of a plaintiff's recovery to 'actual damages'.

Generally, in order for a retraction to be effective, it must be full and frank. In some cases, a hedged retraction has been considered to constitute a second, separate libel or has been considered as a factor enhancing, rather than miti-gating, damages.

Libel reform

The financial enormity of recent verdicts, and the lack of uniformity in state retraction statutes, on the one hand, and the many proof hurdles in the plain-tiff's path to vindication of reputation, on the other, have spawned initiatives designed, their proponents argue, to streamline, if not obviate altogether, libel litigation; to obtain a quick, effective remedy for injury to reputation; and to protect the media from the threat of debilitating damages. These initiatives have assumed various forms, including legislative proposals introduced at federal and state levels, and 'model laws' crafted by study groups hoping to influence legislation. Predictably, in dealing with so volatile an issue, these proposals have spawned great controversy and divisions of viewpoint, from both the plaintiff and defence perspectives.

While each approach to the subject has differed in its details, common to most of the reformers' efforts has been to focus the inquiry solely on whether an allegedly libellous statement is true or false, and, where falsity is proven, to obtain a prompt retraction. The degree of fault on the publisher's part, e.g. whether it acted with 'actual malice', is irrelevant in this process. In turn, individuals who have been falsely defamed cannot recover damage remedies (although they may be able to recover their attorney's fees).

The foregoing approach has yet to find broad, bipartisan support. A somewhat more modest approach, initiated by the National Conference of Commissioners on Uniform State Laws, has, however, been greeted somewhat more favourably by the media. This approach aims to replace the current patchwork of so-called 'retraction' statutes, discussed above, with a Uniform Correction or Clarification of Defamation Act. This model legislation limits a plaintiff's recovery of damages arising out of publication of defamatory falsehoods to provable economic loss (i.e. ruling out punitive damages) where a media defendant, having been requested to do so, prints a correction or clarification of an allegedly defamatory statement within a reasonable period of time.

Protecting sources

Constitutional protection

In the 1972 case of *Branzburg* v *Hayes*,[63] the US Supreme Court addressed the question of whether, and to what degree, the First Amendment permits a reporter to refuse to reveal confidential information. The case involved three appeals in which reporters had declined to provide testimony to, or appear before, grand juries on First Amendment grounds. The Supreme Court ruled against the reporters in all three cases. A four-judge plurality opinion stated that 'the sole issue before us is the obligation of reporters to respond to grand jury subpoenas as other citizens do and to answer questions relevant to an investigation into the commission of a crime'.[64] These four justices declined to 'interpret the First Amendment to grant newsmen a testimonial privilege that other citizens do not enjoy'.[65]

Justice Powell's concurring opinion expressed the view that reporters would have judicial protection against grand jury investigations that were 'not being conducted in good faith', sought 'information bearing only a remote and tenuous relationship to the subject of the investigation' or called for the disclosure of 'confidential source relationships without a legitimate need of law enforcement'.[66]

That concurrence has carried great weight. Most lower courts have interpreted the Supreme Court's opinion in *Branzburg* to hold that a news organization enjoys a qualified privilege not to reveal confidential sources and information. While the specifics of the privilege vary from jurisdiction to jurisdiction, courts generally prohibit litigants from forcing news organizations to reveal confidential sources or information unless it can be shown that: (1) the information sought is relevant to the litigant's cause of action; (2) the litigant has a compelling need for that information; and (3) the information is not available from another source.[67]

State shield laws

In the aftermath of *Branzburg*, over half of the states have enacted reporter's shield laws that provide some degree of protection against the compelled disclosure of sources.[68] These statutes vary greatly from state to state. The most expansive protection is offered by 'absolute' shield laws.[69] These statutes have been interpreted by courts to provide reporters and news organizations with a broad privilege designed to protect confidential sources and information against intrusive subpoenas except in the most exceptional circumstances, e.g. in which a criminal defendant's Sixth Amendment right to a fair trial may be implicated.

Many states have adopted a 'qualified' shield law, similar in concept to the constitutionally based privilege discussed above.[70] In these jurisdictions, whether a reporter or news organization will be required to disclose confidential information (as well, perhaps, as non-confidential, unpublished information) will typically depend on the relevance of the information sought, whether there is a compelling need for it, and the existence of alternative means of obtaining the information.

Breach of contract

In the 1991 case of *Cohen* v *Cowles Media Co.*,[71] the US Supreme Court addressed the issue of whether a media organization can be held liable when it reveals the identity of a source to whom it has promised confidential treatment. The court held that the First Amendment does not prohibit a compromised source from recovering damages (on the facts presented in *Cowles*, under a theory of promissory estoppel).[72]

Issues of privacy

Whereas libel law seeks to balance reputational interests against the media's need to report freely on matters of public interest, privacy law strives to effect a somewhat different, and arguably more ill-defined, balance.

The law relating to invasion-of-privacy claims has developed along four branches, some of which have been incorporated in the statutes and common law of the fifty states. These four categories have come to be described as 'false light'; 'private facts'; 'misappropriation'; and 'intrusion'. It is common for libel lawsuits filed against publishers to incorporate one or more privacy claims as well, and, while a failure of the libel claim typically portends failure of the associated privacy claims, the variety, and outcomes, of privacy litigation have been extremely diverse.

'False light' privacy claims provide, in some jurisdictions, a cause of action to an individual who is placed in a 'false light' to the public, in circumstances where the false light would be highly offensive to a reasonable person and the publisher either knew of, or acted in reckless disregard as to, the falsity of the publicized matter and the false light in which the individual involved would be placed. Notably, and in contrast to the libel cause of action, it is not necessary, to sustain a false-light claim, to demonstrate injury to reputation, as opposed merely to injured feelings. The very similarity of false-light claims to libel claims has led a number of jurisdictions to refuse to recognize this branch of privacy law as creating a separate basis for legal relief.

While the truthfulness of a given published report is a critical aspect of both libel and 'false-light' claims, this is not the case with respect to the 'private facts' branch of privacy law. The gravamen of this cause of action is the publicizing of matter – even if true – concerning the private life of an individual in circumstances where the disclosure would be highly offensive to a reasonable person and is not of legitimate concern to the public. As one might expect, the strong First Amendment protection afforded to truthful reports by members of the media has tended to tilt the balance in such cases in the media's favour – unless the disclosures are so shocking or sensational and unrelated to any arguable public interest as to warrant recovery.

The 'misappropriation' category has also commonly been said to constitute the so-called 'right of publicity'. Involved here is the prevention of the commercial exploitation of the name or likeness of an individual without his or her consent. Statutory embodiments of this cause of action (such as in New York), as well as common-law interpretations, have engrafted important limitations to enable non-consensual uses of names and likenesses in connection with reporting of newsworthy events (generally liberally construed) and, indeed, to authorize a publisher's advertising of such newsworthy publications.

The fourth privacy law branch, 'intrusion', prevents publishers and others from engaging in acts of physical trespass or similarly intrusive behaviour, e.g. electronic surveillance, in violation of the privacy interests of another, provided the intrusion would be highly offensive to a reasonable person. Not unlike the other privacy causes of action, court interpretations of what constitutes 'highly offensive' conduct have varied widely.

Notes

1   *United States* v *Associated Press*, 52 F. Supp. 362, 372 (SDNY 1943).
2   *New York Times Co.* v *Sullivan*, 376 US 254 (1964).
3   *New York Times*, 376 US at 270.
4   *New York Times*, 376 US at 273.
5   *New York Times*, 376 US at 279-80.
6   *St. Amant* v *Thompson*, 390 US 727, 731 (1968).
7   A state-by-state analysis of prevailing libel laws is compiled annually by the Libel Defense Resource Center, a non-profit organization. Copies may be purchased by contacting the LDRC, 404 Park Avenue South, 16th Floor, New York, New York 10016.
8   The distinction between libel and slander retains modern significance in only one respect – as a factor to be considered in the determination of whether a plaintiff must allege and prove the existence of 'special damages' – that is, the loss of something of economic or pecuniary value. At common law, slander was divided into two categories: slander *per se* and slander *per quod*. Slander *per se* was actionable as a matter of law, without proof of special damages. Slander *per quod* was actionable only if the plaintiff could prove actual economic or pecuniary harm. Whether a statement was slander *per se* or slander *per quod* depended on the content of the statement; slander was actionable *per se* if it fell into one of four categories: (1) allegations of criminal conduct; (2) allegations affecting the plaintiff's business, professional or trade reputation; (3) allegations that the plaintiff has a loathsome disease; or (4) allegations that a female is 'unchaste'.

With respect to libel, there is no general agreement among the states as to what statements are actionable *per se* – that is, as a matter of law, actionable without proof of special harm. Courts in some states hold that all libellous statements are actionable without proof of special harm. Most states, however, have adopted the position that if a statement is libellous 'on its face', that is, without reference to facts not included in the statement itself, it is libellous *per se*. If, on the other hand, the reader must know extrinsic facts for the libellous meaning to be conveyed, the statement is libellous *per quod* and the plaintiff must prove actual pecuniary loss – special damages – for the statement to be actionable. To make matters even more confusing, in some jurisdictions libel by extrinsic fact is considered to be libel *per se* if the libel falls within one of the four above-mentioned slander *per se* categories.

These rules are, at best, archaic and, at worst, illogical. Courts constantly misuse the terminology, creating unclear and often inconsistent precedents. Until such time as the distinctions between libel and slander and *per se* and *per quod* are completely eliminated, in favour of examining all relevant factors surrounding allegedly defamatory communications, this will continue to be a confusing and unpredictable subject area.

9   *New York Times*, 376 US at 271.

10   *Rinaldi* v *Holt, Rinehart & Winston, Inc.*, 42 NY 2d 369, 366 NE 2d 1299, 397 NYS. 2d 943, cert. denied, 434 US 969 (1977).

11   *Philadelphia Newspapers, Inc.* v. *Hepps*, 475 US 767 (1986).

12   *Wilson* v *Scripps-Howard Broadcasting Co.*, 642 F. 2d 371, 75 (6th Cir.), cert. dismissed, 454 US 1130 (1981). The Supreme Court has not explicitly decided whether the Constitution shifts the burden of proof as to falsity from defendants to plaintiffs when the defendants are not members of the press. While the issue is acknowledged in *Philadelphia Newspapers, Inc.* v *Hepps*, 475 US 767 (1986), it was not decided on in that case or in any other Supreme Court case since.

13   See *Old Dominion Branch No. 496, Nat'l Ass'n of Letter Carriers* v *Austin*, 418 US 264 (1974) (plaintiff's inclusion in monthly union newsletter on a 'List of Scabs' for not being a member of the union held not actionable in so far as the term was used in a 'loose, figurative sense', and was 'merely rhetorical hyperbole, a lusty and imaginative expression of contempt felt by union members towards those who refuse to join'); *Greenbelt Coop. Publishing Ass'n.* v *Bresler*, 398 U.S. 6 (1970) (local newspaper's characterization of real estate developer's negotiating position with local city council as 'blackmail' held non-actionable in the context presented, as 'even the most careless reader must have perceived that the word was no more than rhetorical hyperbole, a vigorous epithet used by those who considered [the plaintiff's] negotiating position extremely unreasonable').

14   *Gertz* v *Robert Welch, Inc.*, 418 US 323 (1974)

15   *Milkovich* v *Lorain Journal Co.*, 497 US 1 (1990).

16   See, e.g. *Immuno, A.G.* v *Moor-Jankowski*, 77 NY 2d 235, 567 NE 2d 1270, 566 NYS 2d 906, cert. denied, 111 S.Ct. 2261 (1991); *Gross* v *New York Times*, 82 NY 2d 146, 623 NE 2d 1163, 603 NYS. 2d 813 (1993).

17   See, e.g. *Unelko Corp.* v *Rooney*, 912 F. 2d 1049 (9th Cir. 1990).

18   *Moldea* v *New York Times Co.*, 22 F. 2d 310 (DC Cir. 1994).

19   *Pierce* v *Capital Cities Communications, Inc.*, 576 F. 2d 495 (3rd Cir.), cert. denied, 439 US 861 (1978).

20   *Pierce*, 576 F. 2d at 449.

21   *Memphis Publishing Co.* v *Nichols*, 569 SW 2d 412 (Tenn. 1978).

22   *Kimmerle* v *New York Evening Journal*, 262 NY 99, 102, 186 NE 217, 218 (1933).

23   See, e.g. *Moyer* v *Amador Valley Joint Union High School Dist.*, 225 Cal. App. 3d 720, 275 Cal. Rptr. 494 (1990).

24   See, e.g. *Las Vegas Sun* v *Franklin*, 74 Nev. 282, 329 P. 2d 867 (1958), cert. denied, 423 US 882 (1975).

25 See, e.g. *Simms* v *KIRO, Inc.*, 20 Wash. App. 229, 580 P. 2d 642, cert. denied, 423 US 882 (1975).

26 *Church of Scientology International* v *Time Warner Inc.*, 806 F. Supp. 1157 (SDNY 1992).

27 The 'black-letter' definition of 'public officials' is found in the case of *Rosenblatt* v *Baer*, 383 US 75 (1966).

28 *Monitor Patriot Co.* v *Roy*, 401 US 265 (1971).

29 See, e.g. *Curtis Publishing Co.* v *Butts*, 388 US 130 (1967) and its companion case, *Associated Press* v *Walker*.

30 See, e.g. *Hoffman* v *Washington Post Co.*, 433 F. Supp. 600 (DCC 1977), aff'd mem., 578 F. 2d 442 (DC Cir. 1978); *Trotter* v *Jack Anderson Enterprises, Inc.*, 818 F.2d 431 (5th Cir. 1987).

31 See, e.g. *Rosanova* v *Playboy Enterprises*, 580 F. 2d 859 (5th Cir. 1978).

32 *Time, Inc.* v *Firestone*, 424 US 448 (1976).

33 *New York Times*, 376 US at 280.

34 The actual malice standard applies to all public figures, regardless of whether they are all-purpose or limited-purpose. In the case of limited-purpose public figures, however, the actual malice standard applies only to speech that emanates from the public controversy out of which the plaintiff's public status arises, in contrast to the all-purpose public figure, who must overcome the actual malice hurdle in connection with all speech concerning him.

35 *St. Amant*, 390 US at 731.

36 *Masson* v *New Yorker Magazine, Inc.*, 111 S. Ct. 2419, 2430 (1991).

37 *Harte-Hanks Communications, Inc.* v *Connaughton*, 491 US 657 (1989).

38 *Harte-Hanks Communications, Inc.*, 491 US at 684-85.

39 *Prozeralik* v *Capital Cities Communications, Inc.*, 605 NYS 2d 218 (1993).

40 *Gertz* v *Robert Welch, Inc.*, 418 US at 347.

41 *Dun & Bradstreet* v *Greenmoss Builders, Inc.*, 472 US 749 (1985).

42 These states are Alabama, Arizona, Arkansas, California, Connecticut, Delaware, the District of Columbia, Florida, Georgia, Hawaii, Illinois, Iowa, Kansas, Kentucky, Maryland, Massachusetts, Michigan, Minnesota, New Hampshire, New Mexico, North Carolina, Ohio, Oklahoma, Oregon, Pennsylvania, Rhode Island, South Carolina, Tennessee, Texas, Utah, Vermont, Virginia, Washington, West Virginia and Wisconsin.

43 *Taskett* v *King Broadcasting Co.*, 86 Wash. 2d 439, 445, 546 P. 2d 81, 85 (1976). The Restatement of Torts defines the test for actionable negligence in the libel context as 'whether the defendant acted reasonably in checking on the truth or falsity or defamatory character of the communication before publishing it'. The Restatement suggests three factors that courts should consider in applying the negligence standard: (1) time elements; (2) the nature of the interest the publisher was seeking to protect; and (3) the extent of the damage that would be suffered if the communication proved false. In addition, the Restatement suggests that reasonable care is to be measured against professional standards in the community where the defendant operates. Thus, where a defendant is 'a professional disseminator of news, such as a newspaper, a magazine or a broadcasting station, or an employee, such as a reporter', he, she or

it should be 'held to the skill and experience normally possessed by members of that profession.

44 *Chapadeau* v *Utica Observer-Dispatch, Inc.*, 38 NY 2d 196, 199, 341 NE 2d 569, 571, 379 NYS 2d 61, 64 (1975); see also *Naantaanbuu* v *Abernathy*, 746 F. Supp. 378 (SDNY 1990).

45 *Weiner* v *Doubleday*, 550 NYS 2d 251 (1989), cert. denied, 495 US 930 (1990).

46 *Naantaanbuu* v *Abernathy*, 816 F. Supp. 218 (SDNY 1993).

47 NY Civ. Rts. Law Section 74 (McKinney 1976).

48 *Holy Spirit Association for the Unification of World Christianity* v *New York Times Co.*, 49 NY 2d 63, 399 NE 2d 1185, 434 NYS 2d 165 (1979).

49 *Holy Spirit Association for the Unification of World Christianity*, 49 NY. 2d at 68, 399 NE 2d at 1187, 424 NYS 2d at 168.

50 *Edwards* v *National Audubon Society Inc.*, 556 F. 2d 113 (2nd Cir.), cert. denied, 434 US 1002 (1977).

51 *Edwards*, 556 F. 2d at 120.

52 *Cianci* v *New York Times Publishing Co.*, 639 F. 2d 54 (2nd Cir. 1980).

53 *Cianci*, 639 F. 2d at 69.

54 *Cubby, Inc.* v *Compuserve Inc.*, 776 F.Supp. 135 (SDNY 1991).

55 Awards of presumed damages appear still to be available on lower fault standards in cases involving private individuals not involved in matters of public concern.

56 With respect to private plaintiffs not involved in matters of legitimate public concern, as a result of the US Supreme Court's holding in *Dun & Bradstreet* v *Greenmoss Builders, Inc.*, the availability of punitive damages, and the requisite fault showing, are purely matters of state law.

57 *Feazell* v *Belo Broadcasting Corp.*, No. 86-2227-1 (Waco Tex. Dist. Ct., 19 April, 1991).

58 *McDermott* v *Biddle*, No. 00682 Phila. 1993, A. 2d, 1994 WL 323494 (Pa. Super, 8 July, 1994).

59 *Sprague* v *Walter*, 543 A. 2d 1078 (Pa.), appeal dismissed, 488 US 988 (1988).

60 *Prozeralik* v *Capital Cities Communications*, supra n. 39.

61 *Srivastava* v *Harte-Hanks Television, Inc.*, No. 85-CI-15150 (Bexar County Tex. Dist. Ct., 15 May, 1990).

62 At last count, thirty-two states had enacted some form of retraction statute.

63 *Branzburg* v *Hayes*, 408 US 665 (1972).

64 *Branzburg*, 408 US at 682.

65 *Branzburg*, 408 US at 690.

66 *Branzburg*, 408 US at 710.

67 See e.g. *Senear* v *Daily Journal*, 97 Wash. 2d 148, 641 P. 2d 1180 (1982).

68 At the last count, twenty-nine states had enacted some form of reporter's shield statute.

69 See, e.g. PA. CONST. STAT. ANN. Section 5942 (Purdon 1982 & Supp. 1984).

70 See, e.g. PA. STAT. ANN. 12 Section 2506 (West 1994).

71 *Cohen* v *Cowles Media Co.*, 111 S. Ct. 2513 (1991).

72 Under promissory estoppel doctrine, a promise which is expected to induce reliance and does in fact induce such reliance is determined by law to be binding if injustice can be avoided only by enforcing the promise.

2

Australia

Andrew Percival and Victoria Holthouse
of Allen, Allen & Hemsley (Sydney)

The law of defamation in Australia is a body of law primarily concerned with the protection of reputation.

> The plaintiff complained of two articles, headed 'Fergie's sister in marriage split' and 'Fergie antics anger Queen'. These, together with several other publications, imputed that the plaintiff had committed adultery contrary to her moral obligation of marriage. She was awarded Aus.$300 000 (US $228 000) plus Aus.$65 000 (US $49 000) interest.

> An actress and dancer sued a magazine over an article headed 'I was Dylan's sex slave', claiming that the article conveyed imputations including that she was a disgusting publicity-seeking trollop in that she engaged in masturbation and bizarre and erotic behaviour with a well known pop star and told the story to a news publisher. In this action, Gypsy Fire was awarded Aus.$130 000 (US $99 000); an earlier action for criminal defamation, obscene libel and blasphemous libel over the same article had been dismissed.

In Australia, since there are eight different jurisdictions, there are varying attitudes of judge and jury in relation to what is defamatory and how much it is worth. New South Wales is the centre for high damages awards. Other states are unlikely to produce damages awards of more than Aus.$100 000 (US $76 000).

The plaintiff is required to choose a single forum in which to sue in relation to the publication of a defamatory statement in more than one jurisdiction. The rule is that the defamation occurs in the place of publication. Of course, the plaintiff can choose to sue on the publication that occurred within one forum, but claim damages for injury to reputation caused by the publication in other jurisdictions. The plaintiff must specify the different states and territories, because the defendant is entitled to plead the defences of each place of publication relied on.

Under the laws applicable in each of the jurisdictions in Australia, a defamatory statement is, in general terms, a statement which alleges a defect in a person's character. Thus, a defamatory statement is one which is 'likely to cause ordinary decent folk in the community, taken in general, to think the less of'[1] the person about whom the statement is made or one which would 'tend to lower the plaintiff in the estimation of right-thinking members of society generally'[2] or one which exposes the plaintiff to ridicule.

However, in Australia what is defamatory varies from jurisdiction to jurisdiction, that is from state to state or territory (as the case may be). In New South Wales the law of defamation is governed by the common law as amended by the Defamation Act 1974, whereas in Victoria, South Australia and Western Australia the law of defamation is governed principally by the common law. In Queensland and Tasmania, on the other hand, the law of defamation has been codified, while in the Australian Capital Territory and the Northern Territory the position is different again because in both jurisdictions statutes have been enacted amending the common law but in ways different from each other and different from the states.

Consequently, what is defamatory in one state (or territory) may not be defamatory in another. For this reason it is important to note at the outset the similarities and differences in the law of defamation between the various states and territories in Australia.

Variations between states and territories

As indicated above, the law of defamation in Australia may be broken down into the following categories:

- common law: Victoria, South Australia and Western Australia;
- common law as amended by statute: New South Wales;
- codification by statute: Queensland and Tasmania;
- common law and statute: Australian Capital Territory and the Northern Territory.[3]

The resulting similarities and differences are, in summary, set out below.[4]

Common law jurisdictions

In these jurisdictions the distinction between libel and slander is maintained. A libellous statement is a defamatory statement in permanent form (e.g. publication in a newspaper) while slander is a defamatory statement in a transient form (e.g. an oral statement to a third party).

In these jurisdictions, for a statement to be defamatory, it must disparage a person's reputation by imputing behaviour or characteristics for which that person is responsible. The mere fact that a statement may have adverse financial consequences for the person about whom the statement is made is not sufficient.[5]

Truth is a complete defence to a claim that a particular statement was defamatory. This is because the law presumes a defamatory statement to be false.

New South Wales

In 1974 the New South Wales Government enacted the Defamation Act 1974, which repealed its predecessor, the Defamation Act 1958, and reinstated the common law as to defamation but subject to certain modifications. These modifications include the following:

- the distinction between libel and slander has been abolished;
- truth is only a defence in the publication of defamatory statements where the statement relates to a matter of public interest;
- the proceedings of a number of tribunals are protected by absolute privilege.

Code States

In these jurisdictions the law of defamation is governed wholly by statute; that is, in Queensland by the Criminal Code and the Defamation Law of Queensland of 1889 and in Tasmania by the Defamation Act 1957.

In the Code States, the common law concept of what is defamatory has been extended. An 'imputation concerning any person' by which that person is 'likely to be injured in his profession or trade' is actionable as defamation. It is enough that the imputation concerns the person and is likely to injure the person's business.[4]

A newspaper reported that a footballer was overweight, largely due to injury which, through no fault of his own, prevented him from playing at his best.

In the Code States, this would fall within the statutory definition; but it was held not to be defamatory in New South Wales.[7]

A defamatory statement here includes statements made against relatives, whether living or dead, by which the plaintiff's reputation is damaged.

As with the situation in New South Wales, truth is only a defence where the defamatory statement relates to a matter of public interest.

Again as with the situation in New South Wales, the distinction between libel and slander has been abolished.

Australian Capital Territory and Northern Territory

In the Australian Capital Territory, the common law has been modified by the Defamation Act 1901 (NSW) and by the Defamation (Amendment) Act 1909 NSW, with the result that, while the common law continues to apply, it has been modified as follows:

- the distinction between libel and slander has been abolished;
- truth is only a defence where the defamatory statement relates to a matter of public interest;
- fair and accurate reporting of a wide range of proceedings and a number of official publications is protected.

In the Northern Territory the common law has also been modified by statute, in this case by the Defamation Act 1980. As with the situation in the Australian Capital Territory and various other jurisdictions, the distinction between libel and slander has been abolished and protection is afforded to the fair and accurate reporting of its proceedings of various public bodies and of certain specified individuals.

Conclusion

While there are significant differences between the States and Territories as to what is defamatory and how it is treated, there nevertheless is substantial similarity as to what is defamatory, as Deane J. recently noted:

> The law of defamation in most jurisdictions is 'mosaic of statute and common law'. The variations between the six different states are considerable. Subject to one presently unimportant qualification, the broad central proposition of the defamation law is, however, the same in all jurisdictions. It is that a person who publishes an assertion of fact or a comment which injures (or is 'likely' to injure) the reputation of another is guilty of a tort and liable in damages unless he or she can positively justify or excuse the publication in the particular circumstances of the case.[8]

The 'unimportant qualification' referred to by His Honour was the continuation of the common law distinction between libel and slander and the need to prove material injury in an action for slander in some jurisdictions.[9]

The plaintiff's task

Who may sue?

The rules as to those who may sue for defamation are exactly the same as under English law. However, in contrast with the position in England, while the dead or their personal representatives cannot sue for defamation, relatives may be able to do so if the defamatory statement about the dead person reflects upon them as well as upon the deceased. Of course, the relatives may sue in their own right if they are defamed directly.

Who may be sued?

Essentially anyone taking part in the publication of the defamatory statement. As under English law, each person who takes part in the publication of the defamatory statement is jointly and severally liable for its publication and can be sued.

What the plaintiff must prove

In order to succeed in a defamation action the plaintiff must establish:

- that the statement was defamatory;
- that the statement referred to the plaintiff;
- that the statement has been published by the defendant to a third party.

Each of these elements of a defamation action is considered below.

Obviously the plaintiff should obtain a copy of the defamatory matter to assist his or her case. With books, newspapers, magazines and other printed matter, there is little difficulty. However, television and radio broadcasts are more difficult, and the plaintiff may only have heard about the publication and the gist of the defamation from a third party. The Broadcasting Services Act 1992 (Cth) provides that any television or broadcasting licensee which broadcasts material relating to political matters, current affairs and so forth must keep a recording for six weeks from the date of the broadcast (or sixty days from that date if a complaint has been made about the publication). The Act does not provide access to the material, however. In New South Wales, at least, the plaintiff can commence proceedings by pleading the imputations as well as he or she can at the time, and then seek discovery of the material.

In a defamation action, the judge must determine whether the statement alleged to be defamatory was in fact capable of conveying a defamatory meaning. If there are two possible meanings, one innocent and one defamatory, then the judge must leave it up to the jury to decide which meaning to accept. Those statements which are not capable of a defamatory meaning are not submitted to a jury.[10]

What is a defamatory statement?

The tests of what is defamatory reflect almost exactly the English legal position. Accordingly, whether or not the statement in question is defamatory is a question of fact and, in determining whether a statement is defamatory, a court has to determine:

- whether the ordinary reasonable reader would, in fact, have understood the matter complained of as conveying those imputations (that is, the meaning of the words);
- whether the reader would, in fact, have understood such imputations as being such as to cause ordinary decent folk in the community, taken in general, to think less of the plaintiff (that is, the defamatory character of the imputation).

Whether a statement is defamatory depends on the view the ordinary person takes on the meaning of the language and on the standards, moral or social, by which the person judges the imputation. The standards are those common to society generally.[11]

In this regard, it needs to be noted that innocent words may be defamatory and that a statement may be defamatory by reason of its publication to a person with special knowledge of the individual about whom the statement is made or about other extrinsic facts. This is defamation by 'true innuendo'.

> To say that a named person is the owner of a restaurant and has been declared bankrupt is defamatory of the true owner. The named person was the manager, not the owner, of the restaurant.[12]

> A newspaper cartoon which imputed that a secretary to a Minister in the Australian Government had an adulterous affair with the Minister was determined to be defamatory.[13]

> A well-known professional rugby league football player sued a newspaper over an article which asserted that he was 'fat, slow and predictable'. The imputation that the player was fat and slow was held not to be defamatory. The imputation that the player was unfit and therefore playing poorly was capable of being defamatory. The article also conveyed a ridiculous impression of the player which was capable of being defamatory. It displayed the footballer in a 'ridiculous light'.[14]

A photograph of a well-known professional footballer taken in the showers while the team was on tour was held to be defamatory, on the basis that the photograph made him look ridiculous and that his reputation was tarnished because the public may have thought that the footballer had deliberately posed for the photograph.[15]

The following have been considered not to be defamatory:

- the assertion that a horse stud farm was forced to close because of a virus;[16]
- saying that an airline company is exposed to a special risk of hijacking through no fault of its own.[17] This was not defamatory at common law, but was held to be defamatory under a New South Wales statute at the time.

In these cases, there was no imputation which was disparaging of the plaintiff's reputation, and no allegation of carelessness or incompetence of the plaintiffs that led to the closure or risk, respectively.

Sometimes an article or a programme taken as a whole may contain a complete refutation of a defamatory allegation contained in it. The 'bane' of the defamation may be entirely removed by the 'antidote' in the rest of the article. But a simple denial or command to disregard the defamation may not be enough to remove the bane. The court is entitled to see or hear the whole article or programme and weigh up the derogatory allegations against the rest of the programme.

A radio commentator broadcast a commentary on a television interview given by the plaintiff. In his commentary, he described her as 'an immoral adventurer ... who has slept with a variety of notable politicians', and followed that with 'In fact, of course nobody knows any such thing. There is indeed not even the faintest suggestion that she has ever had any such relationship...'. The court found that the effect of the defamatory statement was not overcome by the rest of the programme, and characterized the commentator's approach as 'with friends like this, who needs enemies?'[18]

The test is what the ordinary reasonable person would view as the meaning of the words. Caricatures and cartoons may not be protected if they tend to cast the subject in a 'ridiculous light' and are regarded by the community as having gone beyond a joke. On the other hand, publications which are hyperbolic or 'over the top' may not be seen by the community as anything other than a joke and not taken seriously. The constitutional freedom now available for 'political discussion' (discussed below) would now operate to protect cartoons, caricatures or satirical pieces on political matters.

Identification

In order to succeed in a defamation action, the plaintiff must not only establish that the statement was defamatory but also that the statement was made about him or her. That is, the plaintiff must establish that he or she is the object of the defamatory statement – that the defamatory statement concerned the plaintiff. The standard here is not subjective, that is, whether the defendant intended to identify the plaintiff, but, rather, whether a recipient of the statement would reasonably identify the plaintiff as being the person to whom the statement referred.

If the statement in question is clearly defamatory and identifies the plaintiff in a way that anyone would know to whom the statement referred, then it is not necessary to establish that the persons to whom the statement was published had any special knowledge of the plaintiff.

If, on the other hand, the statement is not clearly defamatory or if it does not clearly identify the plaintiff, it is necessary to establish that the statement was published to persons who, having special knowledge of the plaintiff, would comprehend the statement as being defamatory of the plaintiff. The idea that if a person is not named, they are not defamed, is a fallacy.

> A newspaper report which stated that a contingent of NSW police raped women in Darwin was held not to be defamatory of an unnamed police officer who was part of the contingent. A jury could not hold that the report was published of and concerning the individual police officer. [19]

> In relation to an article on a police investigation into allegations of the theft of wheat from storage bins in west New South Wales it was held that it was open for the jury to identify the plaintiff with the article on proof that readers would know that the plaintiff had contracts at storage sites in New South Wales and was the only contractor able to move quantities of wheat such as that stolen. [20]

The relevant threshold for the plaintiff is whether the plaintiff proves enough facts to establish that the ordinary reasonable reader in possession of those facts would reasonably identify the plaintiff. [21]

Publication

In addition to establishing that the statement was defamatory and that it concerned him or her, the plaintiff must show that the defamatory statement was 'published'.

Publication in this context does not require the statement to be made to the public at large. Communication of the defamatory statement to one person (but not if the only person is the plaintiff) will suffice.

> A defamatory statement concerning a company made only to a servant or agent of that company constitutes publication of the statement. [22]

'Publication' of a defamatory statement means the communication, whether orally or in writing or electronically (e.g. by computer, radio or television broadcast), to a third party capable of understanding the material. 'Publication' of a defamatory statement is not a technical or limited term, and may occur by any means by which people communicate with one another. Signs, posters and effigies can all amount to publication. Each repetition of the defamatory statement is a separate 'publication'.

> A television programme entitled 'This Day Tonight' contained an interview between a member of the staff of the Australian Broadcasting Corporation (ABC) and a political correspondent for the newspapers, the *Financial Review* and the *Sun-Herald*. During the interview an allegedly defamatory statement concerning the then Prime Minister was made. It was held that the broadcasting of the programme throughout Australia resulted in it being published in each place in which the programme was seen.[23]

Republication occurs when a person repeats another person's defamatory statement. Repetition of such a defamatory statement is itself a new and separate defamation; the republisher does not have to adopt or reaffirm the statement. Of course, some republications, such as parliamentary or law reporting, are protected in the interests of a free flow of information in society. Similarly, publishing a rumour can be defamatory:

> The captain of Australia's Davis Cup team successfully sued a newspaper for reporting 'There is no truth in the rumour' that the captain's amateur status was to be investigated. The report that there was a rumour amounted to the repetition of the allegation contained in the rumour itself.[24]

Prefacing a defamatory statement with phrases like 'It is rumoured that' or 'I have been told that' is no safeguard from defamation, because the defendant can be found to have passed on a rumour and, by doing so, given it credence.

Publication on the information superhighway

The publication of defamatory statements on computer networks such as the Internet raises the question of whether the person who posts the statement on a computer is liable for publication of that statement on other computers.[25] If that person authorized the republication of the statement or intended the statement to be so republished or such republication was the natural consequence, then that person may be liable.[26] This, however, may depend upon the location in which republication occurs and the defamation laws applicable to that location. For example, a statement published on a computer network in Australia may amount to the publication of a defamatory statement but the republication of that statement in another country via the computer network may or may not amount to be publication of a defamatory statement in that country.

Republication of defamatory statements on computer networks also give rise to the question of whether a person will be liable for republication if his or her computer is used in the republication. It is likely that in these circumstances the person would be able to take advantage of the defence of innocent dissemination.

The defendant's task

Once the plaintiff has established that the statement in question was defamatory, that it concerned the plaintiff and that it had been published, the burden of proof shifts and the onus is then upon the defendant to establish one or more of the available defences if liability is to be avoided.

Constitutional protection

Until 12 October 1994, there had not been articulated any constitutional protection for freedom of communication. But the High Court, in *Theophanous* v *The Herald & Weekly Times Limited* held that there is implied in the Australian Constitution a freedom of communication[27] in relation to 'political discussion'. The High Court has distilled from the provisions and structure of the Australian Constitution a freedom of communication, although not of expression generally. The implied constitutional protection is based on the fact that the system of representative government depends on a free flow of information and ideas, and that freedom extends to everyone participating in the political debate.

The limit on the constitutional freedom is difficult to define, given the inter-relationship of commonwealth and state powers, and the need for a flow of political ideas across those relationships. However, in *Theophanous*, the relevant publication concerned the performance and the fitness to hold office of a member of Federal Parliament. That is clearly 'political discussion'. The High Court held that 'political discussion' includes discussion of the conduct, policies or fitness for office of government, political parties, public bodies, public officers and those seeking public office. 'Political discussion' would also include the discussion of the political views and public conduct of those involved in activities which are the subject of political debate, such as trade union leaders, political or economic commentators.

The overriding limit on this implied constitutional freedom is the 'efficacious working of representative democracy and government'.[28]

This implication of freedom of communication does have an impact on the existing laws of defamation. It protects political discussion from exposure to liability for defamation. A publication will not be actionable under a law relating to defamation if:

- the publisher was unaware of the falsity of the material published;
- it did not publish the material recklessly, that is, not caring whether the material was true or false;
- the publication was reasonable in the circumstances.

If those requirements are met, then the publication may be said to have been made in circumstances of qualified privilege.

Whether the publisher acted 'reasonably' means that the publisher must show that, in the circumstances, it took some steps to check the accuracy of the defamatory material or establish that it was otherwise justified in publishing without taking those steps. The onus of proof is on the defendant. The publisher must establish that the publication falls within the constitutional protection.

This implication of freedom of communication in relation to political discussion outlined above does override state and territory laws in relation to defamation. The implications are that newspaper publishers in particular will be able to rely on a constitutional protection to publish articles and letters relating to political discussion with some impunity. It means that the publisher will not have to prove that the publication was true, if the publisher can rely on this defence.

It will not then be necessary to rely on the common law or on separate defences in each state and territory where the paper was published, such as qualified privilege, truth or fair comment. Of course, those defences will continue to be relied upon where the matter complained of does not fall within the test set out by the High Court for 'political discussion', or where the publisher cannot establish that the publication falls within the constitutional freedom.

Common law

At common law the three main defences are:

- truth
- fair comment
- privilege.

However, as noted earlier above, not all of these defences will be available in each of the states and territories of Australia. For example, in those states and territories where the common law has been modified or replaced by statute, truth of itself may not be a defence. Rather, it may be necessary to show that the statement complained of was true and related to a matter of public interest. This is discussed below.

Truth

Complete defence

At common law truth is a complete defence. The reason for this is that, at common law, an actionable defamation consists of a 'false' statement impairing another's reputation with the law presuming, until the contrary is proven, that the statement in question is false. In most significant respects, the requirements of the defence – and the standard of proof – are identical to those under English law. The one exception is 'contextual imputation' under New South Wales and, to a lesser degree, Tasmanian law.

The defendant may wish to assert that there is a separate and additional defamatory meaning in the matter complained of to the particular defamatory meaning alleged by the plaintiff. The defendant may seek to justify this separate meaning, the effect of which is so serious that there can be no further injury to the plaintiff's reputation caused by the other meaning alleged by the plaintiff. In New South Wales and Tasmania, this is a form of the defence of truth or justification, called contextual imputation.

The gist of the accusations must be true, but erroneous details which may aggravate the 'sting' can be ignored. For example, if the allegation was that the plaintiff was sentenced to three weeks' imprisonment, it may be justified by proving that the plaintiff was actually sentenced to only two weeks.[29]

Standard of proof

The standard of proof imposed upon a defendant to establish that the statement was true is the usual civil standard – on the balance of probabilities.

However, if the statement complained of imputes that the plaintiff committed a criminal offence, the defendant must then establish beyond reasonable doubt the commission of the offence by the plaintiff in order to succeed on a defence of the truth. At common law, a conviction for the crime is not admissible as evidence, because it is simply an opinion of guilt. Some states have made certain convictions conclusive: for example, in New South Wales conviction by a state or territory or Commonwealth court is conclusive proof of the commission of the offence;[30] but not if the conviction has been set aside.

Queensland, South Australia and the Australian Capital Territory have similar provisions.

Fair comment

In common with many other legal systems, the law in various Australian jurisdictions protects 'fair comment' on issues of public interest. That is, 'fair comment' is a defence to a claim of defamation.

In order for this defence to be made out, the comment must be:

- recognizable as comment;
- based on provable facts;
- on a matter of public interest;
- one that a fair-minded person could honestly make;
- made without 'malice'.

Recognizable as comment

The availability of this defence depends, in part, on it being clear from the context and the circumstances in which the defamatory statement was made that it constituted a statement of opinion or comment and not a statement of fact.

As noted earlier, a defamatory statement which is a statement of fact must be shown to be true in all material respects in order to make out the defence of truth. No claim of 'fair comment' applies, or could apply, to a statement of fact which is untrue.

It is therefore important to distinguish between those statements which are statements of fact and those which are statements of opinion or comment, since it is only the latter for which the defence of 'fair comment' is available.

The defendant published an article giving an abridged report of the address of the plaintiff's counsel to the jury which contained statements defamatory of the plaintiff (namely, that the plaintiff was an oppressive landlord who charged excessive rents but who failed to keep the rented premises in good order). The plaintiff sued for the libel in the article. The court held that the publication was not comment but purported to be statements of fact.[31]

A well-known Sydney food critic wrote a review of a restaurant which was published in a high-circulation Sydney daily newspaper. In his review, the critic described the lobster he ordered as overcooked, the flesh 'dry and tough' and as a 'charred husk of a shell containing meat that might have been albino walrus'.

The court found that this was not fair comment, and that several assertions made about the cooking and the price were untrue. The comments were defamatory and were not based on proper material for comment.[32]

Based on provable facts

In order to succeed in making out this defence, the facts upon which the comment or opinion is based must be proven and, further, the truth or accuracy of those facts must be established. A comment cannot be fair if it is based upon facts which are untrue.[33]

On a matter of public interest

In order to qualify for the defence of 'fair comment', the comment must be on a matter of 'public interest'. As to what are matters of 'public interest', these include:

- national, state and local governmental affairs; and
- matters submitted to public attention, e.g. works of authors, theatrical performances, restaurants and their reviews, and so on.

However, in order for the defence to be available, the comment must be in relation to the subject matter of public interest and not some extraneous matter.

- A politician's private life is not a matter of public interest merely because the politician is a public figure. A statement that a politician was a 'wife beater' was defamatory.[34]
- A famous cricketer's private life about which allegations of adultery and unusual sexual practices were made was not a matter of public interest, unless it either affected his ability to perform his public duties, or he made it a public matter himself.[35]

Fairness

The comment must be one that a fair-minded person could make based on the facts proved. Provided that the comment is a view honestly held, that is, it was not made with malice (see below), and is one which a fair-minded person could make based on the proven facts, it will qualify as fair comment. It need not be reasonable: indeed, it can be exaggerated, robust or prejudiced as long as the defendant genuinely and honestly believed in the truth of the statement.[36]

Malice

A defence of 'fair comment' can be defeated by the plaintiff establishing that the defendant's comment was motivated by 'malice'. To establish 'malice' the plaintiff must show that the purpose of the defendant in making the comment was not to express a view honestly held but, rather, it was to injure the plaintiff.[37]

In attempting to establish 'malice', it is not enough for the plaintiff merely to show that the defendant held some grudge against him or her. A person may hold a grudge against another but yet still be able to express a view honestly held about that person. To establish malice, the plaintiff must go further and show that the comment was motivated by some other purpose than the mere expression of opinion honestly held.

Privilege

Absolute privilege

The occasions where absolute privilege is granted are rare. This is because it effectively precludes a person whose reputation is impugned from any legal redress. The protection is accorded no matter what the publisher intended; it can be malicious, irresponsible and vindictive, but all this is outweighed by the public policy that some publications must be without fear of later legal action. Accordingly, it has only been granted in situations necessary for the proper functioning of all facets of government, that is, the legislature, the executive, and judicial proceedings.[38] A limitation on the defence is the purpose for which the relevant defamatory statement was made and the fact that the defence is available only for a distinct category of publications.[39] Most jurisdictions have set out what types of public bodies and in what circumstances publications made by or to those bodies may be subject to the defence. Also, the defence is available only to the original publisher, not to subsequent publishers (although they may have a defence of qualified privilege).

Parliamentary proceedings

Absolute privilege attaches to oral and written statements made by members of federal and state parliament when made in the course of proceedings of either the House of Representatives or the Senate. In addition, this immunity has been extended by statute to include the broadcasting of parliamentary proceedings and the publication of reports, papers, speeches and the like where such publication is done with appropriate parliamentary authority.

However, republication of members' speeches, even by the members themselves, outside parliament, does not attract absolute privilege, although it may attract qualified privilege (see below).

The executive

Absolute privilege also attaches to internal communications between ministers, between ministers and the Crown and between certain other high officers of state. It does not, however, attach to all communications between public officials and those performing statutory functions.[40]

Judicial proceedings

Absolute privilege also attaches to statements made in judicial or quasi-judicial proceedings (such as tribunals carrying out judicial rather than administrative functions), whether made by a judge, a juror, a witness, a barrister, a solicitor or a party to the proceedings. The privilege attaches not only to statements made during the course of judicial proceedings but also to those made in steps preceding, but in anticipation of, judicial proceedings. Reports of foreign legal proceedings do not qualify for this blanket protection; the only possible claim to privilege is that a particular matter on foot overseas is of very substantial concern to the Australian public.[41]

Qualified privilege

The main categories of qualified privilege are:

- statements made in performance of a duty;
- statements made in furtherance of an interest, public or private;
- statements in protection of a common interest.

Statements made in performance of a duty

Qualified privilege attaches to statements made by a person where the person is under a legal or moral obligation to make the statement and the person to whom it is made has a reciprocal interest in receiving it. An example might be a teacher making a report to a superior about a student or other teacher which contains defamatory statements about the subject of the report.

> A newspaper published a series of statements and cartoons concerning the relationship of a parliamentary minister and his private secretary. The court held that the paper did not have a duty to publish some of the articles or cartoons.[42]

In New South Wales a further defence of qualified privilege provides that the conduct of the publisher in publishing the matter must be reasonable in the circumstances.[43] Either defence may be pleaded.

Statements made in furtherance of an interest

Qualified privilege also attaches to statements made in response to an attack – that is, the subject of a defamatory attack has a right of reply to defend him or herself and will be protected by qualified privilege in so doing.

> A police officer, in reply to serious criticism in relation to his conduct, gave a report containing allegations defamatory of the plaintiff to his immediate superior. The officer was protected by the defence.[44]

The means of reply should reflect the means of attack. If an attack is addressed to the public at large, then the answer can be published in a manner that would reach the public generally.[45]

In order to qualify for qualified privilege, however, the reply must be reasonable and must be in proportion to the original attack. However, a riposte made in reply to a retort to the original attack is not protected by this defence.[46]

Common interest

Qualified privilege attaches to statements where the defendant and the third party possess a common interest in the subject matter of the communication. The 'interest' need not be in the fact which was itself communicated, but simply in the subject matter to which the communication is relevant.[47]

> A Yugoslav club in Australia published an article in a newspaper written in Croatian and distributed to several thousand members of the Yugoslav community which was defamatory of another, smaller Yugoslav club and its president in respect of their political stand over guerrilla tactics during the Second World War. The court held that the two groups did not have a common interest in communicating the argument in New South Wales. The 'interest' need only be a general one, so long as the 'common convenience and welfare of society' dictates that the interest be protected.[48]

Abuse of qualified privilege

Qualified privilege is defeated by proof of 'malice' on the part of the defendant. In this context 'malice' is used to mean not only the situation where the defendant makes the statement for the purposes of injuring the plaintiff and did not have an honest belief in the truth of the statement, but also the situation where the defendant makes the statement for a purpose other than that for which the privilege was granted.

> A television current affairs programme asserted that a person was involved in the murder of a well-known anti-drugs campaigner. The plaintiff (who was not the alleged murderer) was filmed speaking to a reporter and saying 'Yes, I Dominic', which was in fact the first name of the person allegedly involved in the murder. Further film showed the plaintiff violently attacking the camera. The

court found that the defendant was not actuated by malice. The depiction of the plaintiff's violence was directly relevant to the occasion of qualified privilege (the remainder of the television piece).[49]

Protected reports

There is a defence at common law for publication of defamatory material in certain categories of reports. This is a defence of qualified privilege which automatically attaches to specified categories of reports. In Queensland, Tasmania and Western Australia, the categories are specified in the relevant statute. In New South Wales, Victoria, the Australian Capital Territory and the Northern Territory, the common law defence can apply if the statutory provisions do not. As a defence of qualified privilege, the report must be made in good faith (or without malice) for the information of the public, and be fair and accurate. The protection does not extend to publications which amount to a contempt of court.

The common law protects reports of judicial proceedings in open court, and the report must be substantially accurate concerning the proceedings.[50] So a report containing factually untrue statements which were made during the proceedings, but which were fairly reported, would be protected.[51]

The onus of proof that the report is fair and accurate is on the defendant.

Reports of parliamentary proceedings are similarly protected by the common law, and reports of the proceedings of federal parliament are now protected by the Parliamentary Privileges Act 1987 (Commonwealth), which gives absolute privilege to fair and accurate reports of proceedings of meetings of parliament and their committees.

As with court reporting, the report does not have to be verbatim, but the common law requires that the report be fair and accurate. So a 'parliamentary sketch' will be privileged if it is made fairly, with the intention of giving an impression of the impact made on the hearers.[52]

New South Wales

The Defamation Act 1974 (NSW) provides a defence for a 'fair protected report'. The Act lists specified proceedings which are protected, and second-hand reports based on the original protected report, or even on an earlier report which wrongly passed itself off as protected. The publication must be in good faith for public information or the advancement of education.

The proceedings include parliamentary proceedings, judicial or quasi-judicial proceedings, public proceedings of an international organization and proceedings of certain statutory bodies. In addition, the Act provides for a defence for the publication of certain public documents and records and abstracts or summaries of these. Again, the publication must be in good faith and for public information or the advancement of education. Many of the protected public documents and records overlap with reports of the specified proceedings.

Victoria

There is a statutory protection for a fair and accurate report of judicial proceedings in open court, unless the report was made with malice. There is a similar protection for reports of parliamentary proceedings and proceedings of public inquiries. The statutory protection for reports of proceedings of municipal councils has further qualifications, including that the report must be published without malice; it must be published bona fide; it must contain no blasphemous or indecent matter; it must be a matter of public concern; it must be and published for the public benefit. In addition, if the publisher was requested to insert in the publication a 'reasonable letter or statement by way of contradiction or explanation', and refused to do so, then the defence will fail.

However, in Victoria, the common law protection may be relied upon if the publication does not fall within the statutory protection.

South Australia and the Northern Territory

Fair and accurate reports of judicial proceedings are protected, provided the report is published contemporaneously with the proceedings. There is also statutory protection for fair and accurate reports of public meetings, parliamentary proceedings, councils and other statutory bodies, royal commissions, and so on. However, the publications which are protected must take place by newspaper, radio or television; they must not be made maliciously; they must not be blasphemous or indecent; they must be of public concern, and they must be for the public benefit. Again, as in Victoria, the defence is not available if the publisher has refused to publish a reasonable letter or statement by way of contradiction or explanation of the report.

Tasmania, Queensland and Western Australia

Reports of various proceedings are protected provided they are fair, and published in good faith for the information of the public. In Tasmania and Queensland the common law protection is excluded, but in Western Australia the common law is still available if the statutory provisions are not. Again, reports of proceedings which are protected include parliamentary proceedings, court proceedings in open court (unless publication is prohibited by the court or the matter is blasphemous or obscene), various statutory inquiries, and public meetings.

Australian Capital Territory

Reports of proceedings will be protected if they are fair and accurate, made in good faith for the information of the public and are not blasphemous, seditious or obscene. The protection does not extend to reports in the electronic media and is limited to newspaper reports only.

Other defences

Innocent dissemination

Those who are not authors, publishers or printers of defamatory works can use the defence of innocent dissemination. They must have no reason to suspect that the publication contains libellous material; and the ignorance of the libel must not be due to negligence.

> A television station published a programme which was defamatory of the plaintiff. The station was held to have been an innocent disseminator because it was fed the programme under licence by a station in a different city. The defendant was not entitled to change the content, and it was expected to be broadcast unaltered.[53] However, on appeal, it was found that the defence of innocent dissemination was not made out.[54]

Settlement

An agreement to settle a case for an apology or damages will extinguish the claim.

Consent

A plaintiff who consents to the publication of a defamatory statement cannot sue for defamation.[55]

Offer of amends

This is a statutory defence in New South Wales. The Defamation Act 1974 sets out the requirements: the defendant must not have intended the statement to be defamatory; must have exercised reasonable care in relation to its publication; did not know of any circumstances by which the statements may have been defamatory; must have made an offer of amends including an offer to publish a correction and apology; and must give a statutory declaration with particulars of any correction or apology or steps taken before the offer of amends. The defendant must have included an offer to take reasonable steps to notify recipients of the publication that the publication may be defamatory. Tasmania has a similar provision for making an offer of amends.

Where the offer is accepted, the plaintiff may not commence or continue any proceedings against the defendant for damages. In these circumstances, the court may order the payment of the plaintiff's costs arising out of the acceptance of the offer and any expenses the plaintiff may have incurred as a result of the publication of the defamatory statement.

Limitation

The usual rule is that a publication occurring more than six years earlier cannot be the subject of an action for libel or slander. The period may occasionally be extended if, for example, the plaintiff had been unaware of the publication.

Remedies

The legal remedies available in respect of defamation are:

- damages
- injunctive relief

Damages

In all jurisdictions in Australia, compensatory damages may be awarded to a successful plaintiff. Damages are the indicator of the nature and extent of vindication for the plaintiff. In addition, in each jurisdiction other than New South Wales exemplary damages may be awarded. In New South Wales, exemplary damages have been abolished.

Compensatory damages are awarded to compensate a plaintiff for the harm suffered from the defamatory statement. Such harm includes injury to reputation, injury to feelings and health, and special or actual damage (e.g. financial losses, loss of business or trade and the like). Exemplary damages may be awarded to punish the defendant in circumstances where the defendant has been particularly outrageous in making the defamatory statement:

> ... a jury may inflict what are called exemplary, punitive or vindictive damages upon a defendant, having in view the enormity of his offence rather than the

measure of compensation to the plaintiff.... In many civil actions, such as libel, slander, reduction, etc., the wrong done to the plaintiff is incapable of being measured by a money standard; and the damages assessed depend upon the circumstances showing the moral turpitude or atrocity of the defendant's conduct, and may properly be termed exemplary or vindictive rather than compensatory.[56]

The amount of damages payable by the defendant may be mitigated by evidence of the conduct of the parties, whether the defendant offered an apology, or by proof of the bad reputation of the plaintiff.[57]

If the defendant fails to apologize, particularly when requested to do so by the plaintiff, the plaintiff may be entitled to aggravated damages. So, too, may the terms and timing of the apology itself aggravate damages. A poorly placed apology (say, on page 28 of a paper), when the original defamatory material was under a four-inch headline on the front page, will not be adequate.

The highest ever award of damages in Australia was Aus$600 000 (US$450 000) in aggregate, for two actions. The High Court, however, considered the award excessive, and considered that a useful comparison for juries to make while considering the award of damages is the maximum compensation allowable for personal injuries cases.[58]

In New South Wales, the highest award was Aus$350 000 (US$260 000)[59], but the Court of Appeal ordered a new trial on the issue of damages, considering that the jury went 'over the top'. In fact, on 1 February 1995, a second Supreme Court jury at a retrial on damages awarded the plaintiff reduced damages in the amount of Aus$100 000 (US$75 000). It is unlikely, after *Carson*, that a jury will award over Aus$200 000 (US$150 000).

Injunctive relief

Damages may not provide adequate compensation to the injury suffered by a plaintiff from a defamatory statement. In these situations the defendant may prefer to avoid the injury by preventing the publication of the defamatory statement by means of an injunction.

An injunction is obviously most effective if obtained before the defamatory statement is published. However, obtaining an injunction can be difficult, given the balance of the plaintiff's rights to his or her reputation and the defendant's right to freedom of speech. The plaintiff must establish that a subsequent finding by a jury that the published statement was not defamatory would be set aside as unreasonable, and there must be no real ground for supposing that the defendant may succeed on the defence of justification, privilege or comment, and that the plaintiff is likely to recover more than nominal damages. An injunction will not go which will have the effect of restraining discussion in the press of matters of public interest or concern.[60]

A well known Australian cricketer obtained an interlocutory injunction to prevent a television station from broadcasting a programme which asserted that the cricketer had committed adultery or that he had engaged in unusual sexual activities. The judge could not hold that a jury's verdict that the programme was not defamatory would be set aside as unreasonable. However, the private activity of a public figure was found to be a matter of public interest only if that activity had some bearing upon the cricketer's capacity to perform his public activities, or because he made it a public matter himself. The judge granted an injunction, since the potential damage to the cricketer was far greater than any damage the defendant might sustain by not publishing the programme.[61]

Injurious falsehood

The plaintiff may prefer to bring an action for injurious falsehood rather than defamation. The elements of this action are:

- the defendant must publish a false statement to a third person;
- concerning the plaintiff or the plaintiff's goods;
- maliciously;
- the plaintiff must suffer actual financial damage.

Criminal defamation

Common law jurisdiction

Criminal defamation is a common law misdemeanour. Most Australian jurisdictions have also created statutory versions of criminal defamation. The common law criminal defamation is distinguished from the civil action in several ways:

- the offence is limited to libel; that is, defamatory publications in permanent form;
- criminal defamation may be committed even if the libel is published only to the person defamed;
- it is possible to libel the dead; that is, publications which are made with the intention of causing injury to living members of the family of the dead person can be criminal defamation.

At common law, truth is no defence to criminal defamation. However, all Australian jurisdictions have statutorily amended the offence to permit a plea of truth as defence. It is only a complete defence in the Northern Territory. In every other jurisdiction, the publication must be for the public benefit, except in New South Wales, where the defamatory imputation must be true and can relate either to a matter of public interest or be published under qualified privilege.

Although the defamation need not tend to cause a breach of the peace, it must be a serious and not a trivial libel. There are also categories of obscene and blasphemous libel.

New South Wales and South Australia

In New South Wales, the Defamation Act 1974 has abolished the common law misdemeanour. Criminal defamation is defamation with intent to cause serious harm to any person or the publication of defamatory matter where it is probable that the publication will cause serious harm.

An oral defamatory communication can amount to criminal defamation.

Victoria

Here, truth is a defence to criminal libel, provided its publication was for the public benefit.

Queensland, Western Australia and Tasmania

In these jurisdictions, the spoken word can be a criminal libel. Unlike New South Wales and common law jurisdictions, a criminal libel in these Code States requires publication to a person other than the person defamed.

Australian Capital Territory and Northern Territory

In the Australian Capital Territory, statutory modifications have brought the offence of criminal libel into line with the Victorian law.

In the Northern Territory, the Code introduces the element of intention. There must be an intention to cause a breach of the peace, to cause loss, to interfere with free exercise of a political right, to prevent a person from performing any duty imposed by law or to do other lawful things.

In each of these jurisdictions, the offence is punishable by imprisonment or a fine.

Journalistic privilege

'Journalistic privilege' is the special status of the media in relation to disclosure of confidential sources in legal proceedings. This is also known as the 'newspaper rule'. The general rule is that, during the process of discovery in a defamation action, a media defendant will not be required to disclose its sources. However, the rule has never extended to the trial itself. During the trial, if disclosure of confidential sources is necessary and relevant to an issue at trial, then the defendant must disclose its sources.

Obviously, media defendants assert the 'newspaper rule' in the interests of a free press and the rights of free speech. The journalist's code of ethics makes no exception for disclosing his or her sources of information even in the course of a trial, but the courts do not take this into account: 'It is a fundamental principle of our law, . . . that the media and journalists have no public interest immunity from being required to disclose their sources of information when such disclosure is necessary in the interests of justice'.[62]

Journalists face the prospect of jail for contempt if they follow this code of conduct. They now tend to see this prospect as a necessary evil in order to protect their sources.

> The plaintiff complained of an article published in a daily newspaper which included the following statement:
>
> 'One of the leading local US banks maintains that of Philippines' $26 billion foreign debt, the President and close 'cronies' like Coconut King Eduardo Cojuangco and Sugar Baron Roberto Bendicto, not to mention the First Lady, have totally squandered $9 billion of it'.
>
> The plaintiff sought an order that the writer attend court and be examined on any matter relating to the identity or the description of the source of the information to enable him to commence proceedings against the source of the information. The defamatory imputations were attributed to 'a senior American bank official and prominent local businessman'. The thrust of the publication was that the imputations had a solid basis of support in the views of prominent business people. The High Court held that, by identifying their sources in this general way, the newspaper gave the imputations an 'aura of authority and authenticity' which would otherwise have been lacking if the imputations had simply rested on the newspaper's and the journalist's assertions. The attribution of the imputations to apparently authoritative sources is more damaging than any imputation without any reference to sources.[63]

The key issue in relation to the newspaper rule is whether the interests of justice are served by compelling the media defendant to reveal its sources before trial. If the defendant is likely to succeed on a defence of, say, qualified or statutory qualified privilege, the court is more likely to order disclosure.

Statutory qualified privilege in New South Wales will require disclosure of sources in any case to determine whether or not the defendant's conduct is reasonable in publishing the defamatory statement in all circumstances. If the defendant is likely to succeed, then the plaintiff will be left with no effective remedy against the newspaper or the journalist. In those cases, the court can exercise its discretion to allow preliminary discovery so that the plaintiff may have an action against the sources.

Costs

Normally, costs 'follow the event', so the unsuccessful party will usually have to bear the costs of the successful party as well as their own. However, the courts have a wide discretion in relation to costs, and these may be awarded on an indemnity basis where the unsuccessful party has prolonged a case with hopeless defences or with deliberately false allegations.[64]

Restraint of an alleged contempt of court

The man accused of the 'backpacker murders' argued that the publication of his photograph in a high-circulation weekly magazine would prejudice criminal proceedings already on foot. He argued that the publication would have the tendency to poison the minds of potential jurors, so that they would be prejudiced in considering the evidence of the criminal trial. In September 1994, the publisher was found in contempt.

The test is whether there is a real risk of serious prejudice to a fair trial in those proceedings. A lapse of nine or ten months between the publication and the trial would not ordinarily operate to prejudice the minds of the jury.

> A television station proposed to publish a television programme concerning allegations of child sexual abuse made against a person who was a plaintiff in a defamation action brought against a magazine for the publication of very similar material. The Attorney General sought a restraining order, preventing the broadcast of the television programme. The restraining order was refused.[65]

The judge found that, once it had been established that the publication had a tendency to interfere with a fair trial, the defendant may ask the court to weigh the competing public interests in maintaining the fairness of that trial and in permitting the discussion of public affairs, which is vital to the working of an open and democratic society. If the fairness of the trial outweighs the need for open discussion, then a contempt has been committed. However, if the tendency to interfere has not first been established, then the competing public interests need not be balanced.

Privacy

The various jurisdictions in Australia do not protect a 'right of privacy'. 'Privacy' as a concept tends to exist as a nebulous adjunct to some other right, such as illegal physical intrusions (trespass), credit reporting or the appropriation of someone's name or personality.

The Privacy Act 1988 (Cth) is a federal law which prescribes standards for the use of, and access to, private information by federal departments and federal statutory bodies. Complaints may be made to a Privacy Commissioner.

In New South Wales, a Privacy and Data Protections Bill was introduced to Parliament in April 1994. It deals with data protection principles, but does not provide enforcement mechanisms.

Notes

1 *Gardiner* v *John Fairfax & Sons Pty Ltd* (1942) 42 SR (NSW) 171 at 172 per Jordan CJ; *Consolidated Trust Co Ltd* v *Browne* (1949) 49 SR (NSW) 86 at 88 per Jordan CJ.
2 *Sim* v *Stretch* (1936) 52 TLR 669 at 671 per Lord Atkin.
3 Tobin, T.K. and Sexton, M.G. *Australian Defamation Law and Practice*, Butterworths, 1441, paragraph 1020.
4 A full description of the similarities and differences is set out in *Australian Defamation Law and Practice*, Butterworths, 1991.
5 *Sungravure Pty Ltd* v *Middle East Airlines Airliban SAL* (1975) 134 CLR 1.
6 *Sungravure Pty Ltd* v *Middle East Airlines Airliban SAL* (1975) 134 CLR 1.
7 *Boyd* v *Mirror Newspapers Ltd* (1980) 2 NSWLR 449. See also Watterson, R., 'What is defamatory today?' *Australian Law Journal*, **67** (11), 811–827.
8 *Theophanous* v *The Herald & Weekly Times Ltd* (1994) 124 ALR 1 at p. 53.
9 Ibid. Note 173.
10 *Jones* v *Skelton* (1963) SR NSW 644.
11 *Reader's Digest Services Pty Ltd* v *Lamb* (1982) 150 CLR 500 at 505.
12 *Mirror Newspapers Ltd* v *World Hosts Pty Ltd* (1979) 141 CLR 632.
13 *Morosi* v *Mirror Newspapers* (1972) 2 NSWLR 749.
14 *Boyd* v *Mirror Newspapers Ltd* (1980) 2 NSWLR 449.
15 *Ettinghausen* v *Australian Consolidated Press Ltd* (1991) 23 NSWLR 443.
16 *Dawson Bloodstock Agency Pty Ltd* v *Mirror Newspapers Ltd* (1979) 1 NSWLR 16.
17 *Sungravure Pty Ltd* v *Middle East Airlines Airliban SAL* (1975) 134 CLR 1.
18 *Morosi* v *2GB* (1980) 2 NSWLR 418.
19 *Jones* v *Mirror Newspapers* (unreported, NSW Supreme Court, Yeldham J, 24 April 1979).
20 *Steele* v *Mirror Newspapers Ltd* (1974) 2 NSWLR 348.

21   *Steele* v *Mirror Newspapers Ltd* (1974) 2 NSWLR 348.

22   *Traztand Pty Ltd* v *G.I.O.* (1984) 2 NSWLR 598.

23   *Gorton* v *ABC* (1974) 2 FLR 181.

24   *Hopman* v *Mirror Newspapers Ltd* (1961) SR NSW 631.

25   Arnold-Moore, T. (1984) 'Legal Pitfalls in Cyberspace: Defamation on Computer Networks'. *Journal of Information Science* **5** (2), p. 165 at p. 179, and see the cases there cited.

26   *Ibid.*

27   *Nationwide News Pty Limited* v *Wills* (1992) 177 CLR 1; *Australian Capital Television Pty Limited* v *The Commonwealth* (1992) 177 CLR 106.

28   *Theophanous* v *The Herald & Weekly Times* (1994) 124 ALR 1.

29   *Alexander* v *N.E. Railway* (1865) 6 B&S 340.

30   Defamation Act 1974 (NSW), section 55.

31   *Myerson* v *Smith's Weekly* (1923) 24 SR (NSW) 20.

32   *Blue Angel Restaurant Pty Ltd* v *John Fairfax & Sons Ltd* (unreported, NSW Supreme Court, 20 April 1989).

33   *Bailey* v *Truth and Sportsman Ltd* (1938) 60 CLR 700.

34   *Mutch* v *Sleeman* (1928) 29 SR (NSW) 125.

35   *Chappell* v *TCN Channel 9 Pty Ltd* (1988) 14 NSWLR 153.

36   *Gardiner* v *Fairfax* (1942) 42 SR (NSW) 171.

37   *Renouf* v *Federal Capital Press of Australia Pty Ltd* (1977) 17 ACTR 35.

38   Fleming J. G. (1992). *The Law of Torts* (8th edn.), The Law Book Co., p. 558.

39   *Rajski* v *Carson* (1988) 15 NSWLR 84.

40   Fleming, *op. cit.*, p. 562.

41   *Thompson* v *Consolidated Press* (1968) 89 N.W. (Pt 1) (NSW) 121.

42   *Morosi* v *Mirror Newspapers Ltd* (1977) 2 NSWLR 749.

43   Defamation Act 1974, section 22; *Morosi* v *Mirror Newspapers Ltd* (1977) 2 NSWLR 749.

44   *Mowlds* v *Fergusson* (1940) 64 CLR 206.

45   *Loveday* v *Sun Newspapers Ltd* (1938) 59 CLR 503.

46   *Kennett* v *Farmer* (1988) VR 991.

47   *Howe* v *Lees* (1910) 11 CLR 361.

48   *Andreyevich* v *Kosovich* (1947) SR(NSW) 357.

49   *Barbaro* v *Amalgamated Television Services Pty Ltd* (1985) 1 NSWLR 30.

50   *Anderson* v *Nationwide News Limited* (1970) 1 NSWLR 317.

51   *Waterhouse* v *Broadcasting Station 2GB Pty Ltd* (1985) 1 NSWLR 58.

52   *Cook* v *Alexander* (1974) 1QB 279.

53   *Thompson* v *Australian Capital Television Pty Ltd* (unreported, ACT Supreme Court, Gallop J, 20 December 1993).

54   *Thompson* v *Australian Capital Television Pty Ltd* (unreported, Federal Court of Australia, Burchett, Miles and Ryan JJ, 19 December 1994).

55   Compare *Ettinghausen* v *Australian Consolidated Press* (1991) 23 NSWLR 443, where the footballer was held not to have consented to the publication a photograph of him naked.

56   *Uren* v *John Fairfax & Sons Ltd* (1986) 117 CLR 118 at pp. 136-7.

57   *Scott* v *Sampson* (1882) 8 QBD 491.

58   *Carson* v *John Fairfax & Sons Limited* (1993) 178 CLR 44.

59   *Eittinghausen* v *Australian Consolidated Press* (1991) 23 NSWLR 443. Other States and Territories have, historically, had much lower awards: the highest ever Victorian award was Aus$150 000.00; in Tasmania, awards hover at Aus$50 000.00–$70 000.00.

60   *Church of Scientology of California Inc* v *Readers Digest Services Pty Limited* (1980) 1 NSWLR 344.

61   *Chappell* v *TCN Channel Nine Pty Limited* (1988) 14 NSWLR 153.

62   *John Fairfax & Sons Limited* v *Cojuangco* (1988) 165 CLR 346.

63   *John Fairfax & Sons Limited* v *Cojuangco* (1988) 165 CLR 346.

64   *Wentworth* v *Rogers* (No 5) (1986) 6 NSWLR 534.

65   *Attorney General (NSW)* v *TCN Channel Nine Pty Limited* (NSW Supreme Court, Hunt J, 6 July 1990, unreported).

3

Canada

Douglas F. Harrison[1] of Stikeman and Elliott (Toronto)

Despite Canada's geographical proximity to the United States, there are significant differences between Canadian and US defamation law. Most notably, Canadian courts have not adopted the constitutional protections afforded to US defendants as a result of the decision of the US Supreme Court in *New York Times* v *Sullivan*.[2] Canadian defamation law is in large part derived from English law and in many respects resembles the law in other Commonwealth jurisdictions.

While defamation law is within the jurisdiction of the Canadian provinces and territories, as opposed to the federal government, there is a large degree of uniformity across the country.[3] The exception to this is the Province of Quebec, which derives its laws from the French Civil Code. This chapter will focus on the law in the common law provinces and territories. A brief overview of the law in Quebec follows at the end of the chapter.

Essentials of defamation in Canada

What is defamatory?

There is no one accepted definition of what constitutes defamation in Canada. Professor Raymond Brown of the University of Windsor (Ontario) has noted that Canadian judges have used a number of different terms to arrive, essentially, at the same result: 'Does the publication tend to lower the reputation of the plaintiff in the estimation of others, whose standard of opinion the Court can properly recognize or who are commonly referred to as right thinking members of society?'[4]. Unlike in Australia, it is not clear that in Canada holding someone up to ridicule, by itself, amounts to defamation.

A sampling of cases since 1950 shows that Canadian judges have held that it is defamatory to say that someone:

- is dishonest, untrustworthy, disreputable, dishonourable, ungrateful or irresponsible;
- has engaged in conduct that is criminal, disreputable or fraudulent or permits immorality to be practised by others;
- lacks integrity, is cruel, sadistic or inhuman, prejudiced, hypocritical, unpopular or has a social disability;
- abused a position of trust, was incompetent, inefficient, unintelligent, unmotivated, incapable;
- is a charlatan, subversive, insane or senile.[5]

What was once considered defamatory may not be so now and vice versa. Courts are aware of current attitudes and language. In 1968, a judge of the Northwest Territories Supreme Court held that it was no longer defamatory to accuse someone of being a witch. It is unlikely that we will see cases again where someone sues because he or she is accused of being a mountebank or illegitimate.

Humour, satire and parody can cross the line and be considered defamatory:

In a 1981 case involving the Premier of British Columbia, the defendant said that his remarks about the Premier's drinking were intended only in jest. The BC Supreme Court ruled, however, that humour neither justified nor excused the publication of a libel. In a case involving another Premier of British Columbia, a cartoon depicted a caricature of him happily pulling the wings off flies. The BC Court held it was defamatory since it suggested that he had 'the cruel and sadistic nature of one who enjoys inflicting suffering on helpless persons'.

You cannot escape liability for defamation by taking the position that the defamatory words you expressed were an opinion, suspicion or belief. You can also be sued in defamation for repeating a defamatory rumour even if you state that you sincerely do not believe it. You cannot escape the consequences of publishing a defamatory statement because someone else is the author of it and you make that fact known at the time you make the statement.

Even if the words themselves do not convey a defamatory meaning, they may be said to express an innuendo such that by virtue of other facts they convey a defamatory meaning. Innuendo is especially troublesome for the media; for publishers by the juxtaposition of headlines and photographs, the placement of the story or the size of the headline; and for broadcasters by the images or the way the words are spoken. A number of judges have commented on how the words of a script when read in isolation may not convey any defamatory sense at all, but, when viewed as a television programme, the effect is very different.

The distinction between libel and slander

Libel is defamatory material in written form or other permanent form that is visible. To obtain an award of damages in an action for libel, once liability is established it is not necessary for the plaintiff to prove that he or she has suffered any monetary loss; damages are presumed.

Slander is a defamatory statement that is spoken or is otherwise transitory. To obtain an award in damages, the plaintiff must prove that he or she has suffered a specific loss, which can be given a monetary value, as a result of the slanderous statement. However, damages will be presumed where the slander has accused the plaintiff of:

- unfitness to perform his or her business or trade;
- committing a serious crime;
- having a contagious or infectious disease;
- in the case of a woman, being unchaste.

The distinction between libel and slander has been all but abolished by statute in Canada, especially from the point of view of the media. For example, in Ontario, defamatory words in a newspaper or in a broadcast are deemed to constitute libel, and in Alberta, the plaintiff is not required to prove specific loss in order to obtain damages, whether the action is based on libel or slander. In Saskatchewan, however, defamatory broadcasts are still regarded as slander and therefore the distinction between libel and slander remains.

Who can sue for defamation?

The general rule, with exceptions of course, is that any person or entity who has a reputation – personal or business – which is capable of being damaged, may sue for defamation.

Individuals

Any individual may commence a defamation action, including undischarged bankrupts, minors and the mentally disabled.

As a defamation action is personal, defamatory remarks about one person do not allow someone else to sue, no matter how closely related they are, and no matter how embarrassing or upsetting the remarks.

In a 1940 case in Ontario, a court struck out a claim where the plaintiff alleged that he was injured by defamatory remarks about his deceased brother and sister. And in New Brunswick in 1922, a group of siblings were not allowed to sue for defamation where allegations were made that their father was a drunk and that they were placed in a charitable institution because of his neglect. The court found that the remarks did not reflect on the plaintiffs because a 'person may be of the highest character in every way and yet have the misfortune to have a drunken father'.

Similarly, the estates of deceased persons cannot sue for a defamation of the deceased and cannot maintain a defamation action commenced by the deceased prior to his or her death.

Groups/Classes

An attack on a large group of persons does not give any of its members a cause of action unless there is something in the publication which points to a particular member. However, where the group is small, each individual within the group may have a cause of action for defamation.

Recently, the Mayor of Pembroke, Ontario, a town of about 13 500 people, sued an Ottawa newspaper on his own behalf and as a representative of the residents of Pembroke, for libel. A sports columnist had written derogatory comments about fans at a hockey game, suggesting that some of them were from Pembroke. The claim was struck out by the Ontario Court on the basis that the group – the entire population of the town – was too large to give rise to a claim. The judge said that the words in the newspaper column were not capable of referring to the Mayor or the town's residents and there was nothing in the words complained of that specifically identified the Mayor.

Similarly, a former member of the RCAF brought an action on behalf of 25 000 surviving Canadian aircrewmen who served in North-west Europe from 1939 to 1945, for defamation arising out of a film and a book about Bomber Command. The Ontario Court struck out the claim on the basis that individuals in the group, including the plaintiff, were not singled out in the film or the book and that a group of 25 000 could not be libelled.

Corporations

Corporations, including non-profit corporations, may sue for any defamation that affects their property, goodwill or financial position, or that may injure their reputation. By way of example, in an early decision of the Ontario Court of Appeal, a lightning rod company recovered damages in a defamation action after being accused of charging the public exorbitant prices for its product. Personal accusations against the directors may constitute defamation of the corporation if the words reflect upon the corporation. This is especially true where there is one officer and director who is the controlling mind of the company.

The defamation must be capable of affecting the corporation's reputation. For example, it is not possible to defame a corporation by saying it committed murder or rape because corporations cannot, in the eyes of the law, commit such crimes.

Governmental bodies

The BC Court of Appeal has held that municipal corporations may sue for defamation, and an Ontario judge has held that a Roman Catholic separate school board, incorporated under the Ontario Education Act, may do likewise. In both cases, the judges found that the plaintiffs had reputations that deserved protection against defamatory falsehoods. This contrasts with the United States, where the Supreme Court has held that defamatory criticism of governmental entities is constitutionally protected free speech, and at least one state appeal court has held that a governmental entity is not a person and therefore has no reputation that can be defamed.

However, it is unlikely that the BC and Ontario decisions referred to in the above paragraph remain good law today, as they were based in part upon a decision of the English High Court that was overruled by the decision of the House of Lords in the *Derbyshire County Council* case in 1993.

Other entities

Other entities capable of suing for defamation include professional organizations, such as a provincial Law Society or College of Physicians and Surgeons, and trade unions. Religious bodies may also sue, as may partnerships.

Foreign plaintiff suing in Canada

In at least two cases in Ontario, foreign plaintiffs have sued foreign media organizations:

> The Prime Minister of the Bahamas was accused by NBC News of having involvement in the drug trade. In order to avoid the *New York Times* v *Sullivan* rule requiring public figures to show that the defendant acted out of malice in making the defamatory statement, he commenced his action in Ontario rather than New York, where NBC's head office was located. In 1984, a judge of the Ontario High Court permitted the action to proceed on the basis that NBC's

news programme could be seen by television viewers in Ontario who lived close to the US border.

Similarly, in 1990 the American track star Carl Lewis sued a German magazine in Ontario, on the basis that the content of the article had been republished by NBC on its morning news programme, which could be seen by television viewers in Ontario.

Whether this tactic would actually succeed at trial in avoiding the US malice rule is yet to be determined. Commencing an action in Ontario does not necessarily mean that the court will apply only Ontario defamation law. Damages arising from the publication in Ontario are recoverable based on Ontario law. However, with respect to the damages arising from the publication in the United States, an Ontario court would be likely to take the view, based on a 1994 decision of the Supreme Court of Canada, that the defamation took place in the United States. The Supreme Court of Canada has ruled that where a tort, such as defamation, takes place in a foreign country, courts should apply the law of the place where the tort was committed.

A plaintiff who sues a defendant in Ontario while also suing the same defendant in another jurisdiction would face the very real possibility of having the Ontario lawsuit stayed by the Ontario Court pursuant to the Ontario Rules of Civil Procedure. In addition, a foreign plaintiff suing in Ontario is often forced to post security for the defendant's legal costs, in case the plaintiff is unsuccessful in the lawsuit.

Commencing an action

A person who alleges that he or she is defamed may commence an action for damages for libel or slander in any of the Canadian provinces or territories. While it is outside the scope of this chapter, it is worth noting that there are other, related causes of action that a plaintiff could pursue in Canada in respect of words that cause injury, including injurious (or malicious) falsehood (also known as slander of title or slander of goods), misrepresentation, passing-off, breach of confidence or invasion of privacy.

Strict time limits restrict the ability of a plaintiff to sue for defamation resulting from publication in a newspaper or in a broadcast. This affects the length of time a reporter or broadcaster should keep his or her notes and tapes. Table 3.1 outlines the various time limits applicable in the provinces and territories to an action for defamation against a newspaper or broadcaster (for Quebec, see below).

Table 3.1 *Limitation periods in Canada*

Province/ Territory	*Time for giving notice of intention to sue*	*Time to commence action*
Alberta	Within three months after publication of defamatory material has come to plaintiff's attention; plaintiff must give seven days' notice in the case of a newspaper or fourteen days in the case of a broadcast, of his intention to sue	Within two years of publication
British Columbia	No notice requirement	Within two years of publication, but one clear day must elapse between the libel and commencement of the action.
Manitoba	Same as Alberta	Within two years of publication, unless special damages are claimed, in which case within two years after the special damages occurred
New Brunswick	Same as Alberta	Within six months after publication has come to the plaintiff's attention
Newfoundland	Same as Alberta	Within four months after publication came to the plaintiff's attention
Northwest Territories	Within three months after publication of defamatory material has come to plaintiff's attention, plaintiff must give fourteen days' notice in the case of a newspaper or a broadcast, of his intention to sue.	Same as New Brunswick

Table 3.1 *continued*

Province/ Territory	Time for giving notice of intention to sue	Time to commence action
Nova Scotia	Same as Alberta	Same as New Brunswick
Ontario	Within six weeks after the alleged libel has come to the plaintiff's attention	Within three months after publication came to plaintiff's attention
Prince Edward Island	Within three months after publication of defamatory material has come to plaintiff's attention, plaintiff must give five days' notice in the case of a newspaper or fourteen days in the case of a broadcast, of his intention to sue	Same as Manitoba
Saskatchewan	Same as Prince Edward Island	Same as New Brunswick
Yukon	Within three months after publication of defamatory material has come to plaintiff's attention, plaintiff must give fourteen days' notice in the case of a newspaper or a broadcast, of his intention to sue	Same as New Brunswick

It must be remembered that the various statutes contain definitions for 'newspaper' and 'broadcast' or 'broadcasting'. In the case of a defamation allegedly made by a publication that falls outside one of those definitions, different time limitations apply: in Alberta, British Columbia, Manitoba, New Brunswick, the Northwest Territories, Prince Edward Island, Saskatchewan and Yukon, an action for libel and slander must be brought within two years; in Nova Scotia, the time limit is six years for libel and one year for slander; and in Newfoundland and Ontario, the time limit is six years for libel and two years for slander.

Commonly, a plaintiff in a defamation action will sue a number of people or entities, including, in the case of a newspaper or magazine, the reporter or writer, the editor-in-chief, the managing editor, the publisher and the owner. In the case of a broadcaster, the plaintiff will commonly sue the reporter, the producer, the executive producer and the owner of the station or network on which the programme was aired. Naming a number of defendants assists the plaintiff in broadening the scope of the discovery process.

While all persons who are responsible for the publication and distribution of a newspaper, magazine or book may be sued, vendors, distributors and librarians who do not know the content of the publication and have no reason to believe it contains defamatory material would not be held liable. Similarly, in the case of a broadcast everyone who is responsible for the broadcast may be sued. Although the matter has not been decided by a Canadian court, the carrier of a broadcasting signal, such as a cable television operator, is probably in the same legal position as a distributor of written material.

Although the general rule is that you cannot be held liable for the repetition by others of a libel that you published, there are two exceptions that apply to the media business: where you intend or authorize someone else to publish the statement on your behalf; and where the repetition is a natural and probable result of the initial publication.

Under the first exception, those who make a defamatory statement to a reporter will be deemed to have authorized the reporter to publish or broadcast the statement and will be held responsible as if they had published it themselves. The same applies to those who send letters to the editor.

In a case in British Columbia in 1978, a newspaper article containing defamatory remarks was written, edited and published in Ontario. The article was republished by another newspaper in British Columbia. The BC Supreme Court held that the Ontario newspaper was liable for publication in both provinces since the target of the libel resided and carried on business in British Columbia and the republication of the article in British Columbia was a natural and probable consequence of the original publication in Ontario.

Defences

Constitutional: freedom of expression

Section 2(b) of the Canadian Charter of Rights and Freedoms states that there is a fundamental freedom of 'thought, belief, opinion and expression, including freedom of the press and other media of communication'. To date, Canadian courts have refused to extend the provisions of section 2(b) to defendants in defamation actions on the basis that this section applies only to protection of the media from government or government-related action. It does not extend to protect the media from attack by persons who are defamed.

The matter appears to have been put to rest for the moment, by the decision of the Supreme Court of Canada in the case of *Hill* v *Church of Scientology*:[6]

> Hill, a Crown Attorney, was accused by the Church of Scientology and its lawyer of permitting sealed documents to be reviewed by a government official, which was alleged to be a contempt of court. The defendants argued, in part, that the common law of libel infringed the fundamental freedom of expression and freedom of the press as guaranteed by section 2(b) of the Charter. In response to that argument, the Court held that the Charter applied only to government action. In this case, the facts that Hill was a public official, that his legal fees were paid for by the provincial government and that the defamatory statements related to an act he purportedly carried out in the scope of his employment were not sufficient to take the case out of the realm of private action. The court noted that what was at stake was Hill's personal reputation, not the reputation of the Ministry of the Attorney General or of the Government of Ontario.

The court in *Hill* was also unwilling to adopt *New York Times* v *Sullivan* as the law in Canada, despite the defendant's argument that it would make the common law more consistent with the Charter. The court held that the common law of libel strikes an appropriate balance between the twin values of reputation and free expression.

The BC Court of Appeal had previously commented unfavourably on the adoption into Canadian law of *New York Times* v *Sullivan*, in a case involving statements about mismanagement of funds by members of an Indian band. The court said:[7]

> 'The rule in the *New York Times* v *Sullivan* case leaves vulnerable the reputation of all who are or would be in public life, by depriving such people of any legal recourse from defamatory falsehoods directed against them, except in those rare cases where 'actual malice' can be established. Such a rule would be likely to discourage honest and decent people from standing for public office. Thus, the rule destroys, rather than preserves, the delicate balance between freedom of expression and protection of reputation which, as I have already noted, is vital to

the survival of our democratic process of government. For that reason I would
be opposed to introducing such a rule in this country.'

Professor Raymond Brown of the University of Windsor (Ontario) has said
that:[8]

'Unlike their American colleagues, ... (Canadian) judges have weighed more
heavily the value of personal reputation over those of free speech and free press.
Thus there occurs in many of their decisions a careful reminder that these freedoms are ones 'governed by law' and that there is no 'freedom to make untrue
defamatory statements.' This is not intended as an invidious comparison.
(Canadian) judges cherish free speech and a free press no less than their
American counterparts. They just happen to value personal reputation, particularly the reputation of their public servants, more.'

Privilege

Absolute privilege

Statements made in a legislature or a court, or remarks that are made in the
course of performing an executive function, enjoy an 'absolute privilege'
because of the forum in which they are published. The reasoning behind
absolute privilege is to allow those in important government positions to
discuss matters freely without fear of civil suit. This includes parliament, the
provincial legislatures, municipal councils and also various boards. Examples
of reports that will be covered by an absolute privilege include communications between cabinet ministers and reports from senior military officers to
their superiors.

   All judicial proceedings, including administrative tribunals which function
similarly to a court, are protected by an absolute privilege. This privilege
extends to judges, lawyers, witnesses, parties and jurors. It does not matter if
their statements are malicious or irrelevant. Documents filed as exhibits or
admitted as evidence are covered by the privilege. This includes affidavits,
which are taken as read by the court. The protection does not extend, however,
to documents in the court file which are not read in court or taken as read,
including pleadings.

   However, except in limited instances, media reports of occasions covered
by an absolute privilege do not enjoy the absolute privilege themselves,
whether made by a newspaper, a broadcaster or the person who originally
spoke the defamatory words.

   Coverage of court proceedings by newspapers and broadcasters is given
absolute privilege, provided it is a fair and accurate report without comment of

public proceedings, published contemporaneously with the proceedings. The absolute privilege is lost, however, if the newspaper or broadcaster refuses or neglects to insert in its report (or in a report published shortly thereafter) a reasonable statement of explanation or contradiction by or on behalf of the person defamed (other than in British Columbia or in Saskatchewan in the case of broadcasts). The absolute privilege does not extend to protect blasphemous, seditious or indecent matter. While the various statutes generally refer to courts of law, the protection was extended in a Manitoba case to include reports of quasi-judicial proceedings (that case involved a public inquiry before the Board of Transport Commission for Canada). The effect of the absolute privilege is that the claim to privilege cannot be defeated by evidence that the defendant published the report with malice, i.e. out of spite or ill-will towards the person defamed.

Qualified privilege

A 'qualified privilege' protects a variety of other media reports, principally reports of proceedings that are open to the public or on matters of public interest. The qualification is that, in these instances, the privilege is lost if it is proved that the publication was made maliciously.

In Ontario, for example (subject to the qualification of malice), a newspaper or broadcaster may make fair and accurate reports of the proceedings of any legislative body (or one of their committees) in the British Commonwealth, any administrative body that is constituted by any public authority in Canada, any public commission of inquiry in the Commonwealth and the proceedings of any organization whose members represent any public authority in Canada. Other provincial defamation statutes restrict the protection to reports of a particular provincial assembly, or refer to any provincial assembly in Canada and in some instances refer to the Senate and House of Commons. The privilege extends to any report, bulletin, notice or other public document issued by a government department or public official.

Generally speaking, but depending on the province or territory, qualified privilege will also be given to reports of:

- proceedings of a municipal council, school board, board of education, board of health or hospital board;
- proceedings of any board or local authority or committee thereof formed or constituted under Canadian or provincial legislation;
- proceedings of any administrative body constituted by any public authority in Canada;
- proceedings of any commission of inquiry constituted by any public authority in the British Commonwealth;

- commissioners authorized to act by letters patent, statute or other authority;
- a public meeting lawfully held for a lawful purpose;
- findings or decisions of an association or committee thereof, relating to a person who is a member of, or subject to the control of, the association, provided it is a Canadian association relating to arts, science, religion, education, business, industry, professions, sports or games.

The report must be fair and accurate, must be of a matter of public concern and benefit, and the person defamed must be given an opportunity to explain or contradict the report. Protection is not given to blasphemous, seditious or indecent material.

A newspaper or broadcaster also has a qualified privilege regarding reports on matters of public interest, provided there is a duty to publish to the public and an interest in the public to receive the publication. In a 1983 decision, a judge of the BC Supreme Court held that a consumer affairs reporter for a newspaper was protected by a qualified privilege in reporting about the risks associated with the use of the plaintiff's canning lids, since the public would have an interest in knowing about any adverse effects of using the lids.

Truth/Justification

It is a complete defence to a claim for libel if the words complained of are true in substance and in fact, according to their natural and ordinary meaning. However, the defendant must have evidence of the truth at the outset of the lawsuit. If, in response to a defence of justification, the plaintiff requests particulars and the defendant asserts that it intends to obtain the evidence to establish the defence during the examination for discovery of the plaintiff, the defence of justification can be struck out by the court.

Fair comment

It is a defence to a defamation action to say that the words complained of are a fair comment on a matter of public interest. The facts underlying the comment must be true, otherwise the defence is lost. In addition, the comment must not be motivated by malice on the part of the author towards the target of the comment. An opinion can be harsh, and can use vivid language, ridicule or sarcasm, but mere epithets or invective may not be considered fair comment.

What constitutes a matter of public interest is fairly wide-ranging, and includes governmental affairs, the administration of justice, public health and safety, education, political events, elections and sports. The affairs of private organizations that solicit public support or patronage are also matters of public interest, as are the affairs of private organizations regulated by statute. Artistic, literary or other endeavours in the entertainment field are matters of public interest. So, too, are private matters that have a public impact.

Matters that are personal or private to an individual or a relatively small group are usually not matters of public interest. This would include the private life of a public person. Unlike the United States, courts in Canada have historically guarded the reputations of public figures and have cautioned against unwarranted attacks on public officials. The media in Canada is treated like any citizen in terms of its ability to render an opinion – it has no special right to comment on matters of public interest, unlike the constitutional protection afforded in the United States.

Consent

It is also a defence to a libel action to say that the defamatory statement was actively encouraged, solicited or induced by the plaintiff. This consent to the publication of a defamatory statement can be express or implied.

Intention of the writer or broadcaster

It is no defence to say that a defamatory statement was published innocently or unintentionally. Moreover, a defendant cannot escape liability by showing that he or she was encouraged to make the statement by those who ought to have known of its defamatory nature. Where newspapers and broadcasters rely upon wire services, they will still be liable for the publication of defamatory material.

However, where the reporter is shown to have acted out of spite, ill-will or a desire to do harm for its own sake, malice will be proved, and any defence of qualified privilege will be defeated.

A former Deputy Attorney-General of British Columbia succeeded in 1982 in showing malice on the part of a CBC reporter who presented allegations which he knew could not be substantiated but nevertheless made for a more sensational programme.

In 1990, CBC broadcast a consumer affairs television programme which contained a news item on mercury in paint. Colour Your World Corp. was identified as a manufacturer of paint containing phenyl mercuric acetate. During the news item there were pictures and statements about poisoning and deaths from methyl mercury in Japan and Ontario. The programme did not distinguish between methyl mercury and phenyl mercury, which is substantially less toxic than methyl mercury. Colour Your World Corp. sued for defamation in the Ontario Court of Justice. The judge concluded that there was express malice on the part of the show's producers, as they knew and understood the differences between the two types of mercury; that methyl mercury was the cause of the disasters in Japan and Ontario; and that the plaintiff was phasing mercury out of its paint and was applying to use a seal of approval from the federal Department of the Environment. The judge concluded that the defendants had deliberately left these facts out of the programme to make it more dramatic.

Remedies

Damages

The plaintiff in a defamation action is generally permitted to seek an unlimited amount of money as damages, to remedy the harm done by the defamation. There is theoretically no upper limit on damages, and awards have been rising in recent years. In the above-mentioned case of *Hill* v *Church of Scientology*, the jury awarded Hill, a Crown Attorney, C$300 000 (US$217 000) in general damages. Damages can also be recovered for actual monetary losses caused by the defamation, and, as mentioned above, these are generally the only type of damages available in an action for slander.

Certain factors can affect the amount of damages, such as the conduct of the defendant, the extent of the publication, the standing of the plaintiff in the community, and proof of malice. The amount will often be greater if the defendant fails in a defence of justification. In the Hill case, the jury awarded C$500 000 (US$365 000) in aggravated damages because of the malicious nature of the libel and the conduct of the Church of Scientology.

Punitive damages may also be awarded where the court finds that the conduct of the publisher of the defamation was deserving of punishment. Again, in the Hill case, punitive damages of C$800 000 (US$580 000) were awarded against the Church of Scientology. The Supreme Court of Canada upheld the award in part because the Church of Scientology persisted in publishing the libel even after the jury rendered its verdict.

Injunctions: prior restraint

Injunctions prior to publication are extremely rare, but not entirely unknown in Canada. They are difficult to obtain and seldom last beyond a few days. In a leading Ontario case on the subject, the court said that an injunction to restrain publication of alleged libels is an exceptional remedy that should be granted only in 'the rarest and clearest of cases'. It has been suggested by one commentator that an injunction will be granted only where the publication is clearly defamatory and manifestly untrue, or where the defendant is a 'fly-by-night operator of no substance or credibility'.[9]

> In 1993, a BC Supreme Court judge enjoined the CBC from broadcasting a news item about a businessman on a news magazine programme entitled 'The Fifth Estate', because he alleged that the news item would refer to a previous criminal conviction. His concern proved to be unfounded, and the injunction was quickly lifted by another judge. That judge held that the plaintiff's right to keep facts private did not supersede the freedom of the press to report them. The injunction was found to go beyond a prohibition on broadcasting private facts and amounted to an attempt to control the newsgathering process, which was deserving of the court's protection. The plaintiff's interest in suppressing private facts did not outweigh the public's interest in ensuring the integrity of the news-gathering process. Even if some of the reporter's statements were libellous, they did not come within the category of 'rarest' and 'clearest' of cases, those being cases where the court is satisfied that any jury would say that the matter complained of was libellous, so as to warrant an injunction against publication.

However, plaintiffs might not always seek an injunction in respect of a libel. They may seek to restrain a breach of confidence, contract or copyright. In cases of injunctions sought to prevent breach of confidence, Canadian courts have followed the English case law, most notably Lord Denning in *Woodward* v *Hutchins*, where he stated:[10]

> 'If there is a legitimate ground for supposing that it is in the public interest for it to be disclosed, the courts should not restrain it by an interlocutory injunction, but should leave the complainant to its remedy in damages.'

Retraction

Publication of a retraction limits exposure to monetary damages to the actual monetary damages suffered by the person defamed. In other words, the plaintiff must prove that it suffered monetary loss as a result of the defamation.

The retraction must, however, conform with the requirements of the applicable statute. For example, in Ontario the retraction must be full and fair and, in the case of a broadcaster, be broadcast either within a reasonable time or within three days after receipt of the plaintiff's notice of libel. In the case of a newspaper, the retraction must be published in the next issue or any regular issue within three days of receiving the notice. It must also be shown, however, that the alleged libel was published in good faith, did not involve a criminal charge and was published in mistake as to the facts. The retraction provision does not apply to the case of a libel against a candidate for public office unless the retraction is made at least five days before the election. In Saskatchewan, a similar provision calls for the retraction to be published at least fifteen days before the election.

Apology

Even where the statutory requirements for a retraction are not satisfied, a genuine apology for a defamatory publication, which withdraws the original statement and expresses regret for it, made in writing and published at the earliest opportunity, will mitigate to some extent the damages that can be claimed by a plaintiff.

One textwriter set out an appropriate form of apology as:[11]

'In an article published on (date) we referred to certain allegations made by X about Y. Our report was erroneous and we wish to retract the allegation of (impropriety, etc.) on the part of Y. There is no evidence whatsoever of (impropriety, etc.) on the part of Y and we apologize for the publication of the report. Y is a respected member of the community and we regret the embarrassment caused to him.'

Protecting sources

Canadian courts have a discretion not to force a journalist to disclose the source of information during the pre-trial discovery phase of a lawsuit. The practice is not uniform, however. Courts in Ontario have generally not forced disclosure during discovery, while those in British Columbia have done so.

If the identity of the source is a relevant matter at trial, the court may order disclosure. In exercising its discretion, the court will consider whether the source asked for confidentiality, the importance of the source's identity to the lawsuit, whether there are other means of obtaining the information sought and the scope of disclosure requested.

It was suggested, but not confirmed, in a 1989 decision of the Supreme Court of Canada that the court might recognize the right of a journalist to keep the identity of his or her sources confidential if:

1 the information originates in confidence that it will not be disclosed;
2 the element of confidentiality is essential to the full and satisfactory maintenance of the relationship;
3 the relationship is one which, in the community's opinion, ought to be sedulously fostered;

4   the injury that would be caused to the relationship by disclosure must be greater than the benefit to the litigation by disclosure.

To date, the Supreme Court of Canada has rejected claims that the freedom of the press in section 2(b) of the Charter affords protection to journalists seeking to avoid disclosure of the identity of sources. In a 1991 case upholding the validity of a search warrant issued for a CBC news bureau, the court found that there was no evidence that the media would have more difficulty gathering information if sources believed that their identities could be uncovered by police during a search.

Other restraints

Privacy laws

Invasion of privacy is not recognized as a tort at common law by Canadian courts. British Columbia, Manitoba and Saskatchewan have, however, enacted legislation creating a civil cause of action for invasion of privacy, fashioned after the law in the United States. Interpretation of these statutes by the courts has, to date, been limited. In 1986 in British Columbia, a television station was found not to have violated the privacy of a furniture store and its owner by broadcasting film of the premises and the owner's efforts to remove the camera crew from his parking lot, during a period when Teamsters were on strike against another company owned by the same individual. The broadcast was held to be in the public interest and therefore protected. In Manitoba, the Court of Queen's Bench held in 1988 that that province's Privacy Act did not create a tort of placing someone in a false light in the public eye. In that case, the plaintiffs had complained that a newspaper had harmed them by publishing certain tax information that they had submitted to the government and by implying that they were connected with something with which they should not have been connected.

Contempt of court

A newspaper or broadcaster may be cited for contempt where the publication or broadcast would tend to interfere with the fair trial of an action, or other-wise interfere with the judicial process. The question for the court is whether there is a real and substantial risk that publication would make a fair trial impossible in the circumstances and that alternative methods, such as a change in venue, would not suffice. Breach of an express court order banning publication of the judicial proceedings would be contempt, as would speaking to a juror after a trial.

Publication bans are likely to become rarer as a result of the 1994 decision of the Supreme Court of Canada in a case involving a television programme that concerned certain high-profile cases of child abuse by Catholic priests. The court said that such bans should only be issued when (a) the ban is necessary in order to prevent a real and substantial risk to the fairness of the trial, because reasonably available alternative measures will not prevent the risk; and (b) the salutary effects of the publication ban outweigh the deleterious effects to the free expression of those affected by the ban.

Draft guidelines developed by the Alberta Ministry of the Attorney General in early 1993 dealing with contempt of court, principally in the context of pre-trial publicity, set out specific examples of things that would constitute criminal contempt, including:

- publications which state as a fact, expressly or by implication, that an accused is guilty;
- publication of an accused's previous criminal record or general descriptions of an accused's criminal associations or background;
- publication of any out-of-court statement made by the accused;
- publication of a photograph of the accused in a case where identity of the offender is an issue;
- publication of evidence heard in the course of a *voir dire* prior to the evidence being ruled admissible;
- publication of the accused's claims of innocence.

It is not necessary that the person allegedly in contempt intended to interfere with the judicial process – it is sufficient to prove that he or she knowingly published the offending material.

The Alberta draft guidelines also set out the factors affecting a decision by the Crown to charge for contempt for pre-trial publicity:

- the higher the profile of the case, the more likely a charge would be laid;
- the greater the potential for damage from the particular information, the greater the likelihood of a charge (for example, the fact that an accused facing a sexual assault charge had two prior convictions for sexual assault);
- proximity in time between publication and trial;
- prominence given to the story by the publisher.

The draft guidelines also noted that those charged would be likely to include the corporate owner of the publication, individuals such as the publisher, editor, columnist or reporter, or the source of the information, which might be the police or a witness or the accused. At present, it is not known whether these draft guidelines will ever be adopted by the Alberta Attorney General or any other provincial Attorney General.

Criminal charges

The Criminal Code of Canada contains a number of provisions dealing with libel, hate propaganda and spreading false news, although the provisions have been only sparingly used and some have been found by courts to be contrary to the Canadian Charter of Rights and Freedoms and therefore of no force or effect.[12]

Defamatory libel is defined in the Code as 'matter published, without lawful justification or excuse, that is likely to injure the reputation of any person by exposing him to hatred, contempt or ridicule, or that is designed to insult the person of or concerning whom it is published'. A defamatory libel may be expressed directly or by insinuation or irony. A person convicted of publishing a defamatory libel can be sentenced to up to two years' imprisonment, but if he or she knows that the defamatory libel is false the maximum prison sentence is five years. Under the Code, a person is said to publish a libel when he or she (a) exhibits it in public; (b) causes it to be read or seen; or (c) shows or delivers it, or causes it to be shown or delivered, with intent that it should be read or seen by the person whom it defames or anyone else.

Where defamatory material is published in a newspaper, the proprietor of the newspaper is deemed to have published defamatory matter, unless he or she proves that the defamatory matter was inserted in the newspaper without his or her knowledge and not negligently. If the proprietor has given general authority to someone else to manage or edit the newspaper, the insertion of defamatory matter by the manager or editor is not deemed to be negligence on the proprietor's part unless it is proved by the Crown Prosecutor that the proprietor intended to give the manager or editor authority to publish defamatory matter or allowed that individual to continue to exercise general authority after the proprietor knew that defamatory matter had been inserted in the newspaper.

Exceptions to the defamatory libel provisions are made to allow for the publication, among other things;

- of a fair report of, or any fair comment on, the proceedings of parliament or a provincial legislature, or a committee thereof, or a court (other than divorce proceedings), provided it is done in good faith for the information of the public;
- of an extract or abstract of a petition to parliament or a provincial legislature or a paper published by order of, or under the authority of, parliament

or a provincial legislature, provided it is published in good faith and without ill-will to the person defamed;

- of a fair and accurate report, for the public benefit, of a public meeting, if the meeting is lawfully convened for a lawful purpose and is open to the public, provided it is published in a newspaper, in good faith, and the publisher does not refuse to publish, in a conspicuous place in the newspaper, a reasonable explanation or contradiction by the person defamed;
- of defamatory matter that the person reasonably believes is true and is relevant to any subject of public interest, the public discussion of which is for the public benefit;
- of fair comments on the public conduct of a person who participates in public affairs;
- of fair, critical comments about a book, other literary production, publicly exhibited composition, work of art or performance, or other public communication on any subject.

Exceptions also exist in circumstances where the publication of the defamatory matter is invited, is done to answer inquiries or is done to redress a wrong. Truth is a defence to defamatory libel.

There are few examples of prosecutions for defamatory libel. An underground newspaper in British Columbia was convicted of defamatory libel in 1970 for comparing a magistrate to Pontius Pilate. The newspaper unsuccessfully argued that the statement was not meant to be defamatory but was meant as a joke. The court held that the test was an objective one. In Manitoba, a university student was convicted of defamatory libel in 1993 after distributing posters that made rude remarks about his ex-girlfriend. That case is also noteworthy because the judge held that the defamatory libel provisions were, generally, a reasonable limit upon freedom of expression under section 2(b) of the Charter of Rights and Freedoms.

Blasphemous libel is also an offence, punishable by imprisonment of up to two years. There do not appear, however, to be any reported cases of anyone being convicted under this section of the Code.

Advocating the use of force to achieve governmental change in Canada is seditious libel and is an offence under the Criminal Code. It is unclear whether it is necessary for the Crown Prosecutor to prove an intention on the part of the accused to incite acts of violence or public disorder. Commentators have suggested that this provision may be subject to attack under the Charter of Rights and Freedoms.[13] In addition, it is an offence under the Criminal Code to promote disloyalty, insubordination, mutiny or refusal of duty by Canadian military forces.[14]

It was formerly an offence under the Code to spread false news by wilfully publishing information that you knew to be false and that causes or is likely to cause injury or mischief to a public interest. The provision was held to be unconstitutional by the Supreme Court of Canada in 1992, in a case involving an individual who had published material suggesting that the Holocaust was a hoax.

Advocating or promoting genocide is an offence, as is inciting hatred against an identifiable group. In a 1991 case involving an Alberta school-teacher who taught that the Holocaust was a hoax, the Supreme Court of Canada said that these hate propaganda provisions were a reasonable limit on freedom of expression under the Charter.

Libel reform

In Ontario, an advisory committee of prominent media counsel and law professors met in 1989 and 1990 to review the law of defamation. It arrived at consensus on some points but not on others. It did, however, agree that the defence of justification should be easier to use, that the defences of fair report and fair comment should be expanded and that the opportunities for retraction by publishers or for the publication of reply by complainants should be made more accessible.[15]

Despite the continued call by members of the media for Canadian courts to adopt *New York Times* v *Sullivan*, or to extend Charter protection to all private speech, there is little public concern for these matters and no push to move them onto the public agenda. Given the general disaffection in which the media are held by the public, there would seem to be no desire to make it easier for the media to criticize public officials; nor would there seem to be any great desire by those public officials to make it easier for the media to criticize them. Since the courts have refused to make such dramatic changes to the common law, it seems unlikely that the legislatures are going to take up the media's cause in the near future.

The province of Quebec[16]

As mentioned above, the province of Quebec derives its law from the civil law tradition, with the result that there are fundamental differences between the law in the province of Quebec and the law in the common law provinces and territories. At the same time, however, with respect to the issue of defamation, Quebec courts have frequently referred to common law notions, jurisprudence and authors. While this practice has been criticized by some authors[17], it has had the effect of bringing the law of defamation in Quebec closer to the law in the common law provinces.

Fault

In Quebec, civil liability for defamation arises only if the defendant has committed a fault. Unlike the situation in the common law jurisdictions, the publication of false information is not necessarily a fault, nor is it necessary to show that the information was false in order to establish that there was a fault. The cases set out three situations in which the defendant will be held to have committed a fault:

1   Where the defendant made a statement which he or she knew was false;
2   Where the defendant made a statement which he or she should have known was false;
3   Where the defendant made a statement, even if it was true, without proper justification.[18]

The first type of fault is intentional defamation and is the clearest case.

The second type of fault is based on negligence. The court will compare the conduct of the defendant in relation to the conduct of a reasonable person in the same situation. When the defendant is a journalist, the court will examine whether the journalist acted reasonably in preparing the article or the report, and in particular whether he or she took normal precautions in carrying out the background work and used the investigative techniques which were available or which were usually used in such matters. In other words, defamation in Quebec will only be actionable on this basis if there was a violation of the professional standards of inquiry and investigation in journalistic activity.

The third type of fault is based on malice or bad faith. The disclosure of embarrassing information about the plaintiff, even if true, will be actionable unless there is proper justification for disclosure, such as the public interest.

Redress

Generally, commencing an action for defamation in the province of Quebec is barred after one year from publication.[19]

The damages which can be claimed in an action in defamation include damages for physical or psychological injury to the plaintiff and for material injury to the plaintiff, in the form of economic loss.

In addition, the plaintiff can claim damages for 'moral injury',which includes damage to reputation, humiliation, contempt and ridicule. A minority decision of the Supreme Court of Canada appears to have established that a sum of C$50 000 (US$36 500) in 1978 is a ceiling on a claim for moral damages, unless there are exceptional circumstances.[20]

Finally, the court can award punitive damages if the defamation was intentional. Awards for punitive damages in the province of Quebec have tended to be quite small, but the courts have become more generous in more recent decisions.[21]

Press Act

The Press Act[22] limits the liability arising out of a defamation published in a newspaper or other periodical in several ways.

First, it shortens the limitation period to three months following the publication of the article, or three months after the plaintiff had knowledge of the publication, provided, in the latter case, that the action is instituted within one year from publication.

Further, it requires that the complainant give notice to the proprietor of the newspaper before instituting an action. If the newspaper publishes a retraction within two days following receipt of such notice, the plaintiff's claim is limited to physical and material injury. The provisions on retraction do not apply when the newspaper accuses the plaintiff of a criminal offence or when the defamation was directed at a political candidate within three days of the nomination day and up to the polling day.

The Press Act also creates a privilege for the publication of the reports of proceedings of certain public bodies and the courts, and notices emanating from certain government bodies.

Notes

1   The author wishes to thank Stephen W. Hamilton of Stikeman, Elliott (Montreal, Quebec) for preparing the section on the law in Quebec.
2   *New York Times Co.* v. *Sullivan*, 376 U.S. 254 (1964).
3   Alberta: Defamation Act, RSA 1980, c. D-6. British Columbia: Libel and Slander Act, RSBC 1979, c. 234. Manitoba: Defamation Act, RSM 1987, c. D-20. New Brunswick: Defamation Act, RSNB 1973, c. D-5. Newfoundland: Defamation Act, RSN 1990, c. D-3. Northwest Territories: Defamation Act, RSNWT 1988, c. D-1. Nova Scotia: Defamation Act, RSNS 1989, c. 122. Ontario: Libel and Slander Act, RSO 1990, c. L.12. Prince Edward Island: Defamation Act, RSPEI 1988, c. D-5. Saskatchewan: Libel and Slander Act, RSS 1978, c. L-14. Yukon: Defamation Act, RSY 1986, c. 41.
4   Brown, R.E. (1987). *The Law of Defamation in Canada*. Carswell.
5   Brown, above pp. 47-49.
6   (1995) SCJ No. 64, released 20 July.
7   *Westbank Indian Band* v *Tomat* (1992), 88 DLR (4th) 401 (BCCA).
8   Brown, above pp. 5-6.

9   Rogers, B.M. (April 1993). 'Stopping the Story: Injunctions Before Publication or Broadcast', in *Entertainment, Advertising & Media Law* (Law Society of Upper Canada).

10 (1977) 2 All ER 751 (CA) at 754.

11 Williams, J. S. (1988). *The Law of Libel and Slander in Canada*. (2nd edn.), p. 100. Butterworths.

12 Criminal Code of Canada, RSC 1985, c. C-46, sections. 296–315.

13 *Martin's Criminal Code* 1995, p. 97.

14 Criminal Code, section 62.

15 Ontario Ministry of the Attorney General, Advisory Committee on the Law of Defamation, Report, November 1990.

16 This section was prepared by Stephen W. Hamilton of Stikeman, Elliott (Montreal, Quebec).

17 Baudouin J-L. (1994). *La Responsabilité Civile* (4th edn.), para 415. Les éditions Yvon Blais.

18 *Société Radio Canada* v *Radio Sept-Iles Inc.*, (1994) RJQ 1811 (CA).

19 Civil Code of Quebec, *article 2929.*

20 *Snyder* v *Montreal Gazette Ltd.*, (1988) 1 SCR 494.

21 In *Samuelli* v *Jouhannet* (1994) RJQ 152, the Superior Court awarded C$50 000 (US$36 500) exemplary damages. The case is currently before the Quebec Court of Appeal.

22 RSQ, c. P-19.

4

England and Wales

Nick Braithwaite of Clifford Chance (London)

London is a hornet's nest of libel litigation.[1] Awards may be higher in the United States, but there the First Amendment protections for freedom of speech make it hard for many libel victims to succeed. In contrast, litigants swarm around the English[2] courts simply because they offer better chances of success than most other legal systems, and a high level of damages.[3]

Why do libel defendants in England have such a hard time?

Part of the explanation lies in Britain's 'Constitution' – really no more than a set of unwritten conventions, habitually observed. English libel law, unfettered by constitutional constraints or a statutory press code[4], sets a high value upon the protection of private reputation and has traditionally paid mere lip-service to the social utility in freedom of expression. Above all, it has failed to balance this private right with attention to public interest considerations, although there have been signs of a more liberal approach since the seminal case of *Derbyshire County Council* v *Times Newspapers*[5] in 1992.

The posture traditionally adopted by the English common law – judge-made law – in defamation and other areas touching the media, is that journalists are in the same position as any private citizen. The point was brought out by the prosecution in 1992 of Channel 4 Television for contempt of court:

> Channel 4 had screened a programme based on allegations that the Royal Ulster Constabulary had an inner circle linked to Protestant terrorist groups. The Government prosecuted Channel 4 for contempt of court for refusing to reveal the identity of their source – they were specifically obliged to do this under the Prevention of Terrorism Act. Channel 4 argued that it could not comply because of the public interest that similar allegations should be aired and the danger their source would face if discovered. Fining the company £75 000 (US$115 000), the court said it was not for journalists to decide what was in the public interest. They had to obey the law just like any other citizen.[6]

In libel matters, too, the media have few special rights. One exception is the privilege given to newspapers and broadcasters to report certain occasions where the public interest in reporting outweighs any private harm to individuals.

The salient defect in the law is the burden of proving truth. The defendant must prove truth, rather than the plaintiff falsity, and so the dice are heavily loaded in the plaintiff's favour. Time and again, and directly because of the constitutional vacuum, British editors have had to pay damages over stories they know, but cannot prove, to be true.

English libel cases are usually tried by judge and jury – virtually the only civil cases not tried by a judge sitting alone. Juries determine not only issues of fact, but also the size of the award. Plaintiffs' lawyers contend that juries empower the small person against the barons of the press, and that jury trial of a reputation that has been attacked is a quasi-constitutional right. But many media defendants believe that juries are biased against them, and the small number of libel cases they win supports this view.

Juries can be excessively influenced by any massive libel payouts which may hit the headlines in the months before trial. Judges seldom give jurors meaningful guidance on an appropriate level of damages – in a recent case a judge advised the jury not to award 'Mickey Mouse damages'. They thought, quite wrongly, that he was telling them to award a huge amount, and duly obliged.

Some awards in recent years include:

- £500 000 (US$765 000) to a Conservative politician wrongly accused of consorting with a prostitute;
- £260 000 (US$400 000) to a former Royal Navy officer wrongly accused of stealing the log-book of his submarine;
- £1.5 million (US$2.3 million) to a leading businessman who had been wrongly accused of involvement in war-crimes over the forced repatriation of Cossacks at the end of the Second World War;
- £1 485 000 (US$2.3 million) to a husband-and-wife boat building team and their company when their revolutionary boat design was unfairly attacked as 'an expensive white elephant'.

The tendency is ever upwards. Disturbing comparisons can be drawn between the compensation available for personal injuries and for reputation. A car accident victim rendered paraplegic by another driver's negligence could expect to recover much less than a showbiz personality libelled by a national newspaper. But at least the Court of Appeal now has power to substitute a sensible verdict when a jury has gone too far.[7]

Libel litigation is a prodigiously costly pastime. This is due mainly to the expense of legal representation, which may be borne largely by one party or the other at the end of a case. In serious cases, the total legal costs can dwarf the damages recoverable. In 1981, when the *Daily Mail* was being sued by a religious cult, the unsuccessful plaintiff faced a costs bill of £400 000 (US$613 000). Today the equivalent figure could be in excess of £2 million. Successful defendants also face on occasion a real possibility of being unable to recover a significant proportion of their own costs from the plaintiff.

In some countries even a litigant who loses will have to make no contribution to the legal costs of the other side. If successful, the plaintiff's lawyer in the United States, for example, will usually have agreed to accept a 'contingency fee' – no win, no fee – payable out of any damages awarded. In England and Wales, by contrast, the loser normally pays both sides' legal costs.[8] The rationale is to discourage frivolous claims and to promote settlement, but a side-effect has been to make litigation a pastime of the wealthy.

More specifically, the system known as 'payment into court' gives the defendant an effective weapon to force a settlement. It has an important role to play in maintaining a semblance of tactical balance between the parties. However, the unpredictability of jury awards together with a perceived jury bias against the press – if not all media defendants – have reduced the effectiveness of payment into court as a tactical device. This has in turn increased pressure on publishers to settle out of court.

At pre-publication stage, then, one of the considerations to be weighed by investigative journalists will be whether the plaintiff has the resources and determination to sue. So, in the past, many defendant lawyers delayed settling claims until they had tested the plaintiff's mettle and pocket. In the late 1980s the spiralling level of awards induced a more pragmatic and conciliatory attitude on the part of the media, but recently the level of awards appears to have begun to rise again.

The *New York Times* has a policy of fighting every libel case on principle. To take such a stance in the United Kingdom would be foolish. Despite their relatively deep pockets (and sometimes libel insurance cover), the odds are stacked against the media. Add to the factors of cost and jury trial the burden on defendants to show that the words complained of were true, and it is easy to see why they find fighting libel lawsuits all the way to trial a distinctly unattractive proposition.

The plaintiff's task

Plaintiffs do not have it all their own way. Libel actions are not eligible for legal aid, so those without substantial resources may not be able to afford a lawyer. Sometimes a union or employer may be prepared to offer financial assistance. There are also funds set up to assist libel actions – provided, of course, the plaintiff's aims chime with the ideology of the benefactor.

Even for the fairly affluent, undertaking a libel suit without such help is a game for high stakes, given the risk of being saddled with both sides' legal costs. US-style contingency fees are still against English lawyers' professional rules, but a modified version – the 'speculative action' – is permitted in Scotland, and 'conditional fees' have recently been introduced in England and Wales (but not in libel actions).

Libel or slander?

English law distinguishes verbal defamation, termed slander, from publication in 'permanent' form, whether written or broadcast, known as libel. The law presumes that a libel causes loss because of the permanent form of the defamatory statement, and no actual damage need be proven. This legal presumption can help litigants who have suffered no serious damage to their reputation to recover sizeable sums.

With one or two exceptions – the most important being serious criminal offences, and words disparaging a person in a trade or profession – slander requires proof of financial loss. It would be wrong, however, to assume that verbal defamation is not dangerous. A doctor recovered damages of £150 000 (US$230 000) in 1991 when a female colleague accused him, in the full hearing of waiting patients, of sexually molesting her.[9]

Television and radio programmes are deemed by statute to be libel. Electronic publication, exemplified by publication on the Internet, has created many new problems. Is digital transmission publication in permanent form (i.e. libel not slander) if the message is not displayed? Where does publication occur? Is only the sender liable or can computer hosts also attract liability? These await resolution by judicial or statutory intervention.

Who may sue?

Among those who can sue for libel are:

- living persons, including children and mental patients;
- trading companies if the defamation reflects on the company's trading character (a company cannot sue for hurt feelings);
- bankrupts through their trustee in bankruptcy.

The following cannot sue in their own capacity:

- local authorities, and, presumably, government departments;
- the dead or their personal representatives;
- 'enemy aliens';
- unincorporated associations and trade unions.

If a person starts a defamation action and dies before the jury's verdict, the action dies too. So, too, where a defendant dies. The rule reflects the personalized nature of defamation, as well as the importance the common law tradition attaches to oral evidence.

A landmark case in 1992, *Derbyshire County Council* v *Times Newspapers*[10] decided that local authorities cannot, as public bodies, sue for libel in their own right. The same principle would presumably apply to other organs of government, although the precise extent of the prohibition is as yet unclear. (Even though unions and municipal authorities cannot bring a libel action in their own name, members of any group may be able to sue if they can show that the defamatory words refer to them individually.)

The case was interesting because it explicitly approved the principles underlying the US *New York Times* v *Sullivan*[11] case. It leaves the way open for English law to develop a defence analogous to the 'public figure' defence, which has had such a dramatic impact on US journalism since the mid-1960s. The recent decisions in India and Australia espousing the *Sullivan* doctrine now appear to render such a development inevitable.

Who may be sued?

Anyone taking part in the publication of a libel can be sued – editor, author, publisher, printer, distributor, newsagent or bookseller. Innocent distributors (but not printers) can use the defence of innocent dissemination if they can show (in essence) that they were not at fault.

The unsuccessful defendant is, of course, entitled to have the award reduced by the amount of any damages awarded against others liable for the same acts. Moreover, a plaintiff who brings a succession of legal actions for the same publication will be unlikely to recover costs for the subsequent actions.

What the plaintiff must prove

The plaintiff has to prove three facts:

- That the words are defamatory;
- That they refer to the plaintiff;
- That they have been published by the defendant to a third party.

Since damage is presumed in libel cases – although not usually in slander[12] – plaintiffs do not even have to show that the words actually affected their reputation.

What is defamatory?

A statement is defamatory, according to the most widely used definitions, if it:

- exposes a person to hatred, ridicule or contempt, or causes him or her to be shunned or avoided, or has a tendency to injure him or her in his or her office, profession or trade;
- tends to discredit a person by a falsehood;
- tends to lower a person in the opinion of 'right-thinking members of society' generally.

None of these definitions is exhaustive, but the first is the most useful in practice. Some examples of obviously defamatory statements include:

- saying that a person has a venereal disease;
- imputing insolvency or impending insolvency;
- alleging dishonesty or corruption;
- implying that someone is unsuited to a trade or profession;
- (sometimes) saying that a company's products do not work or are dangerous.

It requires no special skill to recognize statements which are defamatory on their face, and with practice most are easily spotted. It can sometimes be difficult, though, to decide whether what is defamatory in one society is equally damaging in another. For example, would it have been defamatory to report that former Israeli premier Menachem Begin had been involved in terrorist activity in British-occupied Palestine? There is no easy answer, but an English court is surely entitled to take into account the values prevailing in a plaintiff's own society. These should in theory be reflected in the level of damages, but in practice a jury's prejudices may be the more important factor.

The essential feature of defamation under English law is damage to reputation, not just financial damage:

> Stephane Grappelli, the jazz violinist, sued his agent for cancelling a series of concerts along with the announcement that 'Stephane Grappelli is very seriously ill in Paris and unlikely ever to tour again'. Although the statement was seriously damaging to his earning capacity, his claim for libel failed because the statement elicited sympathy rather than contempt or ridicule. But he succeeded in his claim for malicious falsehood.[13]

The second highest award ever in the United Kingdom was for a strongly-worded criticism of a revolutionary yacht design in the magazine *Yachting World* [14]:

> The article queried whether the yacht was an 'expensive white elephant' and the jury seemed to show, by its award of £1.485 million (US$2.3 million), that it felt

the article was a devastating attack upon the whole reputation of the boat-building company and its management. The article sent shock-waves through the magazine industry[15], but in reality few risks will attach to objective reports which stick to verifiable facts and make rational recommendations on the basis of those facts.

The judge's role is to determine whether a given statement is capable of the defamatory meaning(s) pleaded, while the jury must decide whether that meaning or those meanings were actually present. There is anecdotal evidence that juries are liable to muddle their role and assume words must be defamatory, when a judge has only ruled that they are *capable* of being defamatory.

Where a statement is not literally defamatory, but a number of implications can be found – some of them defamatory, some perhaps not – the judge has to decide whether the words are capable of supporting the meaning contended by the plaintiff. If he or she decides they can, the jury must decide whether as a matter of fact the harmful meaning was present:

> An article in the *Daily Telegraph* headed 'INQUIRY ON FIRM BY CITY POLICE' reported that the City of London Fraud Squad were 'enquiring into the affairs of Rubber Improvement Ltd. The investigation was requested after criticisms of the chairman's statement and the accounts by a shareholder at a recent company meeting. The chairman is Mr John Lewis, former Socialist MP.' In the libel action which followed, Lewis and the company claimed that the article suggested they were actually guilty of fraud, and succeeded at trial, winning the colossal sum, for 1964, of £100 000 (US$150 000). On appeal, the House of Lords decided that the words were not capable of this meaning, but that they could have the defamatory meaning that fraud was *suspected*.[16]

Mere abuse is not defamatory, provided a reasonable person would not understand the words as conveying truth. Likewise, parody or satire enjoy a wider margin of tolerance than articles intended to be taken seriously:

> A satirical BBC radio programme, *Week Ending*, ridiculed former Fleet Street tabloid editor, Derek Jameson, whose editorial policy, it said, was 'All the nudes fit to print and all the news printed to fit'. The BBC won the libel case Jameson brought, probably on the basis that the words should not have been taken seriously.[17]

But the general rule is that the law reads into a statement the most damaging interpretation that an averagely suspicious person would understand by it.[18] So a cautious approach is fully justified, and if several meanings can be read into a statement or an article as a whole, the best policy is to concentrate on the more damaging interpretations.

Strictly speaking, statements in an article or programme are not defamatory if taken out of context or in isolation from other words countering the sting of the defamation. Thus, reporting a clearly defamatory rumour should not technically be the subject of a successful libel claim, if the article as a whole takes pains to scotch the rumour. On the other hand, if the story leaves real doubt or suggests that there is 'no smoke without fire', it may be defamatory.

If the meaning of a statement is ambiguous, the court will look at the wider context of the article for clarification, and will examine its overall meaning to determine whether it is defamatory as a whole. It is the interplay between the overall meaning and the meaning of individual sections which often taxes the judgement of journalists and lawyers.

Care is needed with the order in which the material is set out, and especially with headlines:

> The *Daily Telegraph* ran an article headed 'TWO MORE IN SCOTT AFFAIR', and went on, 'The names of two more people connected with the Scott affair have been given to the police. One is a wealthy benefactor of the Liberal Party.' There had been allegations of a conspiracy to murder Scott, who claimed to have been the former homosexual lover of the then Liberal leader, Jeremy Thorpe. The article went on to connect the benefactor with obscure payments seemingly bound up with the alleged conspiracy. The plaintiff recovered £50 000 (US$75 000) for libel because the headline created an impression of skulduggery that the rest of the article failed to dispel.[19]

Whether a statement is defamatory or not is a reflection of the views of 'right-thinking members of society' at the relevant time:

> In 1959 Liberace recovered damages from the *Daily Mirror* for describing him as 'a deadly, winking, sniggering, snuggling, chromium-plated, scent-impregnated, luminous, quivering, giggling, fruit-flavoured, mincing, ice-covered heap of mother-love' – meaning, as the jury found, homosexual.[20]

> Thirty-three years later, teen idol Jason Donovan successfully sued the magazine *The Face* for mentioning him in connection with an article on 'outing' closet gays. He claimed that the defamation lay in an implication that he had concealed his sexuality, and did not rely upon any suggestion as to his actual sexuality. Possibly his lawyers were unconvinced – along with a substantial sector of public opinion – that labelling a person as homosexual is defamatory nowadays.

Occasionally, hidden facts are known only to some readers of a story, conveying a defamatory meaning to those readers alone. For example, a hypothetical report that Baroness Thatcher had negotiated a consultancy with a tobacco manufacturer would not by itself be defamatory, but it would if, unknown to the writer, she had been campaigning against the promotion of cigarettes. The term for this is 'innuendo':

A cartoon advertisement in the 1920s depicted, without his consent, a well-known amateur golfer, with a bar of Fry's chocolate poking out of his pocket. The advertisement was defamatory because, although most people would not have drawn any derogatory inference, a restricted circle of golfers knew that amateurs were not permitted to endorse commercial products. This damaged his amateur status, even though most people would not have been aware of any discreditable behaviour.[21]

There is little a writer can do to avoid innuendo based on facts unknown, and the danger is especially great when covering an unfamiliar subject. To some extent it is mitigated by the defence of unintentional defamation. The Defamation Act 1952 introduced the defence of unintentional defamation to meet the problem of accidental defamatory content and identification.[22] The defence, while welcome, unfortunately brought practical difficulties of its own (of which more later), and is rarely used in practice.

So-called 'false' innuendo is the same as a straightforward implication, whose meaning does not depend upon knowledge of special facts.

Identification

The second fact plaintiffs must prove, after showing that the words are defamatory, is that they are referred to as the subject of the offensive statement. No intention on the part of the defendant is necessary, nor does the identification have to be by name:

> One Harold Newstead, a resident of Camberwell, was jailed for bigamy. The *Daily Express* duly reported: 'Harold Newstead, thirty-year-old Camberwell man, who was jailed for nine months, liked having two wives at once ... He said "I kept them both until the police interfered."' There was another Harold Newstead, who also lived in Camberwell and was of about the same age. The fact that the article was intended to refer to the other Newstead was no defence, and the evidence showed that reasonable people could have identified the plaintiff as the subject of the article.[23]

It is enough if, at trial, witnesses are ready to swear that they thought the article referred to the plaintiff, even where they could only identify the plaintiff because they already knew other identifying facts.

The medium chosen is relevant to the issue of identification, for it affects the level of care the reader or viewer is expected to exercise. Photographs in newspapers and chance juxtapositions in films or television programmes are particularly liable to create unintended and damaging connections in the viewer's mind.

It can be just as dangerous, if not more so, to try to avoid libel by not naming a person, since a statement referring to an identifiable group may be read as referring to each member of the group:

> The *News of the World* published an article about a man who had taken hostages because he believed ten detectives from the Banbury police force had raped and assaulted his wife. The newspaper reported his bizarre allegations and ten members of the Banbury force recovered substantial damages, even though no names had been given.[24]

Some groups are so large that it is impossible to identify individual members. Decided cases suggest that a grouping of thirty or more will make identification unlikely, but much depends upon individual circumstances.

Publication

Finally, in addition to proving that he has been defamed, the plaintiff must show that the words have been published, in the narrow sense of being communicated to at least one third party. An insult communicated to the plaintiff, and no-one else, will not amount to publication. But in the case of criminal libel the insult may be so extreme that the law does not require the plaintiff to prove publication to a third party.

There will normally be little difficulty in proving publication against a media defendant. In a libel case – as opposed to slander – damage to reputation is presumed to flow even from a single solitary publication, but wider dissemination, typified by mass media coverage, can be expected to inflate the level of damages. Publication by electronic database or on the Internet raises different issues, many of which are as yet unresolved.

Every repetition of a libel gives rise to a fresh 'publication' and a fresh libel claim. Hence rumours must be treated with extreme caution, for the intention or belief of the person repeating the rumour is irrelevant. In the same way, resuscitating old stories or relying on 'cuts' can be risky, and the fact that the subject did not sue the first time around does not mean that the story is safe to publish.

The defendant's task

Once it has been shown that the words are defamatory, that they refer to the plaintiff, and that there has been a 'publication' – in the technical sense described above – the burden of proof shifts. The defendant then has to establish one of the recognized defences. Any 'constitutional' protection at all for free speech in English law – in the sense of recognition of the public interest in free speech – is embodied in the defences of privilege and fair comment, which attempt to balance public and private interest, with limited success. There are three main defences:

- Truth (or justification)
- Honest ('fair') comment
- Privilege.

Truth (Justification)

The concept of public interest is absent from the defence of truth in a civil libel action.[25] Truth is an 'absolute' defence in that the state of mind of the defamer is irrelevant. So is the public usefulness, or otherwise, of the publication. The grossest invasion of privacy will be justifiable in defamation law if the facts are provably true.

Presumption of falsity

The usual presumption of English criminal law is that a man is presumed innocent until proved guilty. In the law of defamation the presumption is reversed. The burden of proving truth falls squarely on the defendant's shoulders, the presumption being that the words are false. It is not clear in the wake of the decisions of the Indian Supreme Court and the Australian High Court in late 1994, introducing *Sullivan*-type defences, how long English law can persist with this inflexible requirement.

A useful analogy is sometimes drawn between defending a libel action using the defence of justification and prosecuting a person for a criminal offence. This gives some idea of the scale of the task when contemplating a defence of justification – and, of course, unlike the prosecuting authorities, the media have no powers of search and seizure to gather evidence. In deciding whether to publish it is wise to assume, at least where safety is desired, that the stricter standard will apply.

Meaning

Although not necessarily required to show the absolute literal truth of an article, the defendant must prove that the 'stings' are true in substance and in fact:

A story was headed 'False Profit Return Charge against Society'. The subject of the article, a mutual society, had shown in its annual return a capital item which, in the opinion of the regulatory authority, should have been shown as income. The authority had prosecuted the society, with the intention of resolving the issue. The defendants argued that the words of the report were true, which literally they were. But it was held on appeal that the judge had been right to allow the jury to decide whether their meaning was in fact defamatory. The word 'false' was ambiguous, and was capable of conveying knowledge of falsity.[26]

Not only do defendants have to prove that the words are true, but they must prove the truth of every defamatory barb which materially injures the subject[27]:

> In a nineteenth century case, the plaintiff was called a 'libellous journalist'. Although the plaintiff had once been successfully sued for libel, that was not enough for the defendant to establish the defence of truth. To do so, he had to show that the plaintiff was *habitually* a libellous journalist.[28]

So to call a man a fascist, it would not be enough to show that he had once supported fascism. You would have to prove that he is still a fascist.

Standard of proof

It will usually be enough for the defendant to prove truth on a balance of probabilities – the normal civil standard of proof. But the more serious the charge, the stricter the standard. Where a criminal offence is imputed, it approximates to the criminal standard – that is, proof beyond reasonable doubt. Proof of a conviction in the United Kingdom is by statute conclusive proof that the offence was committed.

   Care is needed in reporting that a person has been charged with an offence, or that a writ has been issued alleging some serious civil wrong such as conspiracy, fraud or other dishonesty. The law is unclear as to whether this is defamatory. Certainly, the existence of the writ or a statement of what an action is broadly about can be reported safely provided it is done fairly and accurately, but there is doubt as to how far it is safe to report detailed allegations contained in a writ.

Evidence

A lack of evidence admissible in court will be fatal to a defendant relying on a plea of justification. The English system relies heavily on direct oral testimony, with documentary evidence taking second place.

   It is hard to evaluate the strength of available evidence when faced with tight publishing deadlines. Lawyers' advice will normally be needed where proof depends on the interpretation and admissibility of written evidence, even evidence which may appear conclusive. Some newspapers now make a practice of obtaining sworn statements from key witnesses in advance of publishing a potentially libellous story, or advising journalists to tape-record all telephone conversations. But any defence based on oral evidence necessarily includes an element of risk, not least because oral testimony may collapse in court under close cross-examination.

In normal circumstances, a defendant relying on the defence of justification should be prepared to bring witnesses to London, often at substantial expense.[29] There is, of course, no guarantee that those witnesses will be convincing in court, or even remember what they were so adamant about two or three years before. Statements, affidavits and tape-recordings at least have the effect of crystallizing witnesses' memory, as well as committing them to a version of events.

Journalists need to keep notebooks or tapes for whatever period they or their employers feel is safe, given the three-year limitation period for libel actions. Admissions by the plaintiff are especially useful. Underpinning journalists' evidence in court, contemporaneous notes – which may be referred to – will be crucial in lending a witness credibility.

Defendants do not technically need to have all their evidence in place before publishing, but English barristers will refuse to plead justification without having sufficient evidence to base a plea of truth. There must always be a firm factual basis to work from, but after this, 'discovery' (disclosure of documents ordered by the courts) can help bolster a case, and defendants can rely on evidence collected after publication if this bears out the initial accusation. In reality it is most unwise to assume that it will be possible to scramble around putting a case together after receiving a libel writ. The defendant is obliged to commit to a definitive version of his or her story relatively early in the case, and the court will be hostile to vague and speculative 'fishing expeditions' for evidence under the cloak of discovery, even in the unusual event that a barrister is prepared to plead a speculative case.

Rehabilitation of offenders

The sole instance in civil defamation law where truth is not a complete defence is the reporting of a criminal conviction which is 'spent', as defined in the Rehabilitation of Offenders Act 1974.[30] Because, however, the plaintiff must also show that the defendant 'maliciously' published a 'spent' conviction, and because malice by the media is hard to demonstrate, the Act has had little practical impact on reporting.

Repetition and rumours

A common misconception is that the defence of justification covers the repetition of statements made by third parties, for example that someone, perhaps in a position of authority, has made a particular defamatory allegation. This is *not* the case, and journalists must remember that they have to prove the truth of what other people may have said (or rely on one of the other accepted defences). This may frequently be an impossible task for the person repeating the allegation without personal knowledge of the facts.

Another aspect of the same idea is that unconfirmed defamatory rumours should not be reported until confirmed. Competitive pressures create headaches for journalists and the lawyers checking an item for publication, where an unconfirmed rumour is seeping into the public domain. A lower level of damages should result if defamatory words are framed in unsensational terms. Naming the source of a rumour and proper reporting of 'balancing comment' is supposed to reduce the sting of an article and so the amount awarded by a jury. It may also affect the meaning of an article in the defendant's favour.

It may be worth calculating that an article which, taken as a whole, does not suggest any wrongdoing will not attract a writ. If a libel claim is brought, it should be possible to avoid liability by showing that the thrust of the piece counters the 'sting' of the libel. A determined plaintiff may, however, be able to extract an early settlement and an apology simply because a defendant does not wish to run the risk of a perverse jury finding on the actual meaning.

Innuendo

Where the words used are factually accurate, but carry a defamatory implication or innuendo, the defendant will have to prove the truth of the damaging implication:

> A house that had suffered war damage belonged to a local councillor. It had been noticeably better repaired than another similar house in the area. The councillor's house was then requisitioned by the authorities, along with several others, but shortly afterwards the requisition of the councillor's house alone was cancelled. A newspaper reported these facts accurately. When the councillor sued, it was held the article had implied that the councillor had secured, not merely received, preferential treatment. The newspaper was unable to prove the damaging implication, although it was perfectly reasonable to infer that he had secured preferential treatment.[31]

The case illustrates how dangerous even careful, unsensational reporting can be, if inferential or innuendo meanings can be read into it. In similar cases it can reduce exposure to state that there is 'no question of any improper behaviour by the plaintiff' (many journalists understandably hate such phrases).

Sources

In libel cases it is clearly established that a journalist cannot usually be forced to reveal the source of a defamatory story until trial, and now by statute disclosure will only even then be ordered where necessary in the interests of justice or national security, or for the prevention of disorder or crime. In two major cases in recent years the courts have nonetheless declined to give any special weight to the public interest in preserving the confidentiality of journalistic sources.[32]

Damages

Even if a publisher is convinced that the allegations can be justified, and confident of surmounting the obstacles the law throws in its path, there is a final test of nerve: pleading truth and failing may lead to an award of aggravated damages, to compensate the plaintiff for having the issues thrashed out in the public gaze. It is unsurprising then that media defendants regularly pay sizeable sums to settle claims lacking real merit.

'Fair' comment

In common with many legal systems, English law protects certain comments or statements of opinion. The English protection is qualified, whereas in many countries statements of opinion receive absolute constitutional protection. The defence is useful when you cannot prove a comment is true, or when you do not want to, for example where that might aggravate damages. It is often a difficult defence to get juries to agree upon, but gives wide protection to book reviews and critiques of plays, films and other works of art. It is also a bulwark of the leader-writer's defences.

The comment must be:

- recognizable as comment;
- based on provable facts;
- on a matter of public interest;
- one that a fair-minded person could honestly make;
- made without 'malice'.

Recognizable as comment

The distinction between statements of fact and opinion is often opaque. The nearest to an acid test is whether a fact can be proven by evidence. Thus, to accuse a doctor of negligence is to make a defamatory allegation of fact, even though negligence can normally only be proven in court by the *opinion* evidence of another doctor. But to accuse a politician of political ineptitude will usually be a comment – it is simply unprovable.

It is safer in marginal cases to assume that only the defence of truth will be available. But if the decision is taken to publish relying on fair comment, it should be only because the inference was one that a fair-minded person might draw from demonstrable facts, i.e. there were reasonable grounds for believing the conclusion drawn. Suggestions of dishonesty or improper motive are tricky to defend as fair comment. In cases where dishonesty or impropriety is alleged, the inference must be a reasonable one, and not just one that could be made by a fair-minded person.

To use fair comment as a defence, the comment must be clearly set out, and then the facts upon which the comment is based. The idea is to enable the reader to form a personal assessment of whether the comment is fair and honest. If fact and comment are mixed up, the court may decide that both factual basis and opinion are statements of fact, and the truth of the damaging opinion will have to be proved.

Based on provable fact

Each fact set out as a basis for comment must be proved separately, otherwise the defence will fail:

> A newspaper proprietor, Lord Kemsley, sued Michael Foot for an article headed 'Lower than Kemsley', in which Foot attacked an article in the *Evening Standard* as 'the foulest piece of journalism perpetrated for many a long year'. Kemsley argued that the headline was a statement of fact, that his newspapers were a byword for dishonest journalism. Foot successfully defended the headline as a comment on the fact of Kemsley's newspaper ownership.[33]

Exceptionally, where the facts are protected by privilege – for example, a report of a parliamentary speech – the defendant will only have to establish that privilege applies to the factual basis, and need not prove that the underlying statement was true.

On a matter of public interest

The need for the comment to be on a matter of public interest gives rise to few problems for the media and is easily discharged. Almost any issue in which the public could legitimately show serious interest will satisfy the test.

Fairness

The defence is called 'fair comment', but this is misleading because there is no requirement – except where impropriety or dishonesty is alleged – that the comment should be 'fair' or even very reasonable. The comment must be one that a fair-minded person *could* make based on the facts proved, but the question of the defendant's actual state of mind only arises if malice is alleged.

Without malice

Proving malice can defeat the defence of fair comment, just as it can defeat the defence of qualified privilege.

So long as the belief is honestly held, it does not have to be reasonable. In the leading case on the subject, the House of Lords said:

> Indifference to the truth of what a person publishes is not to be equated with carelessness, impulsiveness or irrationality in arriving at a positive belief that it is true.... But despite the imperfection of the mental process by which the belief is arrived at, it may still be 'honest', that is, a positive belief that the conclusions they have reached are true.[34]

But when the criticism is intemperate, the jury may lose sight of the requirement for the comment to be honest rather than objectively 'fair':

> An accomplished actress was pilloried in a *News of the World* article. It said she 'can't sing, she can't act, her bum is too big and she has the sort of stage presence which jams lavatories'. She recovered £11 000 (US$17 000), defeating a plea of fair comment.

This was an extreme case, where the jury gave the benefit of the doubt to the plaintiff rather than a spiky reviewer. Critics still have considerable latitude to criticize works of art or performances fairly or unfairly, and malice is very hard to prove.

More recently, however, the second highest award ever made in the United Kingdom for libel was for a magazine review of an unusually designed yacht.[35] The case shows that a fair comment defence has to be constructed with care, failing which the defamatory statements may be treated as statements of fact. Unless the award is reduced on appeal, the case may have a chilling effect on product testers, if not on arts critics where the element of subjectivity is more acceptable.

Privilege

In fair comment, English law recognizes the value of free expression of opinion. Similarly, by the defence of privilege it accepts the public or private interest, on certain 'occasions', in the publication of well-defined categories of defamatory statements. The defence protects, for example, court and parliamentary reports, employers' references,[36] statements by chief constables in certain circumstances and government notices, the rationale being that the potential damage to the subject of the defamatory statement is outweighed by the benefit to society in being properly informed.

There are two classes of privilege, absolute and qualified. The only distinction between them is that malice does not defeat absolute privilege.

Absolute privilege

The following are among the more important occasions protected by absolute privilege:

- statements made in the course of UK parliamentary and Commonwealth legislative proceedings;
- contemporaneous newspaper and broadcast[37] reports of UK judicial proceedings;
- official reports of UK parliamentary proceedings;
- reports of the UK parliamentary and other Ombudsmen, of the Monopolies and Mergers Commission and of the Health Service Commissioners;
- statements made in the course of UK judicial proceedings.

Media reports of parliament do not attract absolute, but qualified, privilege. A member of parliament can with impunity in parliament blacken a person's name irrespective of his or her own malice. The only sanctions against abuse of the privilege are parliament's own disciplinary procedures. This is in marked contrast to the protection given to newspaper and broadcast reports of court proceedings which, if the report is fair and accurate and published or broadcast[38] contemporaneously, is absolute. The subject of court reporting is discussed further below.

Qualified privilege

Qualified privilege is distinct from absolute privilege in that it can be defeated by malice. There are five main categories of common law and statutory qualified privilege:

- statements made in performance of a legal or moral duty, provided the recipient has a reciprocal interest in receiving the information;
- statements made in furtherance or protection of an interest, public or private;
- statements in protection of a common interest;
- reports of parliamentary and judicial proceedings;
- statements privileged under the Defamation Act 1952 (statutory qualified privilege).

The first three categories mentioned above hold little further interest for journalists, but, of course, reporting parliament and the courts is a significant part of most newspapers' and broadcasters' daily fare.

Right of reply

An important example of the second category – statements in protection of a private interest – is the privilege of reply to an attack. The subject of a defamatory attack has the right to defend him or herself and will be protected by qualified privilege in doing so. The means used must correspond as far as possible with the channels of attack and be reasonably proportionate to the original attack.

So a newspaper could be protected from a libel suit in relation to a defamatory self-defence appearing on its letters page if the original attack appeared there in the first instance. But if a national newspaper published a reply to an attack originating in the local press, the privilege might be lost.

No public interest defence

Some UK journalists cherish the belief that there exists under English law a privilege for reports on matters of public interest. This is a hazardous illusion (although for some years there was judicial support for a public interest privilege and some European Court of Human Rights cases encourage the belief). In 1984 the Court of Appeal said that such a defence could operate only in restricted situations.[39] There had to be a duty to the public at large to publish the defamatory information, and the public as a whole – not just a section of it – must have a reciprocal interest in receiving it.

Examples might include imminent danger to the public from a cloud of noxious chemicals or the escape of a suspected mass-murderer. Even these instances are still hypothetical since the legal requirements have not been tested in court.

It is to be hoped that the *Blackshaw* case represents the zenith of judicial *laissez-faire* in qualified privilege. There are indications that in years to come appellate judges will be less hostile to common law qualified privilege as a defence in cases of serious public concern.

Statutory qualified privilege

The Schedule to the Defamation Act 1952 sets out a list of occasions which, if reported fairly and accurately in newspapers or broadcasts, attract qualified privilege. For the occasions set out in Part II of the Schedule only, the protection depends on the defendant being prepared to publish a 'reasonable statement by way of explanation or contradiction' from the plaintiff in response to the original article.

The report must be:

- not prohibited by law;
- of public concern;
- for the public benefit;
- fair and accurate.

In summary, Part I covers reports of the proceedings of:

- Commonwealth legislatures;
- international organizations or conferences where the UK is represented;
- international courts;
- Commonwealth courts or British courts-martial held abroad;
- Commonwealth public inquiries.

It also protects extracts from UK public registers and notices published on the authority of a UK court.

Part II statements, where the subject has a reasonable right of reply, protects reports of:

- The findings or decisions of certain UK academic, professional, cultural, trade or sporting institutions;
- UK public meetings on matters of public concern;
- Proceedings of UK local authorities, official commissions, tribunals and inquiries, or other statutory bodies;
- Proceedings at general meetings of UK public companies;
- Officially issued UK government, municipal or police notices.

To ensure that protection is available, it is well worth referring to the actual words of the Schedule. The statute is in evident need of revision. There is no protection in the Schedule, for example, for statements made in any of the

European Community institutions. Of proceedings in foreign countries, only the 'Dominions' – essentially the Commonwealth countries – are covered. So protection might exist for the Jamaican Parliament, but not for the US House of Representatives, although this might well be covered by common law qualified privilege if the subject were of legitimate concern to the British public.

Common law qualified privilege

All fair and accurate reports of UK parliamentary or judicial proceedings are protected at common law. This special media reporting privilege reflects the right of the public to be present during those proceedings. Unlike absolute privilege for court reporting or statutory qualified privilege, there are no restrictions upon the medium in which the article can be published.

In both parliamentary and court reports, the privilege will not apply to matters not strictly part of the proceedings. So in court, abuse shouted from the public gallery would not be protected.

Court reporting

To attract statutory privilege a report of court proceedings must be published contemporaneously, but at common law there is no such requirement. The report must be fair and accurate, but this proviso is mainly honoured in the breach and appears not to be interpreted too strictly, at least in relation to inessential detail.

Common law qualified privilege and absolute privilege apply to all UK tribunals exercising judicial functions, provided that they are open to the public. This contrasts sharply with the limited list of tribunals upon which the Defamation Act 1952 confers protection.

Foreign tribunals only attract the common law qualified privilege if the subject matter is of 'legitimate and proper interest' to the British public – something more than idle curiosity or gossip:

> A man was tried in England for murder and acquitted. Some years later he killed again, this time in Switzerland. During his subsequent trial he admitted responsibility for the first murder and alleged that his first victim had fathered his own wife's child. *The Times* reported his claim, which as the trial took place abroad was not covered by statutory privilege. The killer's wife sued for libel, but the court decided the British public had a legitimate interest in the case and upheld the common law defence of qualified privilege.[40]

This case had a significant connection with the United Kingdom, but care is needed when such a link is missing.

Protection is restricted to what is actually said or done in open court. Reporting pleadings or affidavits is not privileged until they are read out or referred to in court, for until then they are essentially private documents.

Hence the danger, for example, in reporting the launching of a libel action – the writ may be protected, but it is not necessarily safe to report in detail any statement of claim on the writ.

Malice

Both honest comment and qualified privilege can be defeated by showing that the defendant was motivated by 'malice'. It is irrelevant to any other defences which the defendant may put forward, such as truth or absolute privilege.

'Malice' has a wider sense in libel law than in everyday speech. The plaintiff has to prove that the dominant motive of the defendant was to injure the plaintiff. This will be clear if cross-examination reveals a lack of honest belief that a statement was true, whether due to personal antagonism to the plaintiff or some other improper motive. But a refusal to apologize does not by itself show malice.

Other defences

Unintentional defamation

The Defamation Act 1952[41] protects statements:

- not intended to refer to the plaintiff;
- which are not obviously defamatory and where the publisher was unaware of facts making them defamatory of the plaintiff.

The defence requires that the publisher should have taken all reasonable care in relation to the publication. The defendant must promptly make an 'offer of amends' – meaning an offer to apologize or issue a correction, accompanied by a sworn statement showing why the publication was not negligent. Provided that the publication was not 'malicious', the publisher will have a complete defence. The defence is little used, partly because of its procedural complexity, and also because the news media often cannot prove that they have taken reasonable care. It is of greater use to authors of fiction and their publishers.

Problems of this type can often be avoided by ensuring adequate identification of real individuals – for example, reporting the address of a person charged with an offence in addition to his or her name. In choosing fictitious names, exercise either extreme caution or extreme inventiveness: on the principle of safety in numbers, John Smith is a better choice than Horatio Bottomley.

Innocent dissemination

Those who are not authors, publishers or printers[42] of defamatory works can use the defence of innocent dissemination. The distributors must have no reason to suspect that the publication contains libellous material.

Settlement

An agreement to settle a case for an apology or damages will extinguish the claim. As certain technical conditions have to be met, a lawyer should be involved in all negotiations, particularly those relating to apologies or corrections.

A special feature of settling defamation actions in England is the 'statement in open court'. This enables plaintiffs to have their reputation publicly vindicated, usually by an agreed form of words. The advantage for plaintiffs is that the media can report the statement under qualified privilege, whereas otherwise they might have been inhibited from indicating the nature of the original allegations. It can also enable honour to be satisfied without the parties having to reveal an embarrassingly high or low settlement figure.

Consent

A plaintiff who consents to publication cannot sue for libel. To be safe, a journalist needs to have clear written or taped evidence of consent, although oral evidence backed by contemporaneous notes may be adequate, if accepted by the court. The plaintiff's failure to comment upon an allegation, or to seek an injunction to stop publication when shown an article pre-publication, does not amount to consent.

Payment into court

The procedural device of payment into court, to try to force a settlement, is the most powerful weapon in the defendant's armoury. The system of costs has already been outlined. As a case proceeds towards trial, the legal costs on both sides increase dramatically. A defendant can exploit a plaintiff's fear of losing the case by paying into court a sum the defendant thinks is more than the plaintiff will recover at trial. The plaintiff has the choice of accepting the money in settlement of the action and recovering most of the legal costs, or proceeding with the action.

But a plaintiff who refuses to settle, and fails to recover at trial more than the sum paid in – the payment-in being kept secret from the court – will have to pay both sides' costs from the time when the payment-in was made. The use of payment-in can lead to a war of nerves, which sometimes continues right up to the door of the court:

> Dr Dering, a doctor who had operated experimentally on inmates of Auschwitz extermination camp in the Second World War, sued Leon Uris, author of *Exodus*. Uris and his publishers paid the princely sum of £2 into court. Dering technically won his case, but was awarded 'contemptuous' damages of a half-penny and had to pay the entire costs of the trial.[43]

Defendants must remember that, if a payment-in is accepted, the plaintiff can apply to the court to have a statement read out in court in terms approved by the judge. Only if a very small amount is paid into court will a plaintiff not be entitled to have a statement read out in court.

Limitation

The usual rule is that a publication occurring more than three years earlier cannot be the subject of an action for libel or slander. The period may occasionally be extended if, for example, the plaintiff had been unaware of the publication.

Remedies

English judges are said to be reluctant to restrain the publication of defamatory material where it appears there may be a viable bona fide defence, in particular that the publisher will plead justification to a libel action. In principle, they prefer to allow vindication of reputation by an action for damages. Still, a surprising number of emergency injunctions are granted for libel, and in 1994 a government minister even obtained an injunction against a newspaper for slander.

Damages

Damages may be contemptuous, nominal, compensatory or exemplary, the latter being very large sums intended to punish or deter outrageous or cynical conduct. Awards of contemptuous or, conversely, aggravated damages may be made where the jury wishes to mark its disapproval of, respectively, the plaintiff's or the defendant's conduct. Nominal damages are awarded where the plaintiff indicates at trial that he or she only wishes to clear his or her name and is not interested in financial compensation, or where the court concludes that the plaintiff has suffered no real injury.

A defendant can plead various matters in mitigation of damages, such as the plaintiff's general bad reputation in the relevant sector of his or her life[44] (i.e for the kind of conduct the subject of complaint in the libel action), or any apology offered by the defendant, or the conduct of the plaintiff towards the defendant.

Injunctions

A far more attractive and powerful remedy for the plaintiff who really has something to hide is an emergency injunction. This will bypass the risks involved in a lengthy libel action by stifling the problem at source. Where however, a defendant being threatened with an injunction restraining publication files an affidavit saying that he or she intends to use one of the main recognized libel defences – truth, fair comment or privilege – the court as a rule will not grant an order because damages are seen as a sufficient remedy.[45] So journalists should not hold back from seeking balancing comment from the subject of a forthcoming exposé for fear of attracting an injunction for libel.

An injunction may nevertheless be awarded for another civil wrong such as breach of confidence, conspiracy or malicious falsehood:

> Gorden Kaye, the star of a popular television sitcom, was injured by a falling tree. Reporters from the *Sunday Sport* gained access to his hospital bedside as he lay unconscious, and took unauthorized photographs. His family applied for an injunction restraining the ensuing 'exclusive' interview. They could not show defamation – for who would think worse of Kaye for being injured? The court granted an injunction because it was arguable that Kaye was the victim of a malicious falsehood, namely the implication that he had voluntarily sold his story to the newspapers.[46]

A plaintiff who wants to gag publication may be tempted to pursue an injunction for malicious falsehood or breach of confidence. Here the test the court uses is based on the relative financial harm likely to be suffered by the parties if the injunction is granted or refused. Little, if any, weight is attached to the public interest in permitting publication.

A plaintiff may gain a tactical advantage in seeking an injunction, even if the immediate chances of success are slight. Because the defendant has to disclose the nature of its defence in its affidavit, it will be restricted from altering that line of defence in the light of facts emerging subsequently.

Plaintiffs can thus obtain at the very start of the action a fair idea of the case they are likely to meet. Should the defendant later abandon the defence of truth promised in its affidavit, the jury may show disapproval by increasing the award:

> The satirical magazine *Private Eye* alleged that Robert Maxwell had financed trips abroad for the leader of the Labour Party in the hope of obtaining a peerage. The magazine successfully resisted Maxwell's attempt to suppress publication by saying in its affidavit that it would rely on the defence of truth. It turned out that Maxwell had twice rejected a peerage and the magazine's defence collapsed. The jury made an award of £50 000 (US$75 000) in aggravated damages, while valuing the compensatory element of the libel at only £5000 (US$7500).[47]

Sometimes a judge can be persuaded to grant an injunction *ex parte* for a limited period, that is, without notice to the other party and without that party being entitled to argue his or her case. The defendant needs then to make an immediate application for a full defended hearing and stands an excellent chance of overturning the initial injunction.

If a victim of inaccuracy, invasion of privacy or other journalistic sin does not wish to pursue a claim through the courts, a complaint can be made to the Press Complaints Commission or the Broadcasting Complaints Commission. These bodies concern themselves mainly with complaints of unfair or unethical treatment rather than defamation, but may provide a cheaper means of redress for those whose prime aim is a vindication of their reputation rather than recovery of compensation. The attractions for a plaintiff are speed, low cost and the possibility of forcing the newspaper or broadcaster to publish the Commission's adjudication.

Other restraints

This chapter concentrates primarily upon defamation, to the general exclusion of other restraints on freedom of speech. But some other restrictions demand a passing mention.

Contempt of court

Apart from civil libel, contempt of court is the main day-to-day constraint on journalistic activity in the United Kingdom. Under the Contempt of Court Act 1981, strict limits are imposed on the reporting of material, such as old convictions, which may tip the verdict one way or the other. For example, any suggestion that an accused is guilty may be a punishable contempt.

The rule contained in the Act is known as the 'strict liability' rule. Criminal liability may result from its breach within the United Kingdom, although publication outside the United Kingdom will often be safe because the chances of jurors or magistrates reading prejudicial material published abroad are slim. The main danger area is criminal cases tried by juries – judges trying civil cases and Appeal Court judges presiding over criminal appeals claim that they cannot be influenced by press reports.

The requirements are:

- 'active proceedings';
- a substantial risk of serious prejudice;
- publication to the public or a section of the public.

'Active' cases are those where the first formal step has been taken, e.g. an arrest warrant is issued or a person who is helping the police with inquiries is charged. The strict liability rule only kicks in when the active period begins.

Unless the journalist is familiar with the contempt rules, he or she should seek legal advice if inclined to publish prejudicial information and if criminal proceedings are threatened or in progress. Failure to do so can lead to imprisonment and/or fines.

Criminal libel

Libel can, in cases likely to cause a breach of the peace, still be a criminal offence as well as a civil wrong. In this respect, it is essentially a public order offence. It differs sharply from the civil wrong in two ways. First, truth is no defence unless it is shown that publication was in the public interest. Second, it can be a criminal offence to libel the dead. Prosecutions have to be sanctioned by a High Court judge, and are sufficiently rare to enable the media to disregard the offence for practical purposes.

Malicious falsehood

The essence of defamation is damage to reputation. In malicious falsehood, what is important is the untruth of what is said and the defendant's knowledge of that untruth. There are many instances – for example, saying untruthfully that a rival's product is useless – where a plaintiff suffers harm from inaccurate information which does not denigrate his or her character. In these cases the plaintiff has a remedy, but must prove lack of good faith, falsity and financial loss. By contrast, in an action for defamation the burden is on the defendant to show that the statement is true, and in the case of libel (and sometimes in slander) no financial loss need be proven.

Legal aid is available for malicious falsehood and most other civil wrongs, unlike defamation. An interesting recent case showed that the courts will not stop malicious falsehood from being used to achieve the same result as a libel action, if a libel case is too expensive.[48]

Privacy

English law does not protect privacy as such, except as an indirect conse-quence of enforcing some other right, e.g. a matrimonial or commercial confi-dence. If a publisher can establish the truth of a defamatory statement, it is irrelevant that the story also invades the privacy of its subject. In the case of Gorden Kaye mentioned above, the court struggled to categorize what was essentially an invasion of privacy as libel or malicious falsehood.

Blasphemous and seditious libel and obscenity

Blasphemous and seditious libel are archaic common law crimes akin to crim-inal libel. The law of blasphemy recently came under the spotlight with the attempt by Muslim opponents of *The Satanic Verses* to prosecute the author Salman Rushdie for blasphemous libel. The court was unable to do so because the only religion protected by English blasphemy law is Christianity. Naturally, this did not endear the judicial system to the Muslim community in Britain. There have since been calls for equality of treatment for all reli-gions, either by widening the offence or by its abolition.

Seditious libel is a common law crime defined as the publication of words calculated to disturb the peace and good government of the country and published with that intention.

The test of an obscene publication is whether the effect of the subject-matter taken as a whole is to deprave and corrupt those likely to read it.

Prosecutions for these offences are rare, and because of their subject-matter they do not impinge on day-to-day media activity.

Breach of confidence and journalists' sources

The years since 1985 have seen a steep increase in the number of cases brought to restrain a breach of confidence. The courts have so far consistently refused to grant real weight to the public interest in the confidentiality of jour-nalists' sources:

A trainee journalist received a leaked copy of a confidential report concerning a company in financial difficulties. On contacting the company to check the story, he received an injunction for his pains, and was then ordered to reveal the source of his information. The court found him guilty of contempt of court for refusing to do so. The basis of the decision was that the 'administration of justice' required that the company should find out the identity of the 'mole' who leaked the story. But the court indicated that it might have protected the identity of the source if, for example, the report had disclosed wrongdoing of some kind by the company.[49]

It seems then that only a clearly defined public interest will override ordinary commercial confidentiality.

The 'Spycatcher' saga was essentially about the protection of confidential information, in the particular guise of state secrets:

Peter Wright, a former British Intelligence officer, wrote a book alleging certain illegal acts by himself and others. The British Government sought to suppress publication by actions for breach of confidence around the world. The Attorney-General obtained emergency injunctions against *The Guardian* and *The Observer* newspapers to prevent serialization, but *The Independent*, *The Sunday Times* and the *London Daily News* all published extracts, believing that they were entitled to do so because they were not directly addressed by the injunctions. The court decided they were still in contempt since they had deliberately dissipated the confidential subject matter of the action against *The Guardian* and *The Observer*.

As a result of the case it is now routine for the press and broadcasters to be sprayed with copies of injunctions granted in proceedings for breach of confidence, with the aim of suppressing publication. When, just before the 1992 General Election, a sex scandal was about to break around the Liberal leader Paddy Ashdown, he was able by this means to gag the press for some days. The media has no recourse in this situation except to apply to the court for leave to publish, or to hope that the material will enter the public domain outside the jurisdiction.

The international dimension

It is not always realized that publication predominantly abroad can give rise to a libel suit in England, where a tangible connection with the United Kingdom is evident:

The Greek newspaper *Eleftherotypia* was in 1987 ordered to pay a retired naval officer £450 000 (US$700 000) for a series of articles depicting him unfavourably. Only a few copies of the newspaper had been sold in Britain. His reputation was presumably primarily in the United Kingdom.

All foreigners except 'enemy aliens' can sue in the United Kingdom, but may be required to pay money into court as security for the other side's legal costs, should they not succeed at trial. Those without established reputations in the United Kingdom are in theory unlikely to be awarded large sums, although juries are unpredictable in this respect.

The relevant rules as to jurisdiction and applicable law are complex, and what follows is necessarily a rough outline of the position under English law where there is an international element. It is important to keep separate the issues of whether the English court will exercise jurisdiction (a decision based upon the case's connection with England and Wales) and, if it does, which law it will apply.

Jurisdiction

Foreign states, sovereigns and diplomats are immune from suit, as are international organizations such as the United Nations. Apart from these, whether an English court will assume jurisdiction over a foreign defendant depends initially upon whether the proposed defendant is domiciled or not within the European Union (EU).

Defendants domiciled in the EU

The general rule is that EU-domiciled defendants must be sued in their country of domicile, regardless of nationality. The exception relevant for libel purposes is that a defendant can in effect also be sued in the country where damage occurred, i.e. where the material was received or communicated. This means in the case of international publication that the plaintiff may have a choice of countries in which to sue a defendant and can select the legal system most advantageous to his or her case, or, in theory, bring proceedings in more than one jurisdiction.

Defendants not domiciled in the EU

If the defendant is not domiciled in the EU, the issue is determined by detailed rules of court. The court will be prepared to exercise jurisdiction in libel cases, broadly, if either the defendant is present in England and Wales or carries on business there, or if the allegations complained of were published there.[50]

Leave to serve a writ abroad is usually granted where substantial publication by a foreign defendant occurs within England and Wales, although, strictly speaking, an applicant must satisfy a number of distinct criteria. For this reason, many internationally-based organizations with substantial publishing operations in the United Kingdom will be vulnerable to libel actions there, and may then find it difficult to stay proceedings if publication has been substantial within the United Kingdom.[51]

Applicable law

Surprisingly, the English courts will (provided they also have jurisdiction) be prepared to apply English libel rules to a defamatory publication which has taken place abroad, even where there has been no publication in the United Kingdom. The plaintiff has to establish, however, that the words were actionable[52] according to the law of that overseas country. If, for example, a defamatory publication by a British-based news organization takes place *only* in the United States, and if the defendant appears likely to sustain a US 'public figure' or 'public official' defence, the plaintiff's claim is likely to fail.[53]

Foreign judgments

Whether UK judgments will be enforceable abroad, and vice-versa, usually depends on the existence of a convention for reciprocal enforcement of judgments between the relevant countries, provided the foreign law is not contrary to the policy of the domestic law. Judgments of courts in EC countries can generally be enforced in other EC countries, regardless of whether an EC-domiciled defendant is involved.

Reform

Defamation is virtually the only branch of English civil law requiring a defendant to prove innocence, rather than the plaintiff to prove guilt. The *India Abroad* case[54] graphically illustrates how strict liability under English libel law is inimical to the values of those legal systems which place a premium on freedom of expression.

> In 1992 a New York court refused to allow the plaintiff in an English libel suit against the publication *India Abroad* to enforce an English judgment in New York. The court held that to do so would be contrary to the constitutionally enshrined US protection of freedom of speech, because English law placed the burden of proving truth on the defendant.

There is a growing perception among the British media that the law of libel is in need of reform. The complexity of the law and its procedures not only impedes fair treatment of the parties, but multiplies the cost, excluding all but the wealthy from access to justice. In its current state, the law enables money to buy safety from investigative journalism. But many members of the political establishment fear that relaxing the law would lead to an unacceptable trampling of reputations by sections of the press.

Abortive attempts have been made in parliament to introduce a statutory right of reply. Such a right would no doubt give redress to those who are deterred by the expense and rigmarole of an action for damages, but for whom putting forward a complete picture is more important than financial compensation.

In curbing the more extravagant excesses of the press by deterrent awards, libel juries have until now released governments from public pressure to restrict press freedoms. The cost has been the stifling of journalistic inquiry – the 'chilling effect' of libel constraints – and a failure to protect individual privacy.

The Calcutt Committee, set up to review the need for legislation to protect privacy, recommended a probationary period for the British press to 'put its house in order' by means of self-regulation through the Press Complaints Commission, but subsequently reported, to fierce opposition from the press, that it had failed to do so. Legislation has nevertheless not followed, and the government has rejected a tort of privacy.

Several government-appointed committees have, over the years, recommended libel reforms, most of which have been shelved. Most recent is the Report of the Neill Working Group. This contains many valuable suggestions which, while not of a 'root and branch' nature, are nicely judged to redress the balance between plaintiff and defendant. Many of its recommendations now stand a good chance of getting onto the statute book.[55]

The Neill Working Group expressly rejected the introduction of a *Sullivan* – style defence into English law, but this view preceded the judicial development of similar defences in Australia and India which have now somewhat isolated the United Kingdom. Perhaps a heightened awareness of different countries' experience in the defamation field will also, before the emergence of another Robert Maxwell, prompt a deeper reappraisal of the English system.

Notes

1   On 19 July 1995, the UK government proposed reforms to the law of defamation based on the Neill Report. The proposed reforms include a new 'offer of amends' defence; a reduction of the limitation period to one year; a new summary 'fast track' procedure; an extension of statutory qualified privilege to *all* media, and to *inter alia* proceedings of all courts and legislatures *anywhere* in the world. There

are also provisions designed to improve the defence of 'innocent dissemination' which is available to innocent distributors such as retailers or computer bulletin board operators.

2   This chapter is confined to the law of England and Wales, referred to for brevity as 'English law'. Scots defamation law exhibits some marked differences from its English counterpart. Although a discussion of Scottish law is omitted mainly for reasons of space, it is also true that, because of the more draconian nature of English libel law, the latter impacts more severely upon international publication.

3   Scottish libel juries – which are the exception rather than the rule – tend to be more conservative than their English counterparts, and consequently London is a greater attraction to libel plaintiffs.

4   The Press Complaints Commission is a non-statutory body with a Code of Practice.

5   *Derbyshire County Council* v *Times Newspapers Ltd* (1993) 1 All ER 1011

6   *DPP* v *Channel Four Television Co Ltd* (1993) 2 All ER 517.

7   Courts and Legal Services Act 1991 section 8.

8   Sometimes known as 'the English rule'.

9   (1991) *The Guardian*, 26 October.

10 *Derbyshire County Council* v *Times Newspapers Ltd* (1993) 1 All ER 1011

11 *New York Times Co.* v. *Sullivan*, 376 US 254 (1964). See Chapter 1 for a more detailed discussion.

12 In the case of slander 'calculated to disparage the plaintiff in any office, profession, calling, trade or business held or carried on by him at the time of the publication', financial loss need not be proven: Defamation Act 1952, section 2.

13 *Grappelli* v *Derek Block (Holdings) Ltd* (1981) 2 All ER 272

14 (1994) *The Independent*, 9 July.

15 The case is under appeal at the time of writing.

16 *Lewis* v *Daily Telegraph Ltd* (1964) AC 234.

17 (1984) *The Guardian*, 1 March.

18 *Lewis* v *Daily Telegraph Ltd* (1964) AC 234 at 259 per Lord Reid.

19 (1979) *The Times*, 10 November.

20 *Liberace* v *Daily Mirror Newspapers Ltd* (1959) *The Times*, 17,18 June.

21 *Tolley* v *J.S. Fry & Sons Ltd* (1931) AC 333.

22 Defamation Act 1952, section 4.

23 *Newstead* v *London Express Newspaper Ltd* (1940) 1 K 377.

24 (1984) *The Guardian*, 10 February.

25 In criminal libel the defendant must prove publication for the public good in addition to truth.

26 *English and Scottish Co-operative Properties Mortgage and Investment Society Ltd* v *Odhams Press Ltd* (1940) 1 KB 440.

27 The Defamation Act 1952, section 5 dilutes this requirement, and provides that, where several accusations are made, a defendant need not make them all good if the effect of the remaining unproven allegations upon the plaintiff's reputation is trivial, given the truth of the proven allegations.

28 *Clarkson* v *Lawson* (1830) 6 Bing 587.

29   Where witnesses live abroad or subsequently die, any written evidence can usually be put before the court.

30   Rehabilitation of Offenders Act 1974, section 8(5).

31   *Darsley* v *Crystal Publications Ltd* (1946) *West Norwood Times*, 5 July.

32   *Re An Inquiry under the Company Securities (Insider Dealing) Act 1985* (1988) 1 All ER 203; and *X* v *Morgan Grampian Publishers Ltd & Ors* (1990) 2 All ER 1.

33   *Kemsley* v *Foot* (1951) 2 KB 34; (1952) AC 345.

34   *Horrocks* v *Lowe* (1975) AC 135 at 149 per Lord Diplock.

35   (1994) *The Independent*, 9 July.

36   cp. *Spring* v *Guardian Royal Assurance plc & Ors* (1994) 3 WLR 354.

37   Broadcasting Act 1990, section 166.

38   That is, included in a 'programme service', defined in detail in the Broadcasting Act 1990, section 201.

39   *Blackshaw* v *Lord* (1983) 2 All ER 311.

40   *Webb* v *Times Publishing Co* (1960) 2 QB 535.

41   Defamation Act 1952, section 4.

42   The unavailability of the defence to printers is an historical anomaly.

43   *Dering* v *Uris* (1964) 2 QB 669.

44   *Scott* v *Sampson* (1882) 8 QBD 491.

45   *Bonnard* v *Perryman* (1891) 2 Ch 269.

46   *Kaye (Gorden)* v *Andrew Robertson & Sport Newspapers* (1991) FSR 62.

47   *Maxwell* v *Pressdram* (1987) 1 WLR 298.

48   *Joyce* v *Seugupta* (1993) 1 All ER 897.

49   *X* v *Morgan Grampian Publishers Ltd & Ors* (1990) 2 All ER 1.

50   Those not domiciled in an EC country can be sued in England and Wales provided they are available – however fleetingly – for service with a writ within England and Wales. A writ can be served abroad, but only with permission from the court. The court will be unwilling to give leave to serve abroad if the English courts are not the most convenient forum for resolution of the issues, and may subsequently review any decision to grant leave.

51   Defendants incorporated elsewhere but carrying on business within Great Britain are required by law to register the name of a person within Great Britain to accept service of proceedings on their behalf.

52   The precise meaning of 'actionable' is unclear, but the likelihood of the plaintiff bringing a successful suit is plainly a significant factor.

53   Parliament is poised to abolish this so-called 'double actionability' rule with the Private Law (Miscellaneous Provisions) Bill.

54   (1992) *Wall Street Journal*, 16 April.

55   The Government announced late in 1994 that it intends, in the coming parliamentary session, to implement many of the recommendations of the Neill Working Group. This determination will be assisted by the decision of the European Court of Human Rights in 1995 that the award of damages of £1.5 million in favour of Lord Aldington against Count Nikolai Tolstoy was an infringement of his right of freedom of expression under Article 10 of the Convention.

5

France

Joëlle Hannelais of Moquet Borde Dieux, Geens & Associés (Paris)

In France, a defamation (*diffamation*) action is a delicate balancing act. The judge has to juggle the principle of freedom of communication and expression with individual rights and reputation, and the results are often far from conducive to press freedom.

Article 11 of the Declaration of the Rights of Man of 26 August 1789 establishes in clear terms 'free expression of thought and opinion' as one of the 'most precious rights of man'. This right to freedom of expression has had a constitutional dimension ever since the decision of the Constitutional Court (*Conseil Constitutionnel*) of 16 July 1971 incorporated the Declaration of 1789 into the French Constitution of 4 October 1958.

Conflict is, however, inevitable between the Law of 29 July 1881 – which protects rights to reputation – and the constitutionally protected principles of freedom of expression and freedom of the press. The salient features of this Law are not only a restrictive approach on the part of the courts, exemplified by extensive case law, but also a presumption of bad faith which does not feature in the original law.

What is defamation (*diffamation*)?

There are six main elements of defamation under French law:

- an allegation or imputation;
- of a specific and precise fact;
- attacking honour or reputation;
- identifying a particular person;
- publication;
- bad faith.

Allegation or imputation

Although their practical effects are similar, 'allegation' and 'imputation' cover different situations. An 'imputation' is a direct statement of a disparaging fact – the most direct form of defamation. An 'allegation', on the other hand, is essentially an unconfirmed statement. Together with insinuation and allusion, this is the indirect form of defamation.

Analysing the defamatory character or meaning of a statement is not always a scientific process. A judge's analysis may go beyond the literal words used and rely on evidence extrinsic to the words themselves, which may be spoken or written.

Moreover, the courts attach liability not only to the direct publication of a defamation, but also to any 'secondary' publication – any act assisting direct publication – if it is the personal act of the perpetrator.

Some examples of imputations are as follows:

- an accusation that someone is trading in children with a view to their adoption;
- a claim that during the course of a criminal investigation, a family lawyer sold a photograph of a family member's corpse.

'Allegations' can include:

- defamatory words preceded by phrases like 'allegedly' or 'we understand that';
- insinuation or allusion by way of questions, denials, expressions of doubt or 'what ifs';
- hypothesis or suspicion if related to a specific factual context;
- juxtaposition of an article with an accompanying photograph – for example, publishing a photograph of a police officer next to an article accusing the police of protecting 'racist thugs'.

In one case, the Paris Civil Court (*le Tribunal de grande instance*) ruled that the caption to a photograph, suggesting that the subjects were the kind of people who went around carrying Colt 45s, Sten guns and AK47 rifles, was defamatory.[1]

Care in drafting is not always enough to neutralize the defamatory nature of an allegation – the courts tend to see this as a surreptitious way of libelling a person. However, photomontage caricatures of public figures will not be scurrilous provided their manifest aim is not to ridicule that person or bring him or her into disrepute. The journalist had relied on a general liberty to caricature and treat subjects humorously, and the Versailles Court of Appeal ruled: 'A latitude to caricature is traditionally extended to those whose professional activities entitles them to presume implicit consent by those portrayed.'[2]

Specific and precise fact

This second requirement has been clarified by the Cour de Cassation (with the Conseil d'Etat, the highest French court, apart from the Constitutional Court):

> 'Imputations must be neither vague nor general and must arise in the form of statements which can easily be subjected to proof by evidence and argument.'

This definition distinguishes defamation from 'abuse' (*injure*) which is also an offence (*délit*). Abuse does not consist of a precise imputation of specific fact, but only broad allegations of depravity, general defects of character, or a particular state of mind. So calling someone a drunkard or a liar would be mere abuse. But accusing someone of a specific theft would be defamation.

The line between abuse and defamation is often fine. In French classical theatre, 'traitor' is a routine term of abuse. Yet in the aftermath of the Second World War, the term was applied to suspected collaborators. From that specific context it took on a definite defamatory meaning.

The main significance of the distinction is that provocation is no excuse for defamation, unlike abuse. Defamation can be justified by the defence of truth, whereas it is a feature of abuse that proving the truth is impossible.

The two offences of abuse and defamation cannot be pleaded in the alternative, and the plaintiff must resolve this issue at the outset, otherwise the action will be struck out. If an article contains both defamatory and abusive material, it will be classified simply as defamation.

Attacks on honour or esteem

The courts treat attacks on honour or esteem in the same way, although they are distinct concepts. Honour suggests inherent qualities of integrity, loyalty and morality, while esteem stems from social or professional standing.

Attacks on 'honour' include:

- an imputation that a person has committed or been convicted of a crime;
- an imputation of lack of integrity or morality, such as dishonesty or fraud, which is likely to bring someone into disrepute.

The following are examples of crimes which the courts have found to be defamatory:

- being a murderer;[3]
- handling stolen jewels;[4]
- forming a lawbreakers' association.[5]

Equally, suggestions that a person is morally deficient are attacks on honour because they attract society's scorn on the subject. Likewise with allegations that someone is an informer[6] or accusations of helping to draft anonymous letters.[7]

The defamatory attack need not cause actual loss. The absence of loss will be taken into account when calculating the amount of damages, but does not affect liability.

'Esteem' concerns existing, objective reputation in private, professional or political life. Any attack on a person's esteem tends then to cast the complainant in a discreditable light in the eyes of others. The behaviour concerned must relate to one of those three sectors of life i.e. contrary to that which makes a *'bon père de famille'* (perhaps best translated as 'the reasonable man').

But in certain contexts the courts display a degree of flexibility in favour of relatively uninhibited criticism:

- at election time, the courts are more lenient towards the notion of attacks upon esteem, as political debate affords greater scope for controversy;
- when words are cloaked in irony or parody, containing no direct attack. Satirical attacks benefit from this leniency if their tendency is simply to ridicule.

In 1991, on the eve of an election, an article attempted to inform the journal's readership on the ideology and purpose of a political party, without using the words 'Nazi' or 'Neo-Nazi' and without creating any misunderstanding. The Supreme Court of Appeal held that this was not defamatory.[8]

Conversely, later in 1991, the same court said that an article in a weekly journal did attack the honour and reputation of some café proprietors. The article said that no other establishment in town was a better example of a place where mafiosi, lawyers and politicians could clink glasses in a convivial atmosphere than this worshipful society of dubious contacts.[9]

In assessing an attack on honour or esteem, certain factors assume only marginal importance:

- complainants' self-esteem, which is inherently subjective and personal;
- their actual reputation – that the imputed fact is widely known or believed is of little significance;
- isolated criminal convictions for theft do not justify the label of thief.

Identification

Explicit identification is unnecessary. It is enough that the subject can readily be identified. Identification can be inferred from the overall context, including elements outside the article itself, and it may, of course, be made easier by juxtaposition of the article with a photograph. But disguised identification (e.g. by physical description) is just as dangerous once the complainant can readily be identified.

Publication

Publication can be spoken, written or visual. Spoken publication concerns primarily public speeches before a relatively restricted audience. As far as written work and printed matter are concerned, sale is defined as actual delivery to the public – or even simply offering for sale.

Distribution is a form of publication, and involves handing copies to a number of people, or circulating a single copy among several people. Exhibiting defamatory matter by notices and posters in a public place or in a public meeting also amounts to publication.

In the case of distribution, circulation must take place with the knowledge of the author. Publication cannot be attributed to the author if he or she did not authorize it, and responsibility rests therefore with the person who initiated publication.

Bad faith

It is for the plaintiff to prove the first five conditions. However, the sixth – the presumption of bad faith (*mauvaise foi*) on the part of the author – is for the defendant to displace.

Particular consequences flow from 'bad faith'. There is a presumption that defamatory imputations are made with malice (*intention de nuire*), which applies to all those involved in the chain of publication, not just the author.[10] So magazine editors cannot avoid responsibility by claiming ignorance of defamation committed by one of their journalists. They are in effect responsible for everything in the publication.

The presumption of bad faith is by no means conclusive, however, and can be defeated by proof of good faith. This concept is quite distinct from justification based on the defence of the truth (see below). The following are not indicative of good faith:

- belief in the truth of the statement. If you make an imputation, check it. If you do not, you may be committing at least a negligent defamation;
- lack of harmful intent or ulterior motive – a desire to inform the public is not enough;

- that a fact or rumour has already been published (although this can affect the level of damages awarded);
- reporting a theft conviction, other than in the context of legal proceedings, would be defamation;
- provocation is immaterial. In particular, defamation is still defamation even in reply to a defamatory attack. This only affects the level of damages ultimately awarded;
- even if a correction, clarification or retraction is published straightaway, it has no bearing on bad faith. It only suggests remorse and is no safeguard against liability, although again it may have some effect on damages and/or punishment.

The Paris Appeal Court said in one case that a journalist had taken inadequate care when he implicated a famous author in a fraudulent operation. The journalist himself had said that the allegation was unprovable and possibly unreliable. The journalist tried to defend himself on the basis that he had not subscribed to the rumour or attached any credit to it. This defence was brushed aside by the judges.[11]

The Paris Court has declared that journalists enjoy no special privileges.[12] There is nonetheless a wider margin of tolerance 'when the information sought seems weighty and of legitimate enough interest to justify the words used'.

Journalists reproducing notorious facts in the public domain for the purpose of informing readers are well within their rights. But the moment the journalist superimposes an element of polemic or aggression or departs from objective analysis, liability for defamation becomes a possibility.[13]

Who can sue?

A defamation action is subject to a three-month time limit, i.e. it must be tried within that period. This applies both to criminal and civil actions. The period runs from the day of the délit or, where proceedings have been issued, from the last day of those proceedings.[14]

Direct victim

Only those directly affected can sue, as only they can fulfil the requirement that the defamatory imputation must be specifically directed at a person.

Legal entities

Corporations or other entities with legal personality can sue, although where an individual employee or officer is the real target, the company cannot take proceedings.

Multiple victims

Defamatory imputations are sometimes aimed at several people. This affords no protection to the defendant, and each person identified may sue separately.

Indirect victims or victims *par ricochet*

Employers cannot bring criminal prosecutions for defamation of their own employees. But if they can prove direct and personal loss, they will be able to sue in the civil courts. In the same way, when defamatory imputations are made against the leaders of a political party, criminal action is not available to the members, only a civil action for damages.

The dead

Defamation of the dead is not, as such, punishable. It can only give rise to liability if, by means of the attack on the deceased, the defendant's aim is to undermine the honour or esteem of the deceased's surviving family. They can then sue in their own capacity for defamation in relation to the memory of the deceased.

Associations and trade unions

These cannot sue in their own right but their members may, if the defamatory words are aimed at any of their members. By contrast, individual members cannot bring an action where the defamatory words are aimed at a general body or profession, since they cannot show direct personal damage.

> For example, an article on women lawyers will not attract libel actions from each one for reasons of sheer numbers, so long as 'the article does not contain any allegation or imputation of a precise fact or a definite aspect of behaviour which might attack the plaintiff in a direct and personal manner, which might mark her out or draw suspicion upon her'. This argument raised by the journalist was accepted by the Paris Civil Court (*le Tribunal de grande instance*).[15]

Groups without legal status

Where the subject group is too wide, individuals cannot claim to be identified unless singled out in some way. Examples might include:

- general attacks against clergy;
- a pamphlet against freemasons as a group, which does not name specific individuals.

Where, however, because of the vagueness of the statement suspicion hovers over a number of people, each of them is entitled to seek redress. The Paris Appeal Court has allowed actions by individual members of a local council.[16] The attack must, however, be direct and personal.

Ethnic or religious groups

The 1881 Law provides that these groups are defamed where the defamatory words are intended to arouse racial or religious hatred. Here, defamatory intention is inferable from the words used.

Nevertheless, the Paris Appeal Court has held that 'denouncing the arrogance of young Arabs, and declaring that they take advantage of their protection and privilege, is not a defamatory attack, just as a portrait of violent behaviour by Arabs at a demonstration does not identify young Arabs as a class'.

Public officials

Public officials are also entitled to sue in defamation if the attack relates to their official capacity or role. Ministers, members of parliament and civil servants can all sue under this head, as may any public trustees or agents, citizens involved in public service – however transiently – and other public officials.

For example, a member of parliament accused of encouraging terrorism for calling for the abolition of the 'Security and Liberty' law could bring proceedings. So, too, might an Interior Minister accused of keeping a private militia for his own ends.

Opinion

Finally, even a subject who cannot complain of defamation can always sue for a false or offensive attack amounting to an abuse of freedom of opinion.[17] The

Paris Appeal Court once held that a critical appraisal of the educational value of school history books in measured terms cannot constitute an abuse of freedom of opinion.

Similarly, a restaurant critic responsible for providing practical guidance on presentation, quality, price, setting or welcome will be within the bounds of opinion. On the other hand, the privilege dwindles into abuse once allegations of a false and extreme nature are made, for example, comments about the seasoning on the prawn cocktail or the cleanliness of the carafes.

Compensation and remedies

Costs

Legal aid is available for both plaintiff and defendant to an action for defamation, whether civil or criminal. The criteria for granting legal aid are:

- inadequate financial resources;
- the merits of the case – this applies only to the plaintiff.

Individuals as well as non-profit organizations headquartered in France are eligible. Corporate entities headquartered abroad as well as all commercial companies are excluded.

The successful party can ask the other party to reimburse his or her costs of the action. The judge has an unfettered discretion to award all or part of the costs to the successful party.

The advocate's fees are a matter of agreement with the client, either an all-inclusive pre-agreed lump sum, or a fee calculated at an hourly rate and determined by time spent on the file. In principle, contingency fees are forbidden. It is, however, possible to agree a fee increase or supplement in recognition of work done.

Settlement

The costs of a defamation action and the uncertainty of outcome sometimes encourage the parties to reach a settlement. This inevitably involves concessions on both sides, albeit sometimes in different proportions. In practice, this involves the plaintiff abandoning proceedings in return for payment of a certain sum. Although verbal settlement agreements are possible, it is always advisable to draw up a formal document showing that the agreement is a valid settlement and is in full and final settlement of all claims between the parties, so preventing them from reopening the issues later on.

Failing amicable agreement, civil or criminal action is open to the victim. Special consideration should be given to summary proceedings (*action en référé*).

Criminal cases

Defamation prosecutions must be brought by the Public Prosecutor in the following cases, subject to the need for a preliminary complaint from the injured party:

- courts and tribunals
- the army, air force and navy
- state organs
- the government service
- civil servants and persons with public duties
- heads of state or foreign diplomatic agents
- senators and deputies, jurors and witnesses
- private individuals.

When the French President, a foreign head of government or a foreign affairs minister of a foreign government is defamed, there is no need for a preliminary complaint, and the Public Prosecutor can act on his or her own initiative. The same applies to defamatory statements concerning ministers' (or former ministers') competence in the performance of their ministerial office. The law is silent as to foreign parliamentarians and magistrates. Members of foreign governments do not benefit from the same treatment as their French counterparts, even if their country is a member of the EU.

The sole effect of the preliminary complaint is to render action by the Public Prosecutor admissible, who then has discretion to refuse to bring an action, on the basis of the principle of 'expediency' of legal proceedings. Likewise, the complainant may prompt public action by means of a private criminal prosecution or by means of a civil complaint before an examining magistrate (*juge d'instruction*).

Civil action

The victim may choose to sue for civil damages in the criminal courts in tandem with the public prosecution, or separately before the civil courts. That option is unavailable, however, where the civil action is inseparable from the public prosecution e.g. defamation of judges, members of the armed forces, ministers, members of parliament, etc.

The short limitation period of three months for defamation actions applies to both public prosecutions and civil actions, even if brought separately. Conversely, civil action is not subject to the strict procedures under the 1881 Law as to subpoenas and proof of the alleged defamation (see below), and so the ten-day time limit for the defendant to prove the truth of the defamatory facts does not apply in the civil courts. This is a major advantage of civil action for media defendants.

Significantly, even if the plaintiff cannot establish all the elements of defamation required by the 1881 Law, he or she can still recover damages on proof of fault and damage flowing from spoken or written words (i.e. the equivalent of an action for malicious falsehood in Commonwealth countries). In practice, the plaintiff will normally base a civil claim both on the *délit* of defamation and, in the alternative, on breach of duty of care causing loss.

Summary proceedings

These are a rapid, simple and highly effective means of defence against defamatory imputations, available to a plaintiff in an emergency or in particularly clear-cut cases. The procedure involves asking a judge, sitting alone, not only to grant damages, but also impose Draconian measures such as restraining the distribution or sale of defamatory works, or perhaps even outright seizure of the offending material. Note that the ruling in summary proceedings bites immediately and that appeal has no suspensory effect.

Extreme speed is the salient feature of the summary procedure. A few days, or even a few hours, may separate issue of the writ from a hearing before the judge. This speed is a source of difficulty, since in practice the time limit granted to journalists to prove truth is ten days (see below) under the 1881 Law. In summary proceedings, however, a journalist sometimes only has a few hours to bring forward proof.

Fortunately, the Cour de Cassation has recently ruled that the plaintiff cannot, by summary proceedings, bypass the ten-day time limit (which in principle operates only in the criminal courts). On this basis, the court set aside an order made in summary proceedings which imposed an FF80 000 (US$15 000) damages award on the weekly *L'Evènement du Jeudi*. The court held that summary proceedings must not be a way of depriving the magazine of the ten-day period from which it would have benefited had a criminal action been brought.

In summary proceedings plaintiffs can utilize all the defences available against a charge of defamation, either proving that one of the five essential elements of defamation is missing or raising the defence of truth. The jurisdiction of the summary courts is, however, limited, and, if it becomes evident that there is a real triable issue, the judge is supposed to refer the matter back to the trial courts.

Compensation

Criminal

Different penalties apply depending upon whether the victim is a public official or a private individual. Defamation of individuals can lead to up to six months' imprisonment and/or a fine of a maximum of FF80 000 (US$15 000). But if the defamation concerns the victim's membership of an ethnic or religious group, the penalties rise to a fine of up to FF300 000 (US$56 000) and one year's imprisonment. This higher level of penalty also applies to defamation of public officials, heads of state or diplomatic officers (heads of governments, ministers of foreign affairs and ambassadors).

Second offences of defamation do not – exceptionally in French criminal law – attract heavier penalties. Indeed, mitigation can be pleaded, and if this is accepted the penalty cannot exceed half the maximum penalty.

Civil

Vindication has traditionally been the symbolic function of civil damages. This is no doubt because they are intended as compensation for injury to personality rights, which are inherently difficult to value precisely. The only real sanction used to be the obligation to publish the judgment, in whole or in part, the costs of publication being borne by the defendant. So newspapers accepted the cost of inevitable defamation proceedings as an occupational hazard and as part of their overall business costs.

Those halcyon days seem unlikely to return. In recent years, the civil courts have greatly increased the level of awards to victims of defamation. There appears to be a concerted effort to bring to book journalists who stray from the path of thoroughness and objectivity.

For example, in 1991 *L'Evènement du Jeudi* spent approximately FF700 000 (US$130 000) defending five defamation actions. The editor claimed that this figure represented more or less the magazine's entire annual profit. At about the same time, *Le Monde* had to pay an award of FF100 000 (US$18 500) and publish the court's ruling in three newspapers (including *Le Monde* itself). The cost of these publications amounted to FF250 000 (US$46 500).

The record is currently held by the satirical magazine *L'idiot international* which was ordered to pay a French businessman the sum of FF800 000 (US$150 000) in damages. Not all victims of defamation recover awards of this magnitude. But undoubtedly the increasing readiness of the civil courts, as opposed to the criminal courts, to impose heavy monetary sanctions has encouraged litigation.

The summary procedure

The expedited procedure has become something of a bugbear for the media. For example, *L'Evènement du Jeudi* was ordered in summary proceedings to pay FF80 000 (US$15 000) by way of security for defamatory words about an African Affairs adviser to the President of the Republic. (The case went to a second appeal, the first appeal decision having been overturned by the Supreme Court: see above.)

Finally, there is nothing to prevent plaintiffs from seeking special damages provided the loss clearly flowed directly from the defamation. Proof of both liability and quantum is therefore required.

Who is liable?

Criminal

Since publication is the essence of the *délit*, the publisher/proprietor[18] or director of publication/editor[19] and possibly assistant editors of the publication are primarily liable. Liability is a corollary of their supervisory duty.

The strict order of responsibility is: author, printer, and then seller, distributor and bill posters. Where the directors, co-director or editor are implicated, the author is also brought into the proceedings as an accomplice – the so-called 'chain of criminal liability'.

Civil

Where a newspaper or periodical is found guilty of defamation, the 1881 Law declares that the proprietor is liable for any damages, whether the breach was personal or by one of his authors or accomplices as his servant (e.g. journalists). In civil proceedings, the norm is to issue a writ against both editor and author.

Defences

Truth

Strictly speaking, proof of truth does not eliminate the *délit* of defamation but is an absolute justification in the sense that the author escapes criminal or civil liability. It is therefore effectively a defence and available both in civil and criminal actions for defamation, although the criminal procedure is much stricter.

Principal requirement

The defendant must be able to produce clear and conclusive evidence that the defamatory statements are true. In other words, the defence requires truth to be proven in every material respect.

Formal requirement

The defamatory allegation must be shown to have been true at the time of publication, and this is an important discipline within which journalists have to operate. A request for discovery of documents will therefore be refused where this would amount to a 'fishing expedition' by the defendant to find evidence for a defence of truth. In the same way, evidence which has been discovered after publication will not be admissible.

Procedure

Any form of evidence – documentary or oral – is admissible to prove truth, but the procedure is strict and inflexible. No other form of proof, in particular cross-examination of the plaintiff, is admitted.

The defendant has ten days from service of the writ to notify the Public Prosecutor or the plaintiff, at an address chosen by the plaintiff, of:

- the facts set out in the summons, forming the basis of the plea of truth;
- copies of relevant documents;
- names, professions and addresses of the intended witnesses.

The defendant's address must be notified to the *Tribunal Correctionnel.*

These mandatory formalities are not, of course, defences as such. They are there to enable the defendant to bring evidence before the tribunal and to allow the plaintiff to do likewise. Within five days, and at least three clear days before the hearing, the plaintiff or the Public Prosecutor, as appropriate, has to serve the defendant at the address for service with copies of relevant documents as well as the names, professions and addresses of any witnesses.

Examination of the issue of truth is therefore strictly limited to the documents and witnesses disclosed under the above procedure. Documents not so notified are simply not admissible, whether on behalf of plaintiff or defendant.

Exclusion of the defence of the truth

Evidence of truth is not admitted in criminal or civil cases where the matter is:

- protected under the law of privacy;
- more than ten years old;
- subject to amnesty, rehabilitation, limitation or a successful judicial appeal.

*Privacy (*La vie privée*)*

What is not of public, i.e. general, interest is deemed private. Individual prominence determines the test of public interest, and different standards apply to the private lives of private individuals, film stars and politicians.

This is not, however, a blank cheque for journalists, especially in matters of sexual peccadillo. An imputation that a film star – even one whose private life is notoriously scandalous – is homosexual or a prostitute remains protected and truth is no justification.

In one case the Supreme Court of Appeal held that publishing details of a person's life as a prostitute was defamatory because, although the allegations were no doubt true, they belonged to her private life. She had, it seems, been pretending to be an beautician under a false name.

On the other hand, the French courts hold that the electorate has a right to know facts about an election candidate which might not be justified if they concerned a private person. Private matters may also be closely entwined with current events. For example, a scuffle between employer and employee in the context of a union struggle takes on the aspect of a current event and can be justified as true.[20] When imputations concerning private life and public function are inextricably linked, the public aspect is dominant. The defendant can then resort to the defence of truth in relation to the whole story.

Facts going back more than ten years

This is a kind of statutory right to 'let bygones be bygones'. An imputation by the French satirical magazine *Le Canard Enchaîné* of a precise nature, and one, moreover, which went back twenty-seven years, that Jean-Marie Le Pen had personally practised torture, was a clear and damaging attack on his honour. The defendant was barred from bringing evidence of facts more than ten years old, and facts which were, besides, subject to amnesty.[21]

Amnesty, rehabilitation, limitation and appeal

Where the alleged defamation concerns criminal offences, proof of truth is inadmissible after ten years for *crimes*, three years for *délits* and one year for *contraventions*.

Good faith

Defendants not wanting to establish truth – or unable to do so – can bring forward evidence of good faith. This defence is quite separate from the defence of truth outlined above.

Irrelevant factors

Good faith is a term of art in this context, and cannot be shown by pleading:

- belief in the truth of the imputation;
- pressure of deadlines or difficulty in checking facts;
- desire to inform the public;
- the fact that an earlier publication of the same material has not attracted a lawsuit;
- use of the word 'allegedly';
- that it was someone else's idea.

A simple affirmation of good faith is self-evidently not sufficient.

In one case a group of journalists had reported depositions of witnesses, but had added facts which did not form part of the proceedings. The particular allegation was that the police officers had covertly entered a house and planted pieces of cord which, they claimed, the police officers pretended to discover in the course of their search of the premises.[22]

The Supreme Court of Appeal convicted a journalist in one case for republishing defamatory allegations which had already been published. The court rejected the journalist's argument of the public's right to know, the journalist having failed to prove good faith.

On the other hand, one factor to be considered as evidence of good faith, along with other elements, is putting defamatory third party quotations within quotation marks. The Supreme Court of Appeal's decision highlights the journalist's care in telling the story, which showed lack of any guilty intent.

Relevant factors

Journalists must report and analyse society and can show good faith through intellectual honesty, caution, objectivity and, above all, by checking facts. They may, for example, in the course of an investigation into a particular profession uncover certain suspect practices. Proof of good faith will be admissible if their basic analysis is objective. In a nutshell, careful fact-checking and a bona fide desire to inform the public will probably help to establish good faith.

Defamation does not arise in relation to:

- reporting current affairs;
- public interest defence;
- election coverage.

Reporting current affairs

Careful and objective reporting of current affairs, free of opinions or value judgement, will not lead to liability. This defence does not cover over-zealous reporting – however accurate – which in the court's eyes amounts to exaggeration, prejudice or bias. There is, for example, no defamation risk filing a neutral report that someone is under investigation. It makes no difference if the charge is subsequently dropped, particularly if the journalist reports that fact in the same neutral way.

So, for example, where a journalist relates a decision to expel a foreigner precisely and without malice. The Paris Appeal Court discharged a journalist who 'confined himself to informing his readers of an expulsion order made against a person of Moroccan origin, indicating exactly the underlying reasons.'[23]

Likewise, a story headed 'Rapist Arrested' without any tendentious commentary is not defamatory. Indeed, so long as reporters remain objective and informative, and do not seek to inflict harm upon their subjects, they can shelter under the umbrella of a mission to explain.

Conversely, a tendentious report of court proceedings suggesting that a mere witness is guilty of improper conduct, coupled with false information about a previous conviction, could well be defamation.

Public interest defence

A journalist who can show that defamatory imputations are justified in the public interest will escape liability. For example, criticism – violent criticism even – of pornographic publications may be justifiable in the interests of public morality. The definition encompasses matters of national security, public health, public order or the improvement of public services. In this, the journalist must always be astute to avoid any unjustified personal attack.

Election time

There are no special statutory rules for defamation during election time, but the courts do exhibit a more tolerant attitude because of the public's legitimate interest in receiving information about candidates.

This motive of public information may indicate good faith, but the frayed tempers and surges in public opinion inevitable in any election campaign do not justify journalists in writing whatever they like. Good faith ends where legitimate controversy strays into personal vilification.

Privilege

Parliamentary privilege

Speeches in the National Assembly and the Senate are privileged, whatever the content, as are reports and documents printed by order of either of those two Houses. Parliamentary privilege also extends to publication in the *Official Journal* of documents ordered by the National Assembly to be printed for external publication (for example, the minutes of a parliamentary commission of inquiry). It does not extend to private publications, however, even where they reproduce the text of the *Official Journal*.

Similarly, a newspaper review of defamatory material, spoken or written, originated by members of parliament or from parliament itself, creates a potential liability. The subject can sue the journalist for reproducing the words used.

Parliamentary reports

Fair and accurate reports in good faith in the news media[24] of public sessions of the two Chambers benefit from parliamentary immunity. This does not apply to non-political assemblies, nor to words used in commissions or before commissions of inquiry.

Judicial privilege

According to the 1881 Law:

> 'Fair and accurate reports of judicial proceedings, made in good faith, including speeches made or documents produced before the courts, are privileged from any action in defamation, abuse or contempt of court.'

This covers all judicial tribunals and applies to:

- speeches made in court;
- documents brought to the court's attention, whether or not in issue in the proceedings.

For obvious reasons of public policy, statements made and documents filed by litigants and their counsel are protected. Speeches and written words published outside the court – in a newspaper, for example – for purposes other than providing information about the proceedings do not benefit from this privilege.

Judicial privilege is not absolute, and the court can impose reporting restrictions in relation to hurtful, offensive or defamatory speeches and documents connected with the proceedings, and after weighing the arguments for and against. Damages may eventually be awarded on top of the reporting restrictions, effectively giving the plaintiff two remedies.[25]

Finally, defamatory words unconnected with the proceedings may give rise to a defamation action. A victim who is party to the proceedings – whether as plaintiff or defendant – may request the court to consider a defamation claim later on. This does not apply, however where the victim of the defamatory imputation is a third party.

Judicial reports

As noted above, a fair and accurate report of judicial proceedings, made in good faith, is covered by judicial privilege. The privilege is not, however, available for commentary or opinion accompanying the report; nor, of course, does it extend to reports of court proceedings where reporting restrictions have been imposed. Reports of defamation proceedings where the defence of truth is inadmissible – such as, for example, private matters – are not allowed, nor are reports of divorce or judicial separation (*séparation de corps*).

Fairness and accuracy does not necessarily require word-for-word reproduction, and rewriting is allowed in the interests of a readable story. Bias or unfairness, however, will destroy the privilege – an example of bias might be reporting the prosecution speech only, ignoring the defence case.

Finally, automatic privilege attaches only to contemporaneous judicial reports. Where malice amounting to bad faith is the reason for a delay in publication, the privilege may be lost. An author unable to rely on judicial privilege may still have a defence of 'good faith', for example, where the material is of historical interest.

Related concepts

Any treatment of defamation would be incomplete without touching on various related rights. These include attacks which do not amount to actionable defamation:

- insulting a judge or the President of the French Republic;
- the right of privacy;
- the dissemination of inaccurate news;
- false accusation;
- denigration.

Insulting a judge or the French President

There is a special regime for attacks on those in authority or the police, and particularly insults aimed at:

- judges or jurors;
- the President of the Republic.

For example, such an insult might be accusing a criminal judge of favouring an accused with a title out of deference to the nobility.

A contempt of court, whether towards judges or jurors, by speech, gestures, threats – or even sending something insulting through the post – is punishable by up to one year's imprisonment and a fine of FF100 000 (US$18 500). The penalty can be doubled if the insult is made in public.

Under the 1881 Defamation Law, any contemptuous or defamatory slur upon the President of the Republic undermining his honour or dignity in his public duties or in his private life is a separate offence. The penalties are up to a year's imprisonment and/or a fine of up to FF300 000 (US$56 000).

The right of privacy

Where the attack is not upon a person's social or professional life but upon his or her private life, a law of 9 July 1970 represents a further clog upon press freedom. The rule is that 'each person has the right for his private life to be respected'. Apart from a whole raft of offences which are of no concern here, the judge in summary proceedings (*juge des référés*) has available a number of remedies ancillary to a defamation case to protect privacy, including sequestration (*séquestre*) and seizure (*saisie*), as well as the reporting restrictions mentioned earlier.[26] The idea is to forestall or suspend invasions of privacy, leaving open the question of damages.

Are revelations about the personal wealth of public figures an attack upon their privacy? In one case the Paris Appeal Court has said no, given the serious-minded approach of the journalist in writing the story, and the role of the individuals concerned in the economic life of the nation. Contrast the position concerning disclosure of an individual's earnings, which in France is normally considered private. Nevertheless, courts are reluctant to order a journal's seizure. For example, a satirical magazine, which had published the salary of a managing director, was ordered to publish a notice informing its readers of the director's objections to the infringement of his privacy.

Inaccurate news

The massive turnover of editorial material and deadline pressure do not always permit personal fact-checking. The law recognizes this, and only penalizes the publication of incorrect news if four conditions are satisfied.

Publication

This can be by any means, written or spoken.

Inaccuracy

News (*nouvelles*) means statements of fact concerning current events, even if presented as unconfirmed. The term excludes value judgements or statements of opinion which, on principle, cannot attract prosecution under this head. Thus, even the most tendentious commentaries are permissible provided, of course, they are not defamatory.

It is for the Public Prosecutor to prove inaccuracy. The defence of truth is peculiar to the tort (*délit*) of defamation and does not apply to the offence of disseminating inaccurate news.

Breach of the peace

The inaccurate news must be likely to disturb public peace[27] sooner or later. This gives the *délit* a very wide ambit, but, as with criminal libel in England, cases are rare.

Fault

In contrast with the position in defamation, there is no presumption of bad faith. The prosecution has to prove this, and, in its absence, a journalist who in all good faith publishes inaccurate news through over-reliance on a particular information source will escape liability.

> News and expressions of opinion should not be confused. Nor are predictions the same as news. So for an African politician to say: 'Now the whites have no authority, only the RDA deputies ... Those with RDA cards won't pay any more taxes, won't need to build up reserves of wheat, and won't have any more problems ...' was not considered to be false news.[28]

Simple negligence in failing to check accuracy is not by itself evidence of bad faith in this *délit*. A journalist's refusal to reveal a source of information was, in one case, held not to be enough to suggest bad faith.[29] This decision is open to question. Journalists are not, under French law, bound to protect their sources, although a Law of 4 January 1993, which introduced various reforms in criminal procedure, recognizes only that journalists may protect their sources when called as witnesses. Since then, a refusal to reveal sources may at least be evidence of ill will towards the accused, whatever the motives for refusal.

Bad faith can equally be inferred from the deliberate addition of false material showing an intention to exaggerate and misrepresent the facts. A similar conclusion can be drawn from inherently far-fetched news items.

Conversely, journalists can show good faith by the care they take over a story, by stating any reservations they have or by warning that the information given may be unreliable.

The *délit* cannot be the subject of a private prosecution. Penalties include seizure or suspension of the journal for a duration of three months or more, and a maximum of three years' imprisonment and/or a fine of FF300 000 (US$56 000). If the misleading news is calculated to disrupt the discipline or morale of the armed forces or hinder the national war effort, the term of imprisonment is up to five years and the fine FF900 000 (US$170 000).

False accusation

Citizens discovering breaches of the law are under a legal duty to inform the relevant authorities. These accusations must, however, be accurate and not falsely accuse the innocent, hence the law against false accusations, a *délit* comprised of two elements: accusation and slander.

Accusation

Accusation means a verbal or written report of wrongdoing to the relevant investigatory authority. It must take place soon after the person discovers the wrongdoing and must be aimed at a specific or easily identifiable person. Press reporting of wrongdoings could be false accusation because there could still be a report to the relevant authority, as well as to the public at large.

The mischief consists in the possibility that the subject of the report will incur a sanction – criminal punishment in the case of a criminal offence, administrative, as in the dismissal of a civil servant, or disciplinary. In the employment context, the sanction might include loss of chances of promotion, loss of staff accommodation or dismissal. False accusation differs here from defamation where the harm results from an attack on a person's honour or esteem.

Under the *délit* of accusation the recipient of the accusation must typically be of a rank defined by law (generally a high-ranking officer in a particular organization responsible for disciplinary matters, or a judicial official, or an administrative or judicial police officer).

Slander (*Calomnie*)

This term connotes both the false and deceitful nature of the accusation and the malice of the accuser who knows that the facts were false at the time of the accusation. Unlike defamation, where intention is presumed, the prosecutor must prove the falsity of the accusation. Proof is only possible if the relevant authority decides that the person slandered was in fact innocent.

The criminal law provides for penalties of five years' imprisonment and a fine of FF300 000 (US$56 000). The courts have, in addition, the power to order the publication of the judgment in one or more newspapers at the expense of the accuser. The plaintiff must pay the costs of the action if the defendant is acquitted. The victim can also seek damages either before the criminal court which has heard the *délit* of false accusation or before a civil court.

Denigration

Because of their function of informing the public, journalists are free to make relatively severe judgements on the quality of products or services. Journalists publishing comparative tests cannot be liable in damages provided that they show care and objectivity.

The cases show that any criticism must be considered and not malicious.

Those whose products or services are criticized have little chance of succeeding in a defamation action because the imputation must be aimed at an individual or a company. The case law is full of examples of restaurant owners losing defamation actions over critical reviews which did not suggest personal fault.

> For example, an article encouraged readers to give up wearing furs, without any direct attack on the furriers' profession. The Paris Appeal Court rejected a defamation action against the writers.

But defamation can occur if the criticism, ostensibly focused upon the product or service is in fact an attack on the manufacturer or service provider.

> For example, in the case of *Kléber-Colombes* v *L'Union Fédérale des Consommateurs* it was held that: 'The allegations of a journalist that a tyre manufacturer neglected the safety of its users, despite certain risks established by an inquiry, constitute a defamatory allegation likely to undermine his honour and esteem.'

The journalist will be able to escape liability by proving either the truth of the allegations or his or her own good faith. Good faith can be shown if the aim is a legitimate one, such as providing objective information to consumers. A radical line of cases has recently emerged on the idea of the 'good slanderer', especially in the field of health and consumer rights, so called because they are motivated by the public interest.

General conclusion

Although the French right of free expression is based upon principles of liberty, journalists are more aware of the numerous exceptions to that principle flowing from statute and case law.

To avoid civil or criminal liability, a journalist may be required to justify the seriousness of the article, and generally to observe a duty of care over the information that he or she publishes. This is especially important when a controversial story involves a precise allegation or imputation, as it must be provably true.

Defamation and the foreign press

Three situations arise from the Law of 29 July 1881:

- foreign press[30] edited, printed and published outside France;
- foreign press edited or printed in France;
- foreign press edited abroad and introduced into or circulated in France.

Foreign press edited, printed and published outside France

Defamation proceedings may be brought in respect of publications occurring abroad concerning persons residing in France, if they could be similarly sanctioned by the laws of the country where the wrong was committed. However, the victim of a foreign defamation has no jurisdiction to go before a French court by means of direct summons. The action can only be brought at the request of the Public Prosecutor, and must be preceded by a complaint of the victim or an official request to the French authorities by the authority of the foreign country.

Foreign press edited or printed in France

Defamatory publication in a foreign journal edited or printed in France is subject to the jurisdiction of the French courts and the application of French criminal law. So all the provisions of the law of 29 July 1881 regarding offences, penalties, the question of who is liable and specific rules of procedure are then applicable.

In certain cases, the principal author of the defamation will be a foreigner as 'publishing director' (editor) of a foreign magazine edited in France.

Foreign press edited abroad and introduced into or circulated in France

The French law of defamation applies to publication, circulation, distribution or sale of a foreign journal in France. In the case of the press it should be remembered that the *délit* is committed by publication and that determines territorial competence (jurisdiction). As a result, as soon as a journal written and printed abroad is sold or distributed on French territory, French courts have competence to determine questions of defamation under the 1881 Law.

A foreigner publishing in France a piece which is defamatory of another foreigner also resident abroad commits a *délit* subject to the jurisdiction of the French courts. The place of publication determines whether or not the French judge is competent. The same principle applies where the defendant is not resident in France, provided that the defamation has been committed on French territory.

Who is liable?

The 'chain of liability' (see above) does not apply in this context. Indeed, the Cour de Cassation has held that primary criminal liability rests with those who have introduced or sold, i.e. published, the defamatory text in France.

A decision of the criminal division of the Cour de Cassation of 15 February 1894 decided that the principal author of the *délit* of defamation was a book-seller selling an American periodical in France, one issue of which contained a defamatory article.

Given that the person introducing the defamation into France is the primary defendant, all those helping or knowingly assisting in publication in France will be accomplices. In this way, the manager, the editor or the director of the foreign publication as well as the author may face secondary liability.

Execution of foreign judgments

Foreign defamation judgments are only enforceable in France if they have been through the *exequatur* procedure before a French judge. This procedure involves the judge considering the regularity of the foreign judgment but not going into the merits of the dispute. The review is essentially procedural, concerned in particular with the rights of defence and procedural observations as well as the absence of fraud.

Within the member states of the EU and EFTA, two international treaties are aimed at facilitating the enforcement of foreign judgments within the relevant geographical areas: the Brussels Convention of 17 September 1968 and the Lugano Convention of 16 September 1988. These two Conventions provide that execution shall be ordered on request, without the need for an *inter partes* hearing. Where they do not apply (e.g. enforcement of an American judgment), an *inter partes* hearing is necessary.

Finally, a significant number of bilateral treaties have been concluded between France and various countries intended to facilitate the enforcement of judicial decisions. Specific reference should be made to each of these in context.

Notes

1   25 May 1983.
2   31 January 1991.
3   Criminal Tribunal of Saint Denis de la Réunion of 15 May 1984.
4   Court of Appeal; Paris, 4 October 1984.
5   Crim. 14 September 1985.
6   Crim. 23 December 1905.
7   Crim. 21 April 1980.
8   3 July 1991.
9   13 November 1991.
10   The directors and editors are primarily liable, but, failing that, the author/journalist, then the printers, and finally the newsagents, distributors and bill-posters (Article 42 of the 1881 Law). Under Article 43, when the publishing director or editor is the subject of proceedings, authors/journalists may be pursued as accomplices.
11   23 November 1990.
12   Paris, 5 May 1948.
13   Court of Appeal of Douai, 1 February 1904.
14   According to the Law of 29 July 1881, Article 65, trial of crimes, *délits* and contraventions proscribed under that Law is statute-barred three months after the date of commission, the date of investigation or the date of prosecution, if any.
15   3 December 1978.
16   CA, Paris, 28 April 1987.
17   The Civil Code, article 1382. Proof of damage and a causal link between the statement and the damage are necessary. Thus, abuse of freedom of opinion can lead to liability even where an action for defamation would fail.
18   The *éditeur* is generally the publisher or proprietor, not the editor in the English sense.
19   The *directeur de publication* is essentially the editor.
20   Cass soc. 6 January 1972.
21   Paris, 15 January 1986, GP 86.2.701, four judgments.
22   26 November 1991.
23   9 December 1956.

24 The publication must be a straight report of news reproduced exactly and with due objectivity.
25 The Civil Code, Article 1382.
26 Privacy is a distinct right under French law, independent of defamation law.
27 This concept encompasses public order and social harmony in general.
28 *Chambre criminelle* 16 March 1954.
29 With defamation, by contrast, because bad faith is presumed, disclosure of sources will not by itself be enough to displace the presumption of bad faith. What is required is exact checking of the facts coming from those sources.
30 The 1881 Law, naturally enough, only mentions the press.

6

Germany

Bernd Meyer-Witting and Volker Schmits of Clifford Chance (Frankfurt)

The phenomenon of massive libel payouts in celebrity lawsuits has so far passed Germany by. German defamation law – both civil and criminal – is an altogether more pragmatic affair. Although libellous statements do on occasion attract criminal sanctions, the criminal law also dictates in large degree the scope of civil liability.

That is not to say that the German Civil Code is without powerful sanctions, although the level of damages rarely reaches the heights seen in comparable English or US cases. This is partly because the values of honour and reputation have a relatively low place in the pecking order of the Civil Code. But the more important reason is the powerful constitutional protections for freedom of expression enjoyed by the German media.

Constitution

The German Constitution or Basic Law (*Grundgesetz*) is largely concerned with protecting human rights. Natural and legal persons are protected from state oppression, and any statutory or governmental acts or court judgments that infringe the Constitution can be challenged. But these rights are not confined to governmental or state acts, and there is a knock-on effect in areas of private law affecting ordinary individuals.[1] For instance, an employer enforcing a restrictive covenant against an employee needs to take account of the employee's constitutional rights as well as the rights set out under the general law.

Article 5 of the Constitution

Of interest in this context is Article 5 of the Constitution protecting freedom of expression, freedom of information and freedom of the media (press and broadcasting). Together with the freedoms of art and science they form a solid legal foundation for media activity in Germany. The architects of the Constitution had lived through the years of Third Reich totalitarianism, and realized from that experience that the media work best if the law is liberal in relation to content regulation, while keeping a watchful eye on violent attacks on individuals. Article 5 makes no distinction in this connection between nationals and persons of foreign origin.

Freedom of expression

The wording of the right to freedom of expression ('everyone shall have the right freely to express and disseminate opinion by speech, writing and pictures') shows that expressions of opinion attract the greatest protection. Pure statements of fact do not attract such absolute protection, as in principle only accurate facts are regarded as a valid basis for forming an opinion. False statements of fact do not benefit from the constitutional clause. Obviously this is an important distinction, and one keenly felt in German defamation law.

Media freedom

Freedom of the media (press and broadcasting) is treated separately under the Constitution from the right to freedom of expression. The media have entrenched guarantees (such as the right to refuse disclosure of documents) providing the framework they need to function, but no further absolute rights so far as the content of their output is concerned. Press freedom and general freedom of expression are overlapping, not cumulative, rights. Indeed, the price of the special freedoms the media enjoy is that they are expected to adhere to higher standards of care than ordinary citizens.[2]

These entrenched liberties can only be restricted by a general law with an overall policy aim (for example, for the protection of the young or of certain personality rights), provided the law is not aimed at suppressing a particular means of expression.

General personality right

Moreover, certain other constitutionally protected interests limit by their very nature the scope of the freedoms afforded by Article 5 of the Constitution. The most significant instance is the general personality right. Shaped by the powerful Federal Constitutional Court out of Articles 1 and 2 – the corner-stones of the Constitution's protection of an individual's rights to freedom, self-determination and human dignity – this general right of personality weighs the interests of the press against those of the individual.[3]

The general personality right is broader than the English concept of privacy in that it not only protects private life, but also, for example, personal infor-mation and the way a person's character is publicly depicted.

Criminal defamation

German criminal defamation law has three branches,[4] all of them aiming to protect 'honour.' Obviously honour is in part a function of personal circum-stance, but it can be viewed broadly as the sum of personality and moral values,[5] and includes reputation. In assessing liability, the judge must take account of the subject's past conduct – a person of good character deserves greater protection than a convicted thief.

Insult (*Beleidigung*)[6]

Attacks on a plaintiff's honour can attract criminal liability for 'insult'. For this offence there must be wilful communication by speech or action. By contrast with slander (*Üble Nachrede*), insult requires personal communica-tion to the subject.

The 'insulting' statement must tend to lower the victim in the opinion of society in general. The journalist's intention is irrelevant, and the standard of the reasonable person in the particular situation is definitive. Not only do the age, sex and educational background of both parties have to be considered, but also the overall context in which the statement was made. Thus, a statement made in the context of humour or parody is less likely to be regarded as an offence, although this does not necessarily follow.

All natural and legal persons are protected by the criminal law relating to defamation. There are no automatic exclusions as under English law.

The following are some examples of insult:

- a statement that the mother of a dead child was suing the doctor to make money out of her tragedy;[7]
- a photograph of a properly built house illustrating a story on 'cowboy' builders;[8]
- calling a lawfully published magazine fascist propaganda;[9]

- a cartoon of a politician as an eagle (the German Federal Republic's coat of arms) depicted as a swastika, implying that the politician had fascist views;[10]
- a statement that all German soldiers are potential murderers.[11]

Slander (*Üble Nachrede*)[12]

The second category of criminal defamation corresponds closely to the English common law concept of defamation in that it must lower a person in the estimation of right-thinking members of the community, and is limited to statements of fact.

To be punishable, the statement must be communicated to a third party, unlike the offence of insult, where frequently no third party is involved. A publication of third party statements or rumours, even when no credence is given to them, falls within the ambit of slander. If the perpetrator knew that the statement was defamatory, a criminal offence is committed, even without knowledge of falsity.

To escape criminal liability the defendant must prove that a statement is true. Journalists face a particular danger because of this: it is quite conceivable that a journalist could be punished for making a statement that he or she knows is true, but the truth of which he or she cannot prove without breaching the confidentiality promised to a source.

The following are examples of slander:

- an allegation in a well-known news magazine that a former Defence Secretary had received a suitcase full of freshly printed bank notes;[13]
- an allegation that a taxi-driver refused to accept a fare from an obese passenger;[14]
- calling a resistance fighter against the Nazi regime a traitor.[15]

Malicious defamation (*Verleumdung*)[16]

Finally, the offence of malicious defamation (*Verleumdung*) concerns the deliberate and intentional dissemination of false factual statements that are either defamatory or cause harm to the person's creditworthiness. So far as the latter is concerned – as in malicious falsehood under English law – the subject's reputation need not be damaged. Examples include:

- a statement that a judge was, although not bribed, influenced by irrelevant considerations;[17]

- a statement that a company's main clients had cancelled their orders because of their own financial difficulties, without any reference being made to the company's financial position.

The plaintiff must show that the journalist or publisher knew of the falsity of the statement.

Procedure and sentencing

Criminal proceedings for the three criminal offences can only be brought after notice has been served on the Public Prosecutor, who must rule that it is in the public interest for the case to go forward. This formal notice must be served within three months of the subject first becoming aware of the relevant statement.

Under German criminal law, in contrast to the adversarial approach under English law, the court inquires into the truth. Neither plaintiff nor defendant has the burden of proof – it is for the judge to arrive at the truth.

Each of the three defamation offences carries prison sentences of up to five years and/or fines in the discretion of the court. Fines depend on the personal financial circumstances of the defendant, but in practice are not of particular substance, usually between DM500 and 4000 (US$300 and 2500). An additional weapon in the court's armoury is its power to order publication of an apology or retraction.

Civil law

German civil law protects certain basic broad legal interests, and wilful or negligent interference with these can lead to liability. Honour and reputation are not specifically protected as such under this heading, mainly owing to the overriding concept of 'natural restitution'. This reflects the German juridical perception that true compensation means turning the clock back, rather than awarding damages. What might appear a potential loophole in the protection conferred upon plaintiffs is filled by the general personality right and three special rules of tortious liability.

The civil judicial process contrasts starkly with that of the criminal law. In civil cases, plaintiffs must adduce evidence in support of their claim, and it is for defendants to counter that evidence. The judge rules on the basis of the parties' submissions and there is no jury. The editor, the publisher/proprietor and the journalist concerned are jointly liable but can be sued separately. Depending on the context, liability may flow from different rules, either directly from the press and broadcasting laws, from the principle of vicarious liability, or from the concept of primary and secondary liability (i.e. whether a person is originator, indirect agent or instigator).

General personality right

Section 823 of the Civil Code lays down a general principle requiring compensation for damage:

> 'A person who wilfully or negligently unlawfully injures life, body, health, freedom, property or other rights of another is bound to compensate that person for any damage ensuing.'

Honour, reputation and personality rights are thus not specified as such, but the traditional position underwent a change in an important case decided by the Federal Supreme Court.

> A banker had asked in writing for the correction of a false statement made in a newspaper. The letter was not intended for publication. Nevertheless, and this without the consent of the banker, the newspaper published a distorted version in the Letters to the Editor column. The Federal Supreme Court ruled that as the Constitution enshrines human dignity as the highest value, personality rights should enjoy the same protection as property rights.[18]

Although personality rights were recognized as 'other rights' in tort, no specific definition of the content of those rights was given. In fact, its sources – the right of liberty in Article 2 and the right of human dignity in Article 1 of the Constitution – make a clear definition impossible. So the highest German courts have ruled that the general personality right represents only a framework for determining the merits of each case.

Zones of protection

There are different categories or 'zones' of the personality right.

- In the 'intimate' zone, covering inter alia personal beliefs, health and private sexual matters, absolute protection is generally available.
- Facts from the 'private' zone – private and family life – can only be revealed on the basis of compelling public interest. In such cases there is a clear balancing exercise between the different constitutionally protected rights. It is by and large a matter for individual discretion how much of one's private life should be made public.

- In the third zone – the 'individual' zone – the general personality right protects the right of self-determination. This is infringed, for example, if the press falsely attributes political views to a person, or if statements are wrongly attributed, representing that person in a false light. Thus, it is possible to argue that a defamatory statement under civil law involves bringing a person into hatred or contempt or lowering his or her standing in public opinion. The level of sophistication and knowledge of the likely audience is also relevant.

The following are some examples reflecting the range of interests protected:

- damages for unauthorized use of the photograph of a well-known showjumper in an advertisement for an aphrodisiac;[19]
- an injunction banning publication of an illegal transcript of a telephone conversation between two prominent politicians;[20]
- an injunction restraining broadcast of a film on a prisoner's offences shortly before his release date;[21]
- damages for publishing a supposedly exclusive interview which in fact had never taken place.[22]

Predictably enough, the personality right applies only to the living. Traces linger, however, after a person's death and can be protected by the deceased's estate (e.g. if the deceased is portrayed in a way that would impair or destroy the standing and reputation of that person).

Bringing an action is not always a straightforward matter. An element of fault, either intent or at least negligence, must be proven. Unfortunately, this must be proven by the plaintiff who often has to rely on circumstantial evidence only. Usually the question of fault will be decided on the basis of infringing duties of care. Such duties are based on the idea that the more serious the allegations are, the more prudent the journalist must be. The question is, what would one generally expect a journalist to check in such a situation? A journalist should not rely on one source only, neither should he or she print without cross-checking the information.

Infringement of statute

Paragraph 2 of section 823 of the Civil Code is the other major limb of the civil law relating to defamation, providing as it does that a person who contravenes a statute which is intended to protect a third party is liable in damages. This is the crossover point between criminal and civil defamation law, and a person guilty of insult, slander or malicious falsehood may also attract civil liability in this way.

Injuring credit

Another specific tort is created by section 824 of the Civil Code, which is aimed at protecting a person's credit. Thus, a statement about a third party which the defendant knows to be untrue, and which is likely to endanger that party's credit or damage his earning capacity or prosperity, will attract full liability. In practice, the plaintiff bears a heavy burden, since falsity must be proven. However, the courts have a discretion to reverse the burden of proof and oblige the defendant to prove the truth of the statement.

Liability for wilful injury

In an extreme case, a plaintiff can seek damages by invoking a third branch of the civil law. A defendant wilfully causing damage to the plaintiff in a manner offensive to civilized values is liable pursuant to section 826 of the Civil Code.

Identification

To succeed in both civil and criminal proceedings, the victim and plaintiff must be identifiable. This does not mean that the subject needs be named explicitly, but a reasonable person must understand who was meant in the circumstances. For example, a company's legal representative who, without being named, could show that an allegation about the conduct of the company's business could only refer to him would be sufficiently identifiable. The same applies if the article points to a specific person by giving other information. Furthermore, a member of a group which has been defamed as such can sue if it is clear that the person is part of the group, even if not specifically referred to, and if the group is sufficiently small.

Defences

The following concepts apply to both civil and criminal cases.

Truth

Generally, proof of truth justifies statements of fact which on their face appear to be defamatory. If proof is not clearly established, a defendant will be guilty of a criminal offence and possibly civil defamation as well. Belief in or knowledge of truth is not sufficient, and the plaintiff need not prove falsity.

Sometimes not even truth is a complete defence. For example, if the mode of communication is particularly damaging, its content becomes irrelevant. So also with infringement of privacy – intrusion into the 'intimate zone' cannot be justified on grounds of truth.

Legitimate public interest

The plea of legitimate public interest is closely linked with freedom of expression and freedom of press and broadcasting under Article 5 of the Constitution. German courts look kindly on the plea where public interest issues are at stake.

> In one case the public interest in the conduct of a well-known chemical company outweighed the chairman's interest in his privacy.[23] The same principle applied in the context of a historical broadcast about the burning of the *Reichstag* in 1933 and new evidence about the perpetrators.[24] Obviously, in this case not all facts could have been established beyond any doubt, but the public's legitimate interest in historical research outweighed that factor.

The defence applies solely to statements of fact. A different mechanism applies to statements of opinion or comment. Even inaccurate reporting can be protected on grounds of public interest, as long as the journalist took reasonable care. The publisher must honestly believe in the truth of the statement. There are, of course, no set guidelines for what constitutes reasonable care. A relevant factor is the importance of reporting the news. The newspaper must check sources and contact the relevant authorities to get first-hand information instead of rumours. One case illustrates this matter nicely:

> The German press agency (DPA) received an anonymous telex reporting that a well-known businessman had deposited DM 6 million with a Swiss bank to bribe some German Federal Parliament Deputies. The story was totally unfounded, but a magazine republished it. The court held that news of this kind could not be published without establishing a core of reliable fact. The court emphasized that publication cannot be justified simply by arguing that it had accurately reported a third party's statements.

The plea of public interest is not available in the case of *Verleumdung*. Nor does it protect an article about a person under criminal investigation which prejudges the accused's guilt before a final decision has been made in the case. It is important to note that legitimate public interest does sometimes justify coverage of the criminal proceedings themselves, but frequently not the disclosure of the accused's full name. In other situations it can be appropriate to disclose the identity in full.

Although a public official's professional and social standing is protected just like that of any other citizen, German law draws a distinction between private and public figures. Those who actively participate in public affairs or politics must be deemed to countenance a harsher level of criticism. Thus, for example:

- A town councillor of the Green Party who imitated the voice of a horse in a meeting subsequently had to put up with being called 'a green Muppet' in a party political document;[25]
- A powerful press tycoon who attacked the moral weakness of society at large had to endure outspoken criticism of his own moral shortcomings.[26]

The standard of criticism public figures are expected to tolerate also varies according to their own media profile. The more provocative their own utterances, the more criticism they must bear. Even those directly involved in criminal cases – whether as accused, prosecutors or lawyers – are considered public figures, although only for the actual period of the trial.

The plea covers situations where under English law a defendant would invoke qualified privilege, e.g. statements of witnesses in court proceedings.

Comment and critical opinion

There are no restrictions on comment or critical opinion, and therefore no defence is required. Most statements of opinion benefit from absolute constitutional protection, whereas false statements of fact do not. Of course, the distinction between fact and opinion is frequently problematic, especially where the statements straddle both categories. In cases of doubt, the courts tend to regard a statement as an expression of opinion rather than one of fact. This is in stark contrast to the common law tradition, where the opposite is the case.

As political debate is of critical importance in a democratic society, political discourse is generally regarded as opinion, even if technically the factual content outweighs the element of comment. Thus, a 'statement of fact' that the Chancellor would arm Germany for a new war had to be understood as a statement of opinion.[27]

Strong words and incisive criticism are given wide latitude in Germany. But when unreasonable criticism spills over into insulting speech, the limit of an individual's right to freedom of expression has been reached. So a scandalous opinion that is intended to humiliate can give rise to a defamation claim, unless it is clear that the remark was mere hyperbole. Even here, the burden of proof is reversed and, in cases of comment, the plaintiff must prove that the comment exceeded reasonable bounds and so forfeits constitutional protection.

Limitation

Under the civil law, the limitation period is three years from knowledge of the facts, and there is an absolute bar after thirty years from the actions forming the subject of the comment or statement. After expiry of the limitation period no legal action may be brought, unless the plaintiff can prove that he or she did not know or could not reasonably have known the relevant facts. Three to five years is the limitation period for criminal offences in this area, depending on the offence committed.

Remedies

The German courts' attitude to defamation is in sharp contrast to that of the English courts. They do not give precedence to the right to publish or to private rights, but try to hold a balance between the interests of the press and individual rights. The dictum 'Publish and be damned' holds no sway in Germany, and in an appropriate case the court will not hesitate to restrain publication. In the case of defamatory publication, author, editor and publisher are jointly liable.

The courts accept all forms of evidence (oral, documentary and real) and assess their value under the particular circumstances. There are no specific rules of evidence under German law.

Interim injunction

A plaintiff can seek an interlocutory injunction restraining publication. Since both sides can claim a legitimate constitutional interest, the court must balance the conflicting rights and evaluate the possible impact of an injunction restraining publication as against allowing publication to go ahead. Moreover, the court in granting the injunction must be careful not to prejudge the outcome of the main proceedings.

Restraining publication

If a publication infringes an individual's rights, an injunction can be sought restraining further publication,[28] even where publication was initially of legitimate interest to the public, but where that urgency has been lost. In certain circumstances, an injunction may also take the form of prior restraint, but this can only be justified if the offending information would, if published, endanger some real legal interest which could otherwise be irreparably damaged.

Again, the courts in this case must balance the rights of the individual against the constitutional rights of the press. In the case of a statement of fact to which the plaintiff objects, a 'contradiction' can also be ordered. Here the plaintiff can demand publication of a declaration requiring the defendant to desist from further repetition of the insulting statement.

The most common remedy is an undertaking which specifically prohibits further repetition of the allegations and incorporates a penalty clause in the event of a failure to do so.

Damages

German law distinguishes damages for actual loss and for harm which is incapable of precise quantification. Damages are only regarded as a secondary remedy, and the primary emphasis lies on putting right publishing errors rather than on damages.

The 'special' (i.e. actual) damages element consists of either quantifiable financial loss, or loss of future earnings. The plaintiff only has to prove a causal link between the damages claimed and the wrongdoing of the defendant on a balance of probabilities. So a general medical practitioner was awarded DM120 000 (US$80 000) in damages without needing to prove precisely which prospective patients he had lost in the wake of a defamatory publication.[29]

The amount of 'general' damages awarded for non-pecuniary loss or mental stress is generally much lower. General damages are only awarded in cases of serious and comprehensive assaults on a person's dignity which cannot be compensated in any other way. In addition, actual or presumed knowledge on the editor's part of the likely effect upon the plaintiff is necessary to attract substantial damages in this context. Some examples illustrate the approach:

- DM3000 (US$2000) for an article with a picture claiming that a taxi-driver had shot his passenger for not paying his fare – the driver had acted in self-defence and was acquitted;[30]
- DM3000 (US$2000) for a person whose photograph appeared in a newspaper when wrongly arrested on suspicion of being a terrorist;[31]
- DM5000 (US$3250) for describing three named university professors as 'donkeys;[32]
- DM7500 (US$5000) for including a well-known Social Democrat in a brochure of the opposition Christian Democrat party;[33]
- DM10 000 (US$6500) for dubbing a TV presenter 'a lesbian who looked like a barren old goat';[34]

- DM10 000 (US$6500) for a headline falsely attributing paternity to a pop star;[35]
- DM25 000 (US$16 500) for an unproved allegation that a former Defence Secretary accepted a case full of crisp new banknotes;[36]
- DM40 000 (US$26 500) for an allegation by a journalist, who misquoted a famous writer, that the writer had smoothed the path of terrorism. (Every wrong quotation can only be evaluated on its particular facts, whether or not the misrepresentation is calculated to place the subject in a false or defamatory light.);[37]
- DM60 000 (US$40 000) awarded to a tennis player for a passage in an English pop song falsely suggesting that she had committed incest with her father on thousands of occasions.[38]

For a serious case of defamation, the average damages might be between DM10 000 (US$6500) and DM20 000 (US$13 000). Any case can be appealed either on the facts or on legal principle. The Court of Appeal can also modify the award of damages, but it is very rare for the award to be increased. However, very recently the Federal Court quashed an award of damages of DM30 000 (US$20 000) to Princess Caroline of Monaco, on the basis that it was not sufficiently high.[39] Whether this marks the beginning of a new German approach to damages has yet to be seen.

Where a statement is published on different occasions, whether in print or on television, a plaintiff can recover damages for each separate publication. It should be noted that legal entities are only entitled to recover for actual loss. General damages are reserved for human beings – companies have no reputation as such, nor do they benefit from a general personality right. Plaintiffs can indicate that their only interest lies in vindicating reputation, not financial compensation, and in such a case the court can require defendants to buy space for press advertisements.

Right of reply

There is a statutory right of reply for both press and the broadcast media. The right applies to all statements of fact referring to the claimant, whether or not they are flattering and whether or not they are right or wrong. As truth is irrelevant, the requirements are very mechanistic, particularly in relation to the form and content. A publisher can only refuse to print a reply where it contains a statement generally accepted as false or when some formal requirement has not been satisfied (e.g. missing signature or lateness of complaint). In the broadcast media, the reply is read verbatim by an announcer, possibly accompanying the text with pictures. The right of reply is legally enforceable.

The international dimension

International publication does affect publication in Germany, but the issue can arise in an unusual way. In the case of separate publications both in Germany and abroad, the court will ignore any foreign proceedings and will concentrate exclusively on the domestic publication, the critical point being the impact the defamation has in Germany.

In civil law, a case can generally be heard in the German courts if the defendant is domiciled in Germany. Under tort law and criminal law, even this is not decisive, as the place of infringement or criminal activity is the basis for the German court's competence. The nationality of the plaintiff or defendant is of no concern.

Reform

For some years discussion has centred on the issue of individual protection as against the power of the media. The discussion has been fuelled partly by the Federal Constitutional Court's liberal interpretation of press freedom and protection of opinion. As these rights become more entrenched, the clamour for them to be cut back to protect individual privacy has grown in intensity.

The focus of attention has, interestingly, not been the criminal law, and most people view self-regulatory media control and civil law remedies as a more practical solution. So far as self-regulation is concerned, a proposal has been put forward for a committee representing all media interests, similar to the UK Broadcasting Standards Council but not limited to broadcasting. In relation to civil law reform, one idea which has gained currency is adding into the tort provisions some of the judicial developments concerning the general right of personality.

Notes

1   BVerfGE 7, 198 – Lüth.
2   BVerfGE 35, 202 – Lebach.
3   BVerfGE 30, 173 – Mephisto.
4   Sections 185, 186 and 187 StGB.
5   BGHZ 11, 67.
6   Section 185 StGB.
7   OLG Köln, AfP 1972, 223.
8   BGH, GRUR 1971, 417.
9   BVerfG, NJW 1976, 1677.

10   OLG München, NJW 1971, 844.
11   BayObLG, NJW 1991, 1493.
12   Section 186 StGB.
13   BGH, GRUR 1969, 147.
14   OLG Stuttgart, AfP 1972, 332.
15   BGH, NJW 1952, 1183.
16   Section 187 StGB.
17   OLG Hamm, NJW 1971, 853.
18   BGHZ 13, 334 – Leserbrief.
19   BGHZ 26, 349 – Herrenreiter.
20   BGHZ 73, 120 – Kohl/Biedenkopf.
21   BVerfGE 35, 202 – Lebach.
22   BGH, NJW 1965, 685 – Soraya.
23   BGH, NJW 1994, 125.
24   BGH, NJW 1966, 647.
25   LG Arnsberg, NJW 1987, 1412.
26   BGH, NJW 1964, 1477.
27   BGHSt 6, 159.
28   A famous ban on publication was imposed in the case concerning the claim of the adopted son of Gustav Gründgens, a well-known theatre director during the 1930s, that the novel *Mephisto* by the author Klaus Mann defamed his father in the area of sexual privacy – BVerfGE 30, 173.
29   OLG Frankfurt, ZUM 1992, 361.
30   OLG Hamburg, AfP 1974, 93.
31   OLG Hamburg, NJW-RR 1992, 536.
32   OLG Köln, AfP 1970, 95.
33   BGH, NJW 1980, 994.
34   BGHZ 39, 124.
35   OLG München, AfP 1990, 45.
36   BGH, GRUR 1969, 147 – Strauß.
37   BGH, NJW 1982, 635.
38   OLG Karlsruhe, NJW 1994, 1963.
39   BGH, NJW 1995, 861.

7

India

Ashok H. Desai, Senior Advocate
(New Delhi and Bombay)

A journalist who writes a defamatory article faces two distinct risks under the Indian law, namely a civil suit as well as a criminal prosecution. The civil law of defamation is not codified, and broadly adopts the common law of England. India is not a happy hunting ground for plaintiffs claiming large damages in actions for libel. Such suits are infrequent, and awards are relatively modest. The following features of the legal system discourage claims in tort:

- Civil litigation is dilatory. An action claiming damages for libel might take as long as seven years to be decided in the trial court. Thereafter it would travel slowly up the appellate route, by which time the parties may well lose interest.
- India does not have a jury system. Damages are assessed by the detached and rather cold calculation of a judge.
- The quantum of damages is based on the concept of compensation rather than on general sentiment. This reduces the level of damages to a small figure.
- A plaintiff has to pay a certain amount of money calculated as a small percentage of the total claim as court fees to the state before he or she can file the suit.
- Professional ethics forbid contingency fees for lawyers. This discourages speculative claims.

All these factors make a civil action for litigation one of the lesser perils of journalism in India – although the situation may change in the future.

A more vexing problem for a journalist is to face a prosecution for defamation. Defamation is a criminal offence under the rather antiquated provisions of the Penal Code. Truth by itself is not a complete defence in a criminal case. The further risk under the criminal law is that a private prosecution can be launched by any aggrieved person and can be maintained at any place where a copy of the journal is circulated. India is a vast country, and editors and reporters sometimes find themselves attending remote courts to defend charges of criminal defamation. Let us first consider the constitutional guarantee of a free press.

The Constitution

The Indian Constitution adopted in 1950 ensures that a citizen shall enjoy the fundamental right 'to freedom of speech and expression'. There is no express provision for the freedom of the press. But such freedom is necessarily included in the guarantee of free speech which carries with it a right to publish and circulate one's ideas and opinions by resorting to any available means of publication. The judiciary has vigorously asserted the power to invalidate executive action as well as laws which violate such fundamental rights. There is, however, a specific exception regarding the law of defamation.

Unlike the US Constitution, article 19 of the Indian Constitution provides that the right to free speech is not unlimited but is subject to reasonable restrictions. It saves existing laws and enables the legislature to make laws in so far as they impose reasonable restrictions in relation to defamation. Article 21, which protects life and liberty, has also emerged as the basis for a new right of privacy. The Supreme Court has lately moved towards a change in the law of defamation by adopting in part the law of libel in the United States in the matter of public conduct of public officials, including the leading case of *New York Times* v *Sullivan* which was based on the First Amendment.

The difference between the approach in the United States and India is illustrated by two suits filed in the two jurisdictions regarding the same defamatory statement.

> In his book on Dr Kissinger, the author Seymour Hersh made an allegation that a former Prime Minister of India was a CIA agent. In a civil suit filed in Chicago on behalf of the Prime Minister it was held that the plaintiff was a public figure, and that in order to succeed he would have to show malice on the part of the writer. It was not enough to show that the statement was false. It had to be proved that the writer knew that the statement was false or showed reckless disregard for the truth. On failure to do so, the claim was rejected. On the same facts, an Indian court has held that the statement was clearly defamatory and that it would be for the publisher to prove the truth. It has granted an injunction against the circulation of the defamatory statement pending the trial.

However, a public official, in the discharge of his or her public duty, cannot claim damages even if an imputation is false, unless he or she establishes that the publication was made with reckless disregard for the truth. This exception, however, is confined to his or her public conduct.

A magazine announced the proposed publication of the autobiography of one Auto Shankar who was found guilty of committing serial murders. The publication was to set out his criminal links with public officials. The prison officials sought to stop the publication on the ground that the writings were unauthorized and would tarnish the image of responsible public servants. The court refused to grant any injunction on the broad principle of *New York Times* v *Sullivan*.[1]

Rights of journalists

Courts try to balance the interests of a free press against those of the plaintiff's right to his or her reputation. Free speech is recognized as one of the most important safeguards of a democratic society. At the same time, courts take the view that a journalist does not have any special privilege as such in defamation. A journalist, like any other citizen, has the right to comment strongly on a matter of public interest, provided the allegation of fact on which the comment is based is accurate. The very impact of the libel requires a journalist to be more cautious. In practice, however, courts recognize that a journalist may venture into an area where others fear to tread.

A tabloid published a news item under the heading 'Rape in Jail' which relied on a summary of a confidential inquiry held by the Home Secretary. The gist of the story was that the plaintiff, who was a prisoner in jail, had made another prisoner pregnant. The newspaper contended that in view of the inquiry report the prosecution should be quashed without a trial. The court held that a journalist had no greater freedom to ruin the reputation of another citizen, and that in a criminal prosecution the mere truth of an allegation would not conclude the matter unless it was proved as a matter of fact that the publication was made for public good and that the journalist had acted in good faith. After holding that the right to a free press should make a conscientious journalist more responsible, the court remanded the matter for a full trial.[2]

Civil law of libel

Plaintiff's case

The law of libel in India closely follows the common law of England (Chapter 4 of this book is of direct relevance and should be read in conjunction with this chapter). In practice the plaintiff would have to prove the following:

- that the statement is defamatory;
- that the statement refers to the plaintiff;
- that the statement was published.

Sometimes falsity is regarded as a separate ingredient. The law, rather benignly, assumes the good reputation of a plaintiff. Hence, once it is shown that an imputation is defamatory, it would be assumed that it is false, until proved to the contrary.

Defamatory statement

A statement is defamatory if:

- it exposes the plaintiff to hatred, ridicule or contempt;
- injures him or her in his or her trade or profession;
- causes him or her to be shunned and avoided.

To say that a person had amassed wealth by sucking the blood of the poor was abusive but not defamatory. To say that he would give evidence for a price was defamatory.[3]

> The writer described the plaintiff as a Godse. The reference was to a person called Godse who was convicted for the murder of Mahatma Gandhi. The court held that the words conveyed the clear imputation that the plaintiff was likely to adopt methods of political assassination for enforcing his opinion and were defamatory.[4]

Reference to the plaintiff

One of the distinctions between civil and criminal law of defamation is that in civil law a person can be defamed even unintentionally. If a right-minded person can associate the defamatory statement with the plaintiff, the plaintiff would lose his or her reputation even if the defendant did not mean to defame him or her.

It is not a tort to defame a deceased person as such. However, a statement referring to a deceased person may be derogatory of the plaintiff. The suggestion that the deceased was of a loose moral character, in a given context, may amount to a reflection on the legitimacy of a living person.

A company can also be defamed. So can a class of persons, provided that the class is definable and the imputation affects the reputation of the plaintiff.

Publication

In the case of defamation by a journalist, publication may not be difficult to prove. Under of the Press and Registration of Books Act 1867, section 5, every copy of a newspaper has to contain the name of the owner and the editor.

Further, the printer and the publisher are required to make a formal declaration before the Press Registrar. Under the law these provisions support the presumption as to the identity of the editor, the owner, the printer or the publisher, unless the contrary is proved.[5, 6]

Defences

The broad defences of a journalist fall under the following heads:

- Justification;
- Fair comment;
- Qualified privilege;
- Public conduct of a public official;
- Defamation of government.

Justification

This defence is available regarding a statement of fact. Since defamation is an assault on the reputation of a person, truth is a complete defence. Such a statement may relate even to the private life of the defendant. But, if true, it can be published. One of the curious results of the defence is that even, where the statement is made recklessly, the truth of the statement is a complete answer to the civil suit. The statement must be true in substance and need not be true in every particular detail.

> A newspaper carried the story that the plaintiff had shot a wild elephant, stolen the tusks and thereafter set fire to the dead animal. The plaintiff admitted that he had set fire to the carcass, but stated that he had shot the tusker in self-defence on his own estate. The court held that the plaintiff had dishonestly appropriated the tusks. Although technically this was not theft, the plea of justification was upheld.[7]

> A newspaper reported a widespread rumour that the plaintiff was the owner of a particular studio which was taking nude photographs of young girls, and that he was arrested by the police and made to march in handcuffs. The court held that, although some details of the report may not have been accurate, the plaintiff was associated with the studio and the allegations were true in substance. Investigative journalism had a margin of error where the subject was a matter of public concern.[8]

Fair comment

This defence is available to support a bona fide opinion on a matter of public interest. Legitimate criticism, however strongly expressed, is permissible in public affairs. These include the workings of the state, local authorities and public institutions. Strong opinions are also permissible on works of art. The mere fact that the comment is hostile does not negate the defence. However, the fact of actual malice may show that the comment is not made in good faith.

Qualified privilege

This is a defence where the derogatory remark is protected because of the occasion for making it. The privilege is qualified because it does not extend to reports made maliciously. Such occasions include fair and accurate reports of judicial proceedings, parliamentary proceedings and proceedings of public meetings. Even if a statement made in such a report is false and defamatory, the journalist would be privileged unless it can be established that he or she was acting maliciously.

Public conduct of a public official

A recent defence based on constitutional rights is that an action for damages is not available with respect to the acts and conduct of a public official which are relevant to the discharge of his or her official duty. In such a case, the plaintiff has to establish both that the statement is false and also that the journalist had acted with reckless disregard for the truth. Further, it would be enough for the journalist to prove that he or she acted after a reasonable verification of facts. The journalist would be liable for the publication if it were both false and actuated by malice or personal animosity, and would also be liable if the matter were not relevant to the discharge of the duty of the public official.[9]

Defamation of government

A new exception has recently emerged which is close to the *Derbyshire* case in England. The court has laid down that government, local authority and other organs and institutions exercising governmental power, e.g. statutory corporations, cannot maintain a suit for damages for defamation.[10]

Remedies

The final reliefs in a suit for defamation are of two types. The first is an injunction to prevent the article from being published, and the second is in damages.

An injunction would not be granted at an interim stage if the defendant were going to justify the allegation. Such a defence requires that there should be a full trial before the court can determine the issue.

> R. P. & Co. proposed to issue secured convertible debentures. These became the subject matter of various suits and petitions. The conduct of the company was the subject of adverse comment by the *Indian Express*. The company filed a contempt petition and sought to restrain the *Indian Express* from publishing any article on the subject until the debentures were subscribed. The court held that it would have to balance the two interests of great public importance, namely, the freedom of speech and the administration of justice. It held that there was no imminent danger of injury and hence the injunction need not be continued.[11]

Damages

The issue of damages is entirely for the judge to assess. Courts take the view that damages for defamation are normally compensatory and would be punitive only in exceptional cases.

> A newspaper published an article that an industrial house was guilty of violating the control laws, resulting in shortages in the market. It alleged that the company was making sales on the black market on the basis of a false licence and was dishonestly availing itself of an income tax concession. The trial court awarded Rs300 000/- (then the equivalent of US$40 000) as damages. The appellate court held this to be a very large sum in local conditions and described it as almost a bounty. It halved the award. The above figure is from 1970, and now plaintiffs hopefully make much larger claims. But the ultimate awards still remain on the same modest scale.[12]

Disclosure of source

Plaintiffs sometimes seek to discover the sources of information of the newspaper article. Indian courts have adapted 'the newspaper rule', at least in so far as interlocutory matters are concerned. The press cannot be compelled to disclose the source of information at an interim stage in an action for libel.

> *Stardust*, a film magazine, wrote an article entitled 'Queer Quartet'. The article was described to be *per se* defamatory, and the plaintiff sought to administer interrogatories to find out who the informants were. The court held that 'the newspaper rule' prevented disclosure of such names at the interlocutory stage and rejected the application.[13]

Costs

The cost of litigation is a major disincentive to libel litigation in the United States and England. There are two types of costs: the expenses of your own lawyer and the costs of the opposite party (which you will have to pay if you lose and which you hope to recover if you succeed). Fees of Indian lawyers, on the other hand, are on a moderate scale compared to their counterparts elsewhere, although not quite so regarded by their clients. Although the losing party has to pay the costs of the adversary, even these are calculated on a modest scale. The winning party does not really recover anything like the full cost of litigation.

Criminal prosecution

Under section 499 of the Penal Code, defamation is a criminal offence. Any individual who is aggrieved by an article can launch a private prosecution. Although the Penal Code of 1860 is of ancient vintage, the provision has remained unchanged, and the section 499 broadly makes any defamatory statement criminal unless it falls under one of the statutory exceptions. It is noteworthy that truth is not a complete defence in criminal law. It might be helpful to set out the relevant part of the section.

> 499. Defamation – Whoever ... makes or publishes any imputation concerning any person intending to harm, or knowing or having reason to believe that such imputation will harm, the reputation of such person, is said, *except* in the cases hereinafter excepted, "to defame that person." Explanation 4 – No imputation is said to harm a person's reputation, unless that imputation directly or indirectly, in the estimation of others, *lowers* the moral or intellectual *character* of that person, or lowers the character of that person in respect of his caste or of his calling, or lowers the *credit* of that person, or causes it to be believed that the body of that person is in a loathsome state, or in a state generally considered as *disgraceful*.

Intention

A given mental attitude is a necessary ingredient of the offence. It is essential to show that the journalist intended or knew or had reason to believe that the imputation would harm the reputation of the complainant. Under the criminal law such an intention has to be proved by the prosecution.

Truth

Truth is not a complete defence. A statement of fact will be wholly protected in a civil action if it is proved to be true. Under the criminal law the imputation must be one which requires to be made or published in the public good, and it would have to be shown that the complainant required to be exposed. Exposure of the private conduct of a private person would come within the mischief of the section.

Good faith

Various defences under the exceptions are available if the allegation is made in good faith. Under the Penal Code nothing is done in good faith unless it is done with due care and caution.

> In a land dispute, the accused alleged that the complainant was known to be illegitimate and was not entitled to the land. The court held that the mere belief of the accused was not enough. The accused must show that he had rational basis, had acted with due care and was satisfied that the imputation was true.[14]

Clear imputation

Since the proceedings are criminal, the imputation should be clear and bring a particular person into disrepute. An imputation about a whole class may constitute defamation, provided that the complainant can be identified.

> The allegation that all lawyers as a class were 'dispute brokers' and fomented needless litigation would not entitle a given lawyer to file a case. But the allegation that the Public Prosecutors of a town were all corrupt would be defamatory of any Prosecutor of that place.[15]

Exceptions

The principal defence for a journalist would be to fall within the following exceptions:

- Imputation of truth which the public good requires to be made or published;
- Opinion in good faith regarding the public conduct of a public servant;
- Opinion in good faith regarding the conduct of any person touching any public question;

- Substantially true reports of court proceedings and their results;
- Opinion in good faith respecting the merits of a case decided by a court or respecting the conduct of a person as a party or witness in such a case;
- Opinion in good faith respecting the merits of any performance which its author has submitted to the judgement of the public.

It is for the accused to discharge the burden of proving that he or she falls within the exception. But if the exception is available, the burden of proof is lighter. The accused has to prove the probability of his or her defence, unlike the prosecution, which has to prove its case beyond reasonable doubt.

Procedure

- The real hazard of a prosecution is not its frequency but its inconvenience. A case can be filed at any place where the newspaper has been circulated. A journalist may find him or herself facing a criminal prosecution in a distant court where the complainant alleges that the newspaper has been circulated. It also enables the complainant to indulge in 'forum shopping' and to select a place which is inconvenient to the journalist.
- A complaint can be filed directly by a private person. A complaint against a journalist does not have to be filed by a Public Prosecutor but can be filed by a person aggrieved. The test would be whether the complainant's own personal reputation has been harmed by the allegation. There is one exception to this rule – a Public Prosecutor can file a complaint about an allegation made against high officials of the state and public servants.
- The Supreme Court has the power to transfer cases. It has been willing to transfer a case from a jurisdiction inconvenient to the accused to one which is less inconvenient. Such power can be exercised when there is a real danger of substantial prejudice or non-availability of competent legal service or the absence of congenial atmosphere for a fair and impartial trial.
- The maximum punishment for libel defamation is two years' imprisonment or a fine. This is the outer limit, and sentences are rarely Draconian. The real punishment is to go through the criminal trial.

Contempt of court

Contempt of court is not directly related to libel, although it may be regarded as a species of defamation of the judiciary. A journalist commits criminal contempt of the court when his or her article scandalizes the court or tends to interfere with the administration of justice. The court has the summary power to punish for contempt. It is a special jurisdiction where a court can be a judge in its own cause and impose imprisonment of up to six months. The usual cases under this head relate to allegations against the impartiality and honesty of a judge. Any such attack can be subversive of public confidence in the judiciary. The court is concerned not so much with the conduct of the given judge as the impact the attack can have in bringing the whole system into disrepute.

One of the curious results of this approach is that truth is not accepted as a defence in the matter of criminal contempt. This is an area which requires reform because the exposure of a corrupt judge is itself in the interest of the judiciary. Judges do accept that they are subject to public criticism and scrutiny, but they are sensitive to a reflection on their impartiality. Another type of problem is an attack directed not against a judge individually but against the whole judiciary. It is in this area that the courts have tended to accept criticism with greater grace.

> In 1967 the Marxist Chief Minister of Kerala attacked the judiciary as an instrument of oppression. He said that judges were dominated by class hatred, and denounced the judiciary as a part of the ruling class which worked against the peasants and workers and essentially served to exploit them. The Supreme Court took a dim view of the statement and held that it was calculated to weaken the authority of law and law courts. It therefore imposed the sentence of a nominal fine.[16]

> In 1988 another political leader attacked the judiciary by asserting that the Supreme Court was ruling in favour of rajas and maharajas and that anti-social elements had found their haven in the Supreme Court. Interestingly, the judges took the view that 'times and climes' had changed and that, however unsound, the attack did not amount to contempt of court.[17]

Right to privacy

The law of privacy in India is in evolution. The English common law, which applied until recently, does not accept the concept of privacy as such. In a recent judgment the Supreme Court of India has recognized privacy as implicit in the constitutional right to life and liberty. A citizen has a right to safeguard his or her own privacy, together with that of his or her family, marriage, procreation, motherhood, child bearing and education, among other matters. No-one can publish anything concerning the above matters without his or her consent, whether truthful or otherwise and whether laudatory or critical, otherwise they will be liable in an action for damages. The court has carved out the following exceptions:

- If the publication is with consent;
- If a person voluntarily thrusts him or herself into controversy or voluntarily invites or raises a controversy;
- If the publication is based upon public records, including court records. In such a case the matter becomes a legitimate subject for comment by the media. But this is subject to the exception that a victim of sexual assault, kidnap, abduction or a like offence should not further be subjected to the indignity of his or her name and the incident being publicized in the media;
- In the case of public officials, the right to privacy is not available with respect to their acts and conduct relevant to the discharge of their official duties. In matters not relevant to the discharge of his or her duties, the public official enjoys the same protection as any other citizen.

In the recent case of *Auto Shankar* referred to above, the court held that, even if the publication was unauthorized, the media had a right to publish the life story of Auto Shankar, a condemned prisoner, without his consent or authorization, insofar as it appears from the public records, without invading his right to privacy. In any event, the state or its officials cannot prevent or restrain the publication.[18]

Notes

1   *R. Rajgopal* v *State of Tamil Nadu* (1994) 6 SCC 632.
2   *Sewakram Sobhani* v *R. K. Karanjiya* AIR 1981 SC 1514 (1519).
3   *Purshottam Lal Sayal* v *Prem Shanker* AIR 1966 All. 377 (379,380).
4   *S. M. Narayanan* v *S. R. Narayana Iyer* AIR 1961 Mad. 254 (257).
5   *State of Maharashtra* v *Dr R. B.Chowdhari* AIR 1968 SC 110 (111).
6   *K. M. Mathew* v *State of Kerala* AIR 1992 SC 2206 (2208).
7   *Nellikka Achuthan* v *Deshabhimani Printing & Publishing House Ltd, Kazikode.* AIR 1986 Ker. 41 (43).
8   *Dainik Bhaskar* v *Madhusudan Bhargava* AIR 1991 MP 162 (166).
9   *R. Rajgopal* v *State of Tamil Nadu* (1994) 6 SCC 632.
10   *R. Rajgopal* v *State of Tamil Nadu* (1994) 6 SCC 632.
11   *Reliance Petrochemicals Ltd* v *Indian Express Newspapers Bombay Pvt Ltd* AIR 1989 SC 190 (195).
12   *R. K. Karanjiya* v *K. M. D. Thakersey* AIR 1970 Bom. 424 (423).
13   *Nishi Prem* v *Javed Akhtar* AIR 1988 Bom. 222.
14   *Sukra Mahto* v *Basudeo Kumar Mahto* AIR 1971 SC 1567 (1569).
15   *Narottamdas L. Shah* v *Patel Maganbhai Rerabhai* (1984) Cr. L. J. 1790, 1808.
16   *E. M. S. Namboodiripad* v *T. N. Nambiar* AIR 1970 SC 2015 (2024).
17   *P. N. Duda* v *P.Shivshankar & Ors* AIR 1988 SC 1208.
18   *R. Rajgopal* v *State of Tamil Nadu* (1994) 6 SCC 632.

8

Japan

Koichiro Nakada of Clifford Chance (London) and Makoto Shimada of Shimada, Seno, Amitani and Hirata Law Office (Tokyo)

Defamation plays an important role in Japanese society, and, as in many aspects of Japanese life, balance (*hikaku koryo*) is key. The law attempts to balance freedom of expression, protected by Article 21 of the Constitution, with honour and esteem (*meiyo*), of which reputation (*meisei*) is a specific element. The right to individual happiness ('personality right') is protected by Article 13, which acknowledges that human rights are circumscribed by the public interest.

The Japanese media seem to accept that they have to strike this balance. The concern for the rights of the individual can be seen in the public interest element of the truth defence and in the need for statements of opinion to be reasonably based on true facts:

> In the *Showa Electric Power* case, a journalist alleged that another journalist writing for *Yomiuri Shimbun* had received a bribe to conceal certain facts. The court found the first journalist liable because he had used a number of particularly insulting words about the complainant, and because he had been unable to show that publication was in the public interest.[1]

In the case of politicians, public interest is presumed, and the only issue remaining is truth:

> A journalist alleged that a politician had lied about his past and had failed to disclose criminal convictions. It transpired at the trial for defamation that the politician had not lied about his past, but he had concealed criminal convictions. Although the court found that the first journalist had failed to establish truth, he was not held liable. He had taken reasonable care in that there was a reasonable basis for the allegation that the politician had lied about his past.[2]

Article 233 specifically protects the trading reputation of a corporation by means of a criminal offence.

Japanese litigants are more interested in extracting an apology than in recovering damages, and the court has a discretion to order an apology or a correction.[3] Only the most serious cases go to court, and the compensation is relatively small (generally up to ¥1 000 000 (US$10 000).

There is no set yardstick for the quantum of defamation awards. This is in the discretion of the court and depends on all the circumstances, but relevant factors include the status of the plaintiff and the seriousness of the libel. It is relatively difficult to predict awards because of the small number of defamation cases brought to trial, particularly as many settle out of court.

Likewise, no legal costs are awarded at the end of a case, each side bearing its own costs. Nor is there any contingency fee system, as in the United States, but the court does have a discretion to allocate court fees, which are usually nominal. Legal aid is available in Japan for personal injury cases and other essential litigation, but not for defamation cases. In any event, the legal aid budget is very low compared with some other countries.

Japanese litigants are by disposition inclined to settle before trial, avoiding the need for mechanisms such as payment into court to force a compromise of the action. Stamp duty is payable at the beginning of litigation, and this operates as a disincentive to frivolous litigation. Nevertheless, the net result of the lack of any system for allocating costs on disposal of a case is that quite a few frivolous or undeserving lawsuits are brought.

Who can sue or complain?

Anyone can sue, in principle, including individuals and corporations. Corporations can suffer defamation, but for obvious reasons cannot recover compensation for injury to their feelings. They can, however, recover damages for actual financial loss. So far as damage can be assessed by the courts, compensation can be recovered by companies, and, of course, an apology can be ordered. Unincorporated associations can bring proceedings for defamation,[4] as can trade unions. The civil law does not recognize the right for the dead to sue for defamation, but injury to the feelings of the family is recoverable.

Who can be sued or prosecuted?

Anyone who has inflicted an injury to honour or reputation can be sued or prosecuted, that is, anyone responsible for publication, such as a journalist, editor or newspaper proprietor.

Elements of defamation

The Japanese criminal law[5] defines defamation as the identification of a person in public while damaging that person's honour or reputation. The civil definition of defamation is less strict. No mental element is required for the civil wrong. There is also a criminal offence of publishing inaccurate facts, which need not damage a person's reputation.[6]

The defendant must have alleged specific facts affecting the plaintiff's honour. The four requirements are:

- damage to reputation
- publication ('before the public')
- specific factual allegations
- identification.

Damage to reputation

Whether a statement is defamatory depends on whether a reasonable person would understand the words as seriously damaging the honour or reputation of an individual. Humorous or malicious intent both affect the subtle question of an article's meaning. The question is always whether the words would be reasonably understood to damage a person's honour or esteem.

> It was alleged that it was defamatory to omit the title San from the name of an accused person in reporting court proceedings. The court refused to hold that this could be defamatory.[7]

Whether or not an allegation is defamatory depends in large part on the circumstances of publication and the intention of the publisher. Reporting a damaging court judgment or an arrest might not be considered publication by themselves, but if prompted by an intention to harm or invade a person's privacy they could be considered defamatory.[8]

Publication

'Publication' has to be to the public, under the criminal law only.[9] In civil cases, publication to the public is not crucial, and a single publication to a third party is sufficient. The key point is that publication even to a few people may be enough to found liability, provided that there is a possibility of wider dissemination as a result.

Needless to say, damages will be greater in the case of widespread publication. Mere repetition of a libellous story gives rise to liability in the same way as an original publication. It is unsafe, therefore, to dredge up long-forgotten stories, as each new publication could be defamatory.

Specific factual allegations

Statements of opinion are protected under Article 21 of the Constitution. Genuine statements of opinion cannot be allegations in the sense required by the criminal and civil law of defamation, but the right to free opinion is limited by the requirement of reasonableness. Provided:

- a substantial part of a statement of fact, upon which the opinion is based, is true or there are reasonable grounds for believing so;
- the opinion is honestly held;
- the opinion is on a matter of public interest;

the maker cannot be liable.[10]

> A journalist called a doctor a misogynist for criticizing a woman. It turned out that the journalist had misinterpreted the doctor's comments, and was unable to rely on the opinion defence because he had got his facts wrong.

Identification

Identification by group or implication is not enough. The plaintiff has to be specifically identified, although he or she need not be named. So if you said that all of fifty or sixty people were liars, they could each claim to be identified, whereas this would not be the case if you said that there was one liar amongst the fifty or sixty. If a person is accidentally identified, and the writer has not been at least negligent, there is no liability.

Defences

Lack of fault

Japanese defamation law is subject to an overarching requirement of fault (i.e. negligence at least) on the part of the defendant. Moreover, it is invariably for the defendant to disprove fault. So far as journalists are concerned, the requirement of fault covers a multitude of situations where reportage might otherwise require specific protections.

A novel referred to the lives of a family which bore a striking resemblance to those of a real family of paper distributors. The authors and publishers of the book were not held liable for defamation, because the reference to the family had been purely accidental and there had been no negligence on their part.[11]

The courts expect certain standards of care on the part of journalists and publishers. The precise standard of care required depends both on the context and the media of publication employed. It is not possible to say that a comment should invariably be sought from the subject of an article, but this is a counsel of prudence, as it is the easiest way of finding out whether a claim is true or not.

The burden of proof of the above four elements falls initially on the plaintiff's or prosecutor's shoulders. The latter has to prove defamation identification and publication, and it is then for the defendant to establish an excuse or defence.

Truth

The prosecution has the initial burden of establishing falsity on a balance of probabilities after which the burden shifts to the defendant. But for the defence of truth, proof of truth is not enough. The defendant must also show that publication was in the public interest.[12] Disproving fault is an alternative defence if truth cannot be established.

The Supreme Court has held that truth must be proved conclusively in criminal cases, not on a balance of probabilities, the normal civil standard of proof.[13] Most criminal law academics are critical of this, for it is a heavy burden for a defendant to discharge. Here, documentary evidence is the most potent, but there is no obligation to disclose all documents and disclosure of documents is in the discretion of the court.[14] However, the courts can make very specific orders for disclosure of certain documents or categories of documents, generally on application of the parties.

Journalists cannot be required to reveal their sources as these are constitutionally protected, although such rights may be limited by the public interest. Of course, they may find themselves in difficulties in establishing truth if they cannot call their sources to give evidence.

Proof of a criminal conviction will not by itself be enough to establish truth, since a defendant must demonstrate the truth of the allegation and show that publication was in the public interest. The nature of the crime and the intention of the person reporting the alleged crime are very important.

Public interest

There is a public interest defence in the form of a public official/public servant defence, and this is frequently used in proceedings brought by politicians. Case law has an important part to play here. In criminal cases and cases concerning officials, public interest is presumed.[15]

For example, it might in a given case be regarded as in the public interest for a journalist to expose a politician as dishonest, as public interest would be presumed. The position could be different, however, in relation to a sportsperson or an actor, where the democratic interest in disclosure would be much less. The position of someone in business is equally unclear.

Privilege

If a participant in court proceedings lies or otherwise abuses his or her privilege of freedom of speech in court, he or she may be liable for defamation.[16]

Article 21 of the Constitution guaranteeing protection for freedom of speech probably protects reports of parliaments, courts, conferences, inquiries and proceedings of international organizations, but there is no explicit protection. Article 21 is generally interpreted as entitling journalists to report these occasions, but there must be doubt about the safety of reporting foreign proceedings unless these are of direct interest to the Japanese public.

As far as press conferences, meetings of companies, public health warnings, police statements and professional bodies findings are concerned, there is again no specific protection, but a journalist who relied in good faith on such official warnings would probably escape liability for defamation because there would be no evidence of fault, an essential component.

The protection for reporting statements of or about public officials at national level is virtually absolute. This does not exist at local level, where there is more of a balancing exercise, and the point at issue is whether good faith and care in reporting are relevant to the presence or absence of fault.[17]

> A local politician criticized the head of a prefecture, alleging that he had been incompetent in supervising the local police. He escaped liability for defamation when the head of prefecture sued, because the court held that there were reasonable grounds for making the statement.[18] In another case involving a head of prefecture, the defendant was found liable for defamation, because he had abused the reporting privilege.[19]

Statements of public officials are not necessarily protected. If a public official such as a police officer announces that a certain person is being sought in connection with a particular crime, are the media safe to report that statement?

A fair and accurate report in good faith will be protected, but if the privilege is used as a cloak to cover some ulterior or devious motive, the privilege will not apply. In other words, a responsible approach is all-important.

Pleadings and court documents are regarded as private documents until they are read out in court. The judgment is regarded as the only reliable court document for this purpose:

> A reporter was found guilty of defamation for reporting that the parents were implicated in the death of their three-month old-child.[20] This is a good example of the dangers of reporting court cases prematurely, especially criminal cases. A contrary example is of a journalist who wrote a report of election malpractices, based on the report of an official investigator into the alleged wrongdoing. It was held that he was entitled to rely on the official report, as he then had reasonable grounds for believing it was true.[21]

> A local Japanese news agency reported, based on a police report, that someone had stolen sixty-seven rails from a railway. Although it turned out in the end that the police could not prove the theft, and thus the reporter could not prove the theft, he was held entitled to rely upon the police report as giving good grounds for believing that the story was true.[22]

> In the *Hokkai Times* case, a photographer took a picture of the accused in court and was fined by the court. He challenged the decision, but the Supreme Court ruled that this was a reasonable restriction on his right to take photographs. He had this *prima facie* liberty under Article 21, but this had to be balanced against the accused's right of privacy and the court's interest in maintaining order in court. The matter was subject to the discretion of the court.[23]

Limitation

A limitation period of three years on bringing civil proceedings applies from the time when the plaintiff first became aware of the alleged defamation, and an absolute time bar of twenty years from the event, i.e. any occurrence which took place more than twenty years ago is beyond the reach of the civil courts. Thus, journalists' notebooks should be kept for at least three years.

Under the criminal law, complaint must be made within six months of the event, and no prosecution may be brought after three years from the event complained of.

Litigation and remedies

There is no need to mark correspondence 'without prejudice', and it is unlikely that any correction or retraction would be taken as an admission of liability. There is no system of payment into court or other means of forcing a settlement, but a foreign company or individual can be required to pay money into court by way of security for costs.

Financial loss is not presumed and is relatively unimportant for infringements of personality rights such as defamation. The plaintiff's honour (in the subjective sense) is protected and so he or she has to prove the seriousness of his mental suffering.

The Appeal Court reviews both the facts and the legal issues, while the Supreme Court (which is the final court of appeal), looks only at the legal issues. People appeal mainly in order to have damages reduced, and there are tactical advantages to doing so in that, by increasing the costs exposure and expenditure of time, defendants can sometimes obtain a more advantageous settlement.

Under the criminal law, the maximum term of imprisonment is three years and the original maximum fine was ¥500 000 (US$5000). There is no limit to the amount of civil damages which can be awarded, but causation of loss must be strictly proven. This applies to damage to reputation, and particularly to proof of economic or financial loss.

As far as prior restraint is concerned, the court will balance the worth of the story with the interest which the plaintiff is trying to protect, and in the event that the court grants an injunction the plaintiff will be required to pay a substantial deposit as security against any losses the defendant may suffer.

Other rights

Article 13 of the Constitution protects the right to life, freedom and the pursuit of happiness, and prevents any interference with these which is not required in the public interest. This amounts to a generalized personality right, and privacy may be protected as a function of this.

Foreign elements

Publication in Japan will normally give rise to liability in Japan if the material is defamatory. If no publication takes place in Japan there is probably nothing over which the court can assume jurisdiction, although there may conceivably be some physical act which could be construed as aiding or abetting publication. In the case of publication both in Japan and abroad, the court may be able to take account of damage to reputation held abroad. A foreign defendant domiciled in Japan could be sued there for a publication in Japan.

Notes

1 Tokyo High Court, 21 February 1953.
2 Supreme Court, 23 June 1966.
3 Civil Code, section 723.
4 Supreme Court, 28 January 1964.
5 Criminal Code, section 230.
6 Criminal Code, article 231.
7 Nagoya High Court, 13 February 1990.
8 Nagano District Court, 8 February 1989.
9 Supreme Court, 7 May 1959.
10 Tokyo District Court, 12 July 1972.
11 Gifu District Court, 28 March 1959.
12 Supreme Court, 9 December 1955.
13 Supreme Court, 9 December 1955.
14 There is no provision for compulsory pre-trial discovery, although under the Code of Civil Procedure a defendant can be forced to produce certain types of document. An order for the preservation of evidence is also available.
15 Criminal Code 233-2.
16 Supreme Court, 7 March 1952.
17 Criminal Code, section 35.
18 Supreme Court, 1 September 1930.
19 Supreme Court, 21 February 1935.
20 Supreme Court, 16 November 1972.
21 Supreme Court, 23 June 1989.
22 Sendai District Court, 21 May 1959.
23 Supreme Court, 19 February 1958.

9

Libel laws compared:
Towards a benchmark?

Journalists writing for global circulation face a daunting task in charting disparate legal hazards around the world. To decide in what country or countries a libel suit is likely, it is necessary to look initially at whether suing in a particular country offers a real chance of success to the plaintiff – broadly, a plaintiff can sue in any country or state where substantial publication has taken place.

This chapter focuses on how the eight countries covered here deal with various issues of practical concern to the media, principally libel. A rough-and-ready attempt is made to distil a universal baseline requirement for international publishing, before summarizing the local legal position. At the end of the chapter, aspects of those countries' laws are compared in tabular form.[1]

What is defamatory?

Broadly, a statement will be defamatory if it:

1 Damages reputation by
   ● exposing a person to hatred, contempt, shame and, usually, ridicule
   ● making a person likely to be avoided or shunned.
2 Attacks a person's honour.
3 Injures someone in their trade or profession, or a company in its trading reputation.
4 Accuses someone of
   ● criminal activity, dishonesty, cruelty or hypocrisy
   ● incompetence, inefficiency or stupidity.

United States

A defamatory statement is, broadly, a false statement of fact printed or broadcast about a person that tends to injure that person's reputation. The exact definition of what is defamatory varies from state to state. In New York, for example, a defamatory statement must 'tend to expose one to public hatred, shame, obloquy, contumely, odium, contempt, ridicule, aversion, ostracism, degradation, or disgrace, or to induce an evil opinion of one in the minds of right-thinking persons, and to deprive one of their confidence and friendly intercourse in society'.

Australia

The position is approximately the same as under English law, but varies from state to state. In Victoria, South Australia and Western Australia, a defamatory statement must impute behaviour or characteristics for which the subject is responsible, while in the Code States it is enough that the statement is likely to injure a person in his or her profession or trade.

Canada

The essence is lowering the plaintiff in the estimation of right-thinking members of society. It is defamatory under Canadian law to say that someone:

1   is dishonest, untrustworthy, disreputable, dishonourable, ungrateful or irresponsible;
2   has engaged in criminal, disreputable or fraudulent conduct or permits immorality to be practised by others;
3   lacks integrity, is cruel, sadistic or inhuman, prejudiced, hypocritical, unpopular or has a social disability;
4   abused a position of trust, was incompetent, inefficient, unintelligent, unmotivated, incapable;
5   is a charlatan, subversive, insane or senile.

England and Wales, and India

The definitions are not exhaustive, but include:

1   A statement about a person that exposes him or her to hatred, ridicule and contempt, or which causes him or her to be shunned or avoided, or which has a tendency to injure him or her in his or her office, profession or trade.

2   A false statement about someone to his or her discredit.

3   Words which tend to lower the plaintiff in the estimation of right-thinking members of society generally.

4   Damage to reputation is of the essence, but this need not involve any moral fault, as, for example, in the case of a contagious disease.

Statements of opinion, in the sense of statements that cannot be proven by factual evidence, can be defamatory under English law.

France

Under French law, a defamatory attack is an imputation or allegation which attacks a person's honour or esteem. Honour comprises inner, personal qualities, while esteem has to do with objective reputation and standing in society. Vague, general statements and statements of opinion are excluded, although these may give rise to different heads of liability. Moreover, the allegations must be specific and precise.

Germany and Japan

All three branches of German criminal law protect 'honour', and in general the opinion of right-thinking members of society will be determinative. Past conduct and general character may well determine the degree of protection the law affords. Japanese law is very similar.

Humour, parody and satire

The question is one of objective meaning, not intended meaning. If a joke would not be understood seriously by a reasonable person, there is generally no defamation.

United States

Parody, satire and other forms of humour are usually understood as such, conveying no serious factual sting, however annoying or embarrassing. Courts do realize, however, that humour can be used as a cover for defamatory meaning, and have on occasion found such statements to be libellous.

Australia, Canada, England and Wales, and India

The fundamental question is how a reasonable person would understand the humorous or satirical statement. Generally, the lack of any serious intent is clear enough. Often enough, however, a judge would leave such questions to the jury (but not in India), thus introducing an element of risk into the use of barbed humour.

France

French courts treat irony and parody with a certain leniency, provided the effect is to ridicule rather than to attack the target's honour or reputation.

Germany and Japan

The position is broadly the same as in France.

Identification

The question is whether the plaintiff is reasonably identifiable. Could a single reader or viewer could work out who the subject is? Disguising identity is dangerous because it can widen the circle of potential plaintiffs.

United States

The statement must be 'of and concerning the plaintiff'. The publication need not specifically name the plaintiff, although it is essential that some readers at least could reasonably conclude that the statement refers to the plaintiff.

Generally, individual members of a large group cannot sue for statements about the group as a whole. For the writer to escape liability, the group must be large enough for the defendant to be able to claim legitimately that the individual members are not identifiable.

Australia, Canada, England and Wales, and India

Plaintiffs must show that the words complained of refer to them, and the defendant's intention is irrelevant. Individual members of a large group (say fifty or more) could probably claim not to be individually identified, and so may not be able to sue for defamation.

Liability may be established even where most people would not identify the plaintiff. All that is needed is for a restricted number of people in possession of key information to be able to identify the plaintiff.

France

The plaintiff need not be identified explicitly. It is enough if the subject can readily be identified. As in England and Wales, identification can result from the overall context, including elements extraneous to the article itself.

Germany

The subject need not be named explicitly, but must be reasonably identifiable from the circumstances. Any member of a group referred to as a group can sue, provided there is an element of individual identification.

Japan

The plaintiff must be specifically identified, although the reference need not be explicit. A group of fifty or sixty people could not sue over a defamatory allegation about one of them, but all could sue for an allegation about all of them.

What is 'publication'?

Is every fresh repetition a publication?

Although in civil law jurisdictions 'publication' connotes wider dissemination than under common law systems, in practice the differences are not significant. The crucial distinction is between countries which permit the media to rely upon authoritative sources in matters of public concern (the United States, France, Germany and Japan), and those which do not (the Commonwealth countries).

United States

As in other systems based on the common law, showing or reading a written document to a third party is a technical publication. Thus, repetition of false defamatory rumours or old stories can give rise to fresh causes of action.

In a few states, however, the press are protected by the neutral reportage privilege which protects accurate reports of newsworthy charges against public figures or officials made by prominent and responsible non-governmental sources.

United States law also recognizes that news organizations must be able to rely on articles published by other prominent news organizations, unless they have good reason to doubt the accuracy of the original publication. The status of the subject, the pressure of deadlines and the reliability of the source will all be factors in assessing potential liability.

Australia, Canada, England and Wales, and India

The fundamental position is the same as under US law, in that each fresh publication to a third party is a new cause of action. However, there is no neutral reportage defence or republication privilege, and it is potentially unsafe to repeat old stories or rumours.

If a republication is attributed to a named source, and that source is joined into any defamation action, the court can allocate liability as between the originator and the republisher. Liability in damages should be reduced if the defendant did not originate the libel, but the unpredictability of the jury system makes this prospect tenuous and unreliable in practice.

France

Every fresh publication can lead to liability. In particular, reliance upon an old story or rumour that journalists believe is in the public domain will not establish good faith. However, proper professional fact checking may avoid liability for defamation.

Germany

The position is similar to that in France. Each publication or quotation of defamatory material can attract liability.

Japan

The position in Japanese civil law is as in Germany, while at criminal law publication must be to the public at large.

Proof of falsity/defence of truth

Despite the generosity to media defendants of US law in requiring the plaintiff to prove falsity, the international media must be able to prove truth. The position appears to be changing slowly, with the emergence of public official defences in Australia and India. The fact remains, however, that only truth is an absolute defence in the majority of countries. For complete safety, publication should also be in the public interest.

It is not safe to assume that evidence will be discoverable after publication. Most common law jurisdictions restrict 'fishing expeditions' through the process of disclosure of documentation, and French law prohibits reliance on any evidence other than that available at the time of publication. Note also the French, Japanese and German restrictions upon publication of true private matters.

United States

Since the landmark 1964 *Sullivan* case, public officials have been required to establish falsity. In the *Hepp*s case in 1986, the Supreme Court made clear that both public figures and private plaintiffs must establish falsity at least where the defamatory remark involves an issue of public concern. This requirement is based on the First Amendment and effectively renders the defence of truth, inherited from the common law, obsolete.

Moreover, there is emerging law making foreign libel judgments difficult to enforce in the United States on grounds of US public policy, where fault by the defendant was not a requirement in the forum in which the matter was tried. The decision in the *India Abroad* case shows the New York courts' suspicion of foreign judgments inimical to the US Constitution – the absence of any requirement under English law for the plaintiff to show fault was fatal to enforcement.

Australia, Canada, England and Wales, and India

The defendant must establish truth. Falsity is presumed once the plaintiff has established identification in published defamatory material. Under Indian and English criminal libel law, truth is not a complete defence.

Falsity is presumed upon the plaintiff discharging an initial minimum burden of proof. The defence of justification requires the media defendant to establish truth 'in substance and in fact' of each and every defamatory meaning that the plaintiff can establish. This is a heavy burden, particularly as the standard of proof – the degree to which the tribunal must be convinced of truth – increases with the seriousness of the original allegations.

For example, where a person is suspected of committing a crime, it is almost certainly not enough to show that the suspicion exists. At the very least, evidence must be adduced that there were reasonable grounds for suspecting that person that had committed the crime. Possibly the only safe course is to have evidence of actual commission.

Even where a plaintiff has a generally bad reputation, the defendant cannot mitigate damages on that basis unless the bad reputation is in the relevant 'sector' of the plaintiff's life. 'Relevant sector' means the aspect which is the subject of the allegations.

Australian law is generally identical to English law. In New South Wales, the defence of 'contextual implication' enables a defendant to show that the words complained of do not significantly damage the plaintiff's reputation.

The defence of truth in both criminal and civil libel actions is hard to establish. Defendants must have their evidential material in order at the time of publication, otherwise they risk having their case struck out when pleading justification.

In the case of criminal libel, the defendant must also prove that publication was for the public benefit. In Canada, in the case of criminal libel, publication of defamatory matter that the person reasonably believes to be true, and which is relevant to any subject of public interest, will not attract liability, provided that public discussion is for the public benefit. In an Indian criminal defamation action, the imputation must additionally have been made or published in the public good. Unless defendants can establish one of the exceptions showing good faith, the offence may be made out.

France

Falsity is not presumed, but there is a presumption of bad faith. The defendant has a choice whether to establish the defence of truth or good faith, in any case where truth or falsity is in issue. As the defence of truth is subject to rigid evidential controls, it may be easier in practice to seek to displace the presumption of bad faith.

Truth is an absolute defence in France, even in the presence of bad faith, but it is particularly hard to establish. In particular, the defendant is limited to those sources specified in the initial defence, and is unlikely to be able to uncover incriminating documentary evidence through the process of discovery.

Clear and conclusive proof of the truth of every material aspect is a defence in France, both criminal and civil. Its scope is, however, circumscribed in several respects. First, truth at the time of publication must be shown. Second, truth is not available as a defence in respect of matters more than ten years old, for matters subject to amnesty, rehabilitation, limitation or appeal. And finally, in criminal matters, the defendant has only ten days from issue of proceedings to set out the different sources of evidence to be adduced. The Cour de Cassation has recently ruled, however, that this ten-day rule should apply to civil matters as well.

Germany

Under the criminal defamation provisions, the burden is neutral, with the court acting as inquisitor. Under the civil law, it is for the defendant to establish truth.

Truth is generally a complete defence, but where the circumstances of publication are especially offensive, or in cases of intrusion into privacy, the defence is unavailable.

Japan

Again, in Japan truth is not in itself a sufficient defence. Once the prosecution or plaintiff has established fault of some kind (normally negligence), the defendant must show, in addition to truth, that publication was in the public interest.

Proof of fault

Unlike US law, neither English, Canadian nor French law requires the plaintiff (or prosecutor, as the case may be) to show fault, in the sense of a culpable state of mind. The state of mind of the author is strictly irrelevant in the Commonwealth jurisdictions, although under French law it is a defence to show 'good faith' i.e. lack of fault. This means that reliance upon accepted journalistic practice will not necessarily lead to safety.

United States

The First Amendment has shifted much of the burden onto the plaintiff to show some degree of fault. Even if a plaintiff demonstrates falsity, liability will not follow unless the plaintiff can prove a degree of fault. This involves proof not only of falsity, but also of a failure to meet an objective standard.

In the case of public officials and public figures, the plaintiff, must by clear and convincing proof, show that the defendant published the statement with 'actual malice', meaning 'knowledge of falsity or reckless disregard as to truth or falsity'. The standard applicable to private plaintiffs varies from state to state, but some degree of fault by the defendant is constitutionally required. Most states have applied a negligence standard for private figures.

Australia, Canada, and England and Wales

Truth (justification) is an absolute defence, and the state of mind of the publisher or author is immaterial. So evidence discovered subsequently to publication may be admissible in the resulting libel action. On the other hand, persisting with an unsuccessful plea of justification can aggravate the damages awarded.

France

Bad faith is presumed against the defendant, and so in effect it is for the defendant to show truth or good faith.

Germany

Under the criminal defamation provisions, the burden is neutral, with the court acting as inquisitor. Under the civil law, it is for the plaintiff to establish fault.

India

The provisions of Indian law are broadly the same as English law, but it should be noted that truth is not a complete defence to criminal libel proceedings. The defendant must also show that the statement was made or published in the public good, i.e. that the conduct in question required to be exposed.

Japan

It is for the defendant to disprove fault, i.e. that due care was exercised. This requirement is superimposed on any defence or justification that the defendant may put forward.

Public figure and public interest defences

Because of the sporadic availability and varied scope of public official/figure and public interest defences, public interest or the status of the plaintiff should not be determinative at pre-publication stage in international publishing. The primary focus should be upon the nature of the evidence and upon risk management.

United States

The *Sullivan* case gave defendants a minimum standard of protection by imposing on public officials the burden of proving fault in a libel suit. The standard of fault required is 'actual malice' – knowledge of falsity or reckless disregard of the statement's truth or falsity.

The requirement was subsequently extended to public figure plaintiffs, namely those figures who 'have assumed a role of special prominence in society'. Such figures may be all-purpose public figures (including major corporations) or limited-purpose public figures, essentially those who have voluntarily injected themselves into the vortex of a particular public controversy.

The *Sullivan* defence enables media defendants to escape liability, even where public official and public figure plaintiffs can show that they have published a false and defamatory statement, unless actual malice is proved. Although there is strictly no public interest defence as such, the *Sullivan* defence effectively embodies a public interest notion – providing journalists with greater leeway in writing about persons involved in public affairs.

Australia

In the 1994 *Theophanous* case, the High Court held that 'political discussion' includes discussion of the conduct, policies or fitness for office of government, political parties, public bodies, public officers and those seeking public office. A publication will not be actionable in defamation if:

1 the publisher was unaware of the falsity of the material published;
2 it did not publish the material recklessly, that is, not caring whether the material was true or false;
3 the publication was reasonable in the circumstances.

Canada

A newspaper or broadcaster has a qualified privilege regarding reports on matters of public interest, provided there is a duty to publish to the public and the public have a corresponding interest in receiving the publication. In this, Canadian law is more generous than the laws of other Commonwealth countries.

England and Wales

English law has no generalized public interest defence to speak of, except for a residual privilege, still ill-defined, to report on serious dangers to the public at large. For practical purposes, no such defence is available. Privilege is largely limited to specific occasions, such as parliamentary and court reporting, where the public interest is deemed to override private interests in reputation.

Local, and probably national, governmental departments cannot sue for defamation in their own right as a result of the *Derbyshire* case. This is the only serious inroad upon the principle that public interest is irrelevant to the right to sue for libel.

France

'Good faith' can be established by proof that publication was justified in the public interest (*intérêts supérieurs*). Because the burden is on the defendant, the public interest defence offers journalists unreliable protection.

Germany

The public interest defence applies only to statements of fact. The defendant must:

1 have taken reasonable care;
2 honestly believe in the truth of the statement.

Logically enough, the defence is not available in the case of malicious defamation.

India

The position at civil law is the same as in England and Wales. Under Indian criminal law, the defence of good faith by itself refers more to the standard of care expected of the journalist. The many exceptions include potent elements of public interest, which are for the defendant to establish.

Japan

There is a public interest defence, in the sense that, in order to establish the defence of truth, it is necessary in addition to prove an element of public interest. Such additional public interest element is presumed, and not required in matters relating to public officials and candidates for election to public office.

Statements of opinion

Statements of honest opinion upon matters of public concern will normally be protected, provided no irrelevant or malicious motives are present. There should be reasonable grounds for the opinion. It is always wise to set out (and be in a position to prove) the facts upon which the opinion is based.

United States

Only statements of fact are actionable; pure opinions which neither state nor imply facts cannot serve as the basis of a libel case. The difficulty lies in deciding what is a statement of fact and what is a statement of opinion. In the *Milkovitch* case the Supreme Court complicated the analysis by ruling that an additional question must be resolved as to whether the opinion states or implies undisclosed defamatory facts. If so, it is actionable.

Australia, Canada, and England and Wales

Fair comment, or honest opinion, is in law a qualified defence to a defamation claim – qualified in the sense that it can be defeated by proof of malice. The comment must be honestly held, based upon provably true facts, and upon a matter of public interest. Of these, proving that the facts underlying the comment are true is likely to be the most problematical issue for journalists. Thus, to establish the opinion defence a preliminary truth test must be satisfied.

The court is more likely to classify a statement as comment if the underlying factual basis is clearly set out. This enables the reader to decide whether the opinion is justified on the basis of the facts set out. The opinion does not have to be reasonable (except in allegations of crime or dishonesty). If the statement is so outrageous or vicious as to cast doubt on honesty, the defence may be lost.

France

Opinion is protected under the French Constitution, and genuine statements of opinion cannot be defamatory allegations or imputations, which are factual in nature. There is, however, a separate *délit* of abusing the right to express free opinions.

Germany

Statements of opinion (provided that is genuinely what they are) benefit from absolute constitutional protection. In cases of doubt as to whether a statement is one of fact or opinion, the courts tend to construe in favour of opinion.

India

The civil defence of fair comment is the same as in England and Wales. Under the criminal law, there are specific exceptions for opinions in good faith:

1   on the conduct of a public servant;

2 on the conduct of any person touching any public question;
3 on the merits of a court decision or the conduct of parties or witnesses;
4 on the merits of any performance submitted to the judgement of the public.

These exceptions are not especially hard to establish.

Japan

The position is broadly similar to that under German law. Statements of opinion are protected under Article 21 of the Constitution. In order to attract protection, however, the opinion must be based upon reasonable grounds.

Reporting privilege/immunity

It is dangerous to generalize from the very different local rules. It is safe to say, however, that relatively few countries permit the reporting of foreign court proceedings. Reporting foreign courts and legislatures is sometimes protected in Commonwealth countries, but journalists need to rely primarily upon risk management in this area: it would be strange (but not unheard of) for plaintiffs to sue abroad concerning reports of court or parliamentary proceedings in their own country.

United States

Fair and accurate reports of judicial, legislative and executive proceedings are generally protected under US common law. State laws vary as to the types of proceedings covered by the privilege. There are also discrepancies as to whether the privilege is absolute or qualified. No restriction exists upon the medium employed, provided the report is fair and true.

There is no explicit privilege for reporting foreign courts and at least one important case has rejected such a privilege.

Australia

In significant contrast with the position in England and Wales, there is no privilege for reporting the speeches of members of parliament. There is, however, privilege for reporting domestic judicial proceedings.

Canada

Coverage of domestic court proceedings is protected by absolute privilege. By way of exception, in British Columbia and Saskatchewan, the person defamed has the right to insert in the publication a reasonable statement of explanation or contradiction.

Qualified privilege extends to a number of bodies whose proceedings are open to the public, including Commonwealth legislatures and commissions of inquiry, and Canadian public authorities (with provincial Acts sometimes diluting these protections). Public notices are also protected.

England and Wales

The rules are complex but, generally speaking, fair and accurate contemporaneous press and broadcast reports of the courts are absolutely privileged by statute, malice being irrelevant. At common law there is an additional qualified privilege for non-contemporaneous court reporting, which is not limited to newspapers and broadcasters.

United Kingdom parliamentary reporting is covered by qualified privilege at common law, provided it is fair and accurate.

The Schedule to the Defamation Act 1952 also gives statutory qualified privilege to fair and accurate press and broadcast reports of a number of different occasions. These include reports of Commonwealth court and legislative proceedings.

France

Fair and accurate reports in good faith of public sessions of the National Assembly and the Senate are privileged. Likewise, fair and accurate reports in good faith of speeches made and documents produced before the courts are privileged.

There is no privilege for reporting foreign courts, but presumably the defence of good faith would be available if the matter were of interest to the French public.

Germany

A specific statutory privilege protects speeches of deputies in the Federal Parliament and accurate reports of the Federal Parliament. Statements made in court are not *per se* privileged, but will always be justified under the public interest defence.

Reports of court proceedings can only shelter under the public interest defence. In view of the personality rights at issue in such cases, the German courts scrutinize closely the reporting of criminal proceedings.

India

The position is broadly as in England and Wales. Commonwealth court and legislative reports are covered.

Japan

Article 21 of the Constitution is generally thought to entitle journalists to report court and parliamentary proceedings fairly and accurately. The point has not been tested in the courts, however. Reports of foreign legislatures or proceedings will almost certainly not be covered.

Hyperbole, abuse or insult

Mere insults will generally not be defamatory in the strict sense, since there is no tendency to damage reputation. As with cases of parody and humour, the issue is how a reasonable person might understand the exaggeration or terms of abuse. However, in France, Germany and Japan insulting a person can be a separate criminal offence.

United States

United States law generally takes the view that colourful speech is not intended to be taken literally. Much depends upon context. The less the context suggests that vituperative speech should be taken literally, the less likely that the statement will be actionable.

Australia, Canada, England and Wales, and India

'Mere abuse' is not defamatory, but allegations of fact or opinion are, in precisely the same way as they are in the United States. The test is whether the words would be taken seriously.

France

Abuse (*injure*) is a separate offence (*délit*) in France, but insults cannot be defamation unless they carry an imputation or allegation of fact. Insults to judges and jurors, and to the French President, are also distinct offences.

Germany and Japan

Abuse (*Beleidigung*) is a separate offence in Germany, and consists in wilful communication to the subject of defamatory material. An equivalent provision exists in Japan. Mere insults, which no-one would take seriously, are not abuse in this sense because they are not factual.

Must the plaintiff prove financial loss?

Loss will, in most countries, be presumed for general damage to reputation, but particular financial losses will have to be proven.

United States

At risk of gross over-simplification, if a statement is libellous on its face, damage cannot, without showing of malice, be presumed in most states. If the meaning is hidden, financial loss ('special damages') will have to be proven.

Australia, Canada, England and Wales, and India

Whereas in verbal defamation (slander) proof of loss is normally required, in the case of written and broadcast defamation (libel) damage to reputation is presumed ('general damages'). Special damages can be recovered in addition upon proof of financial loss.

France

Plaintiffs must prove either financial loss or personal damage. Financial loss would include unemployment or loss of profits resulting from loss of trading reputation, while personal loss might be an attack on honour, which is hard to assess in purely financial terms.

Germany and Japan

Financial loss need not be proven, but in practice the sums awarded for general damage to reputation are modest. There is, by contrast, no theoretical limit to the amount that can be awarded in cases of actual provable loss.

Protection of sources

None of the countries surveyed, except perhaps Germany, affords absolute protection to journalists' sources. Broadly, sources should be protected unless there is some overriding public interest requirement (e.g. of justice, crime prevention or national security), and the information cannot be obtained in any other way.

United States

Many lower courts in the United States have interpreted the leading decision of the Supreme Court in *Branzburg* as giving reporters a qualified privilege to protect their sources, unless it can be shown that:

1 The information sought is relevant to the litigant's cause of action;
2 The litigant has a compelling need for such information;
3 The information is not available from another source.

There is, however, a contrary view that rejects such a privilege and a majority of states have also enacted shield laws, which vary considerably from state to state. Some give reporters almost absolute protection, while in others the shield mirrors the constitutionally based privilege set out in *Branzburg*.

Australia

Australian journalists do not even have the formal protections available in England and Wales. The key question is whether the interests of justice will be served by ordering disclosure.

Canada

Canadian courts have the power to order disclosure of sources, but the discretion to do so is exercised differently in different provinces. The court will consider all the factors, including whether the source requested confidentiality, the need for the information, and the scope of disclosure.

England and Wales

English law, and UK law generally, offers journalists theoretical protection over and above that extended to ordinary citizens. The protection is qualified in that no-one may be required to reveal their sources unless the court is satisfied that disclosure is necessary:

1   in the interests of justice or national security;
2   for the prevention of disorder or crime.

Unfortunately, these provisions have not been interpreted liberally in favour of journalists. On at least two occasions reporters have found themselves on a collision course with the courts, which have refused to extend special consideration to the public interest in protecting sources.

In libel proceedings, plaintiffs will in any event be unable even to attempt to force disclosure of a source until trial, and the cases where the above conditions could be satisfied in the context of a libel suit will be relatively rare.

France

In one case, a journalist was not held to be guilty of bad faith for refusing to reveal a source of information. While French law does not require journalists to protect their sources, a law of 4 January 1993 only protects journalists from revealing their sources when called as witnesses. Refusal could lead to an inference of bad faith in defamation proceedings.

Germany

The press cannot be forced to reveal confidential sources, in recognition of the need for investigative journalists not to be limited to publicly accessible sources of information. A journalist wishing to invoke the privilege cannot select material for disclosure (the "all-or-nothing" rule). The privilege does not extend to pictures and photographs.

India

There is qualified protection for journalists' sources.

Japan

Journalists in Japan cannot be required to reveal their sources in the absence of justifiable grounds, a right protected by the Constitution.

Costs

The relevance of costs is the level of financial exposure at which a plaintiff can pursue litigation. In this respect, wealthy plaintiffs and substantial corporations are the most obvious threat in any jurisdiction. In the United States, however, the availability of contingency fee funding for litigation, coupled with jury trial and the possibility of high damages awards, can make a private plaintiff of modest means a formidable opponent.

United States

There is no state subsidy for litigation in the United States, and the winner does not normally recover costs from the losing side. The contingency fee system often funds plaintiffs' costs, and effectively shields them from financial risk arising from litigation.

Australia, Canada, England and Wales, and India

The winner is usually entitled to costs, at the discretion of the court, on a standard basis. Currently, in England and Wales a winning party might recover up to about 75 to 80 per cent of the costs payable to its own lawyers. The 20 per cent (at least) shortfall represents a strong incentive to compromise an action.

In Australia, costs may be awarded on an indemnity basis where the losing party prolongs a case with hopeless defences or deliberately false allegations.

In Canada, a successful party should expect to recover up to 50 per cent, in some cases up to about 75 per cent, and occasionally 100 per cent of costs incurred. In Ontario, legal aid is no longer available for civil defamation claims.

France

It is for the court, whose discretion is unfettered, to award costs upon resolution of the case. The losing party must pay all the essential costs, which are controlled by the court. The court also has a discretion to award other inessential costs based on considerations of fairness and the means of the paying party.

In principle, contingency fees are prohibited, although an uplift in recognition of work carried out is permitted. Legal aid is available, based on the litigant's resources and the merits of the case.

Germany

The loser must pay all legal and extra-legal costs, controlled by the court, whether the case goes to trial or settles out of court. Costs and fees are proportionate to the value of the dispute, seldom exceeding 10 per cent of the sum in issue. Legal aid is available, and defamation is frequently covered under insurance policies.

Japan

Legal aid is not available for civil defamation cases, and there is no system for awarding costs at the end of a case.

Privacy

France, Germany, Japan and some US states have privacy laws which penalize disclosure of private facts. Where facts from public or private figures' private lives are to be disclosed, it is wise to check the legal position.

United States

Privacy law has manifested itself under four main heads:

1   'False light'claims;
2   'Private facts';
3   'Misappropriation';
4   'Intrusion'.

Of most interest to journalists is the second head, but private facts and intrusion is becoming a significant issue. This inhibits the reporting of true facts where it would be highly offensive to a reasonable person and not of legitimate public concern. First Amendment protections have rendered slight the impact of this provision upon the media.

Australia

No privacy rights have been introduced as such, although the Federal Privacy Act 1988 restricts the use of and access to private information by federal departments and statutory bodies.

Canada

No common law privacy right exists, but British Columbia, Manitoba and Saskatchewan have enacted a civil privacy right along the lines of several states in the United States.

England and Wales

At the time of writing, there is no overt protection for privacy under English law. Political pressure grew for legislation following invasions of the privacy of the Royal Family, but has now receded. The only protections *de facto* for privacy are the law of confidentiality, which depends upon an initial relationship of confidence, the laws of trespass, and various laws restricting phone-tapping.

France

French privacy law (protection for *la vie privée*) is probably the most stringent of any country surveyed. Plaintiffs in France can restrict publication of facts which are damaging but true. Nevertheless, some public figures may find that public interest enables journalists to publish details of their private lives, much more latitude being given to revelations about financial probity than to sexual scandal. Different standards apply to different public figures.

Germany

Three categories or 'zones' are protected by the general personality right, the intimate, the private, and the individual. The intimate zone is absolutely protected, while private interests can be outweighed by public interest considerations. Protection for the individual zone corresponds loosely to the 'false light' privacy protection in some US states.

India

Indian law has developed a concept of privacy distinct from its English antecedents. There are exceptions for consent, voluntary participation in controversy and public records. Public officials cannot sue for breach of privacy in respect of matters not relevant to the discharge of their official duties.

Japan

There is constitutional protection under Japanese law for a generalized personality right, and privacy may be protected under this head.

Inaccuracy

Simple inaccuracy will not in general be subject to liability. If, however, the journalist knows that the allegation is false or may not be true, there may be a risk of criminal or civil liability.

United States

As mentioned above, some states prohibit 'false light' invasions of privacy, where:

1   these would be highly offensive to a reasonable person;
2   the publisher acted in reckless disregard of the falsity and of the false light in which the individual would be placed (although the precise standard of care required is unsettled).

The First Amendment requires the plaintiff to prove these facts, and so responsible journalism has not in practice been much impeded.

Australia, Canada, England and Wales, and India

The tort of malicious or injurious falsehood dispenses with the requirement of damage to reputation. The plaintiff must show:

1   falsity;
2   physical or financial damage;
3   malice, normally meaning knowledge of falsity or recklessness as to truth or falsity.

The similarity to the actual malice standard in the US *Sullivan* defence is apparent, the salient difference being the absence of damage to reputation. Legal aid is available in the United Kingdom for malicious falsehood claims, and in some cases this may be the only available means of redress for impecunious victims of press attacks.

The tort is peculiarly suited to protecting the commercial interests of trading corporations and their shareholders. Equally, it is frequently relied upon where a plaintiff claims that its product has been unfairly criticized in the press. However, the omnipresent difficulty of showing malice is a major clog on such claims.

France

Outside the realm of defamation, French law penalizes false information in three main ways.

Dissemination of inaccurate news

The key components are inaccuracy, a likely breach of the peace, and fault (which means something more than negligence). Private prosecutions cannot be brought, nor can civil actions, as this is essentially a public order offence.

False accusation

Those discovering breaches of the law are under a legal obligation to inform the relevant authorities. These accusations must, however, be accurate, as the law penalizes false accusations. Accusation means a verbal or written report of wrongdoing to the relevant investigatory authority. Press reporting can be a false accusation on the basis that the relevant authorities could thereby learn of the alleged wrongdoing.

Denigration

This is a branch of defamation covering attacks on products or services, which, of course, do not themselves have a reputation.

If the attack is, in reality, upon the product or service provider, the media may be liable for defamation, unless they can show truth or good faith. An important line of cases in the field of consumer rights and health has developed the concept of the 'good slanderer' in connection with the good faith defence.

Germany

There is no such right of action. All three branches of the criminal law require a tendency to damage reputation, and falsity by itself is not enough to ground liability.

Japan

There is no specific offence or tort providing redress for inaccurate statements which do not damage reputation, and general principles of tort apply.

Comparative tables

Pages 209–19 contain comparative tables for Chapter 9.

Note

1   These overviews are by definition simplistic statements of the legal position. They should be treated with caution, and as a means of increasing awareness of risk, rather than as a source of legal advice. For a more detailed overview, please refer to the relevant chapters on the individual countries' laws.

Table 9.1 *General*

Applicable law	Is there any constitutional protection for free speech?	Can defamation be a criminal offence?	Range of damages awards in practice	Is proof of financial loss necessary?
United States	Yes	Technically yes; practically unlikely	Very wide, from nominal to multimillion dollar	Generally need to demonstrate 'actual injury' – a low standard; occasionally need to show special damages, involving proof of financial loss
Australia	Yes, see Chapter 2	Yes, in most jurisdictions	To Aus.$350 000 (US$270 000)	Only in verbal defamation (slander)
Canada	Yes, but it does not affect defamation	Yes, rarely	To C$1.6m (US$1.16m) including punitive damages	Only in verbal defamation (slander)
England and Wales	No	Only exceptionally	To £1.5m (US$2.5m)	Only in verbal defamation (slander)
France	Yes	Yes, and a civil wrong	The record is FF800 000 (US$150 000)	Not in criminal jurisdiction
Germany	Yes	Yes, and a civil wrong	Low, rarely exceeding DM30 000 (US$19 000)	No, except in a claim for specific compensation
India	Yes	Yes, and a civil wrong	Low	Not for written defamation
Japan	Yes	Yes, and a civil wrong	Low	No

Table 9.2 *Non-defamatory statements, publication and rumours*

Applicable law	Are inaccurate non-defamatory statements safe?	What constitutes 'publication'?	Is it safe to repeat rumours?
United States	Not always – privacy claims can be brought in some states	Single publication to a third party	Generally no
Australia	No – injurious falsehood (same as malicious falsehood in English law)	Single publication	Generally no
Canada	No – malicious or injurious falsehood	Single publication	Generally no
England and Wales	No – malicious falsehood	Single publication	Generally no
France	No – (1) Publication of inaccurate news; (2) false accusation	Spoken, written or visual. Single publication may not be enough	Generally no, subject to the defence of good faith
Germany	No, although mere inaccuracy does not lead to liability	Communication to the plaintiff, to a third party or intentional dissemination	Generally no, subject to the defence of legitimate public interest
India	No – malicious falsehood and cp. privacy law	Single publication	Generally no
Japan	Yes, unless they injure credit, honour or feeling or cause wilful injury	Single publication sufficient in civil cases	Generally no

Table 9.3 *Truth, falsity and proof*

Applicable law	Proof of truth/falsity	Type of evidence admissible	Is proof of conviction conclusive?	Standard of proof
United States	Plaintiff must prove falsity	All	Yes	Public officials/figures – 'clear and convincing evidence'. Others – preponderance of evidence
Australia	Defendant must prove truth	All (primarily oral)	Yes, in some states including NSW, but not at common law	Balance of probabilities (but greater in serious cases)
Canada	Defendant must prove truth	All (primarily oral)	Generally yes	Balance of probabilities (but greater in serious cases)
England and Wales	Defendant must prove truth	All (primarily oral)	Generally yes	Balance of probabilities (but greater in serious cases)
France	Defendant must prove truth	Not cross-examination or subsequently discovered facts	Yes	Conclusive proof in criminal cases, balance of probabilities in civil
Germany	Plaintiff has proof of falsity in civil cases; because of neutral burden in criminal cases, defendant must prove truth	All	Yes	Conclusive proof in criminal cases, balance of probabilities in civil

Table 9.3 (continued) Truth, falsity and proof

Applicable law	Proof of truth/falsity	Type of evidence admissible	Is proof of convictions conclusive?	Standard of proof
India	Defendant	All (primarily oral)	Generally, yes	Balance of probabilities (but greater in serious cases)
Japan	Plaintiff/prosecutor initially	All	No. Public interest must also be proven	Conclusive proof in criminal cases, balance of probabilities in civil

Table 9.4 *Who can sue?*

Applicable law	The dead	Public figures	Trade unions	Children (normally via a representative)	Unincorporated associations
United States	No	Yes, subject to proof of constitutional malice	Yes	Yes	Yes
Australia	Yes (see text)	Yes, subject to emergent public interest privilege defence	No	Yes	No
Canada	No	Yes	Yes	Yes	Yes, in limited circumstances
England and Wales	No	Yes	No	Yes	No
France	Yes (see text)	Yes	No	Yes	No
Germany	Yes	Public figures must put up with harsher criticism	Yes	Yes	Yes
India	No	Yes, subject to emergent public official defence	Yes	Yes	No
Japan	The estate	Yes	Yes	Yes	Yes

Table 9.5 *Who can be sued?*

Applicable law	Journalist/Author	Editor	Distributor	Printer	Retailer
United States	Yes	Yes	Yes (but very limited liability)	Yes (but very limited liability)	Yes (but very limited liability)
Australia	Yes	Yes	Yes*	Yes	Yes*
Canada	Yes	Yes	Yes*	Yes	Yes*
England and Wales	Yes	Yes	Yes*	Yes	Yes*
France	Yes	Yes	Unusual	Unusual	Unusual
Germany	Yes	Yes	Unusual	Unusual	Unusual
India	Yes	Yes	Yes	Yes	Yes*
Japan	Yes	Yes	Unusual	Unusual	Unusual

*Subject to defence of innocent dissemination

Table 9.6 *Substantive defences*

Applicable law	Truth	Good faith	Neutral reportage	Public interest	Opinion	Reporting privilege
United States	Yes	As embodied in constitutional fault standards	Yes, in some states	Not *per se*	Yes	Yes
Australia	Yes, but not a complete defence[1]	No	No	Yes, provided justification, absence of malice (see text)	Yes	Yes
Canada	Yes	No	No	Yes (see text)	Yes	Yes (see text)
England and Wales	Yes	No	No	No	Yes	Yes
France	Yes	Yes	Yes (good faith)	Yes (good faith)	Yes	Yes
Germany	Yes	No	No	Yes	Opinions are not defamatory	Public interest
India	Yes	Yes, regarding public conduct of public officials	No	Yes, regarding public conduct of public officials	Yes	Yes
Japan	Yes	No	No	Yes	Yes	Public interest

[1]Note defence of contextual imputation in New South Wales

Table 9.7   Time bars

Applicable law	Limitation period	Timebar for reporting past facts (amnesty)
United States	Varies by state: 1–3 years	None
Australia	6 years from publication	None
Canada	From 3 months to 2 years	None
England and Wales	3 years	None
France	Trial must take place within 3 months	10 years
Germany	Civil – 3 years from knowledge of attack and an absolute bar after 30 years. Criminal – 3–5 years depending on the offence	None
India	Civil – 1 year. Criminal – 3 years	None
Japan	Civil – 3 years from first awareness; absolute bar after 20 years. Criminal – complaint within 6 months of event and bar on prosecution after 3 years	None

Table 9.8 *Reporting privilege (1) – Qualified unless otherwise stated*

Applicable law	International organizations	Parliaments		Courts	
		Domestic	Foreign	Domestic	Foreign
United States	Not generally	Absolute	Varies by state	Absolute	Varies by state
Australia	Yes, in NSW	Federal and state parliaments	No	Yes (qualified)	No
Canada	Commonwealth commissions of inquiry	Yes	Yes – Commonwealth only	Absolute, generally	No
England and Wales*	All those of which UK Government is a member	Yes	No, except Commonwealth	Yes (absolute and qualified)	No, except Commonwealth and cases of overwhelming interest in UK
France	Only legitimate public interest	Yes	Probably not	Yes	Probably not
Germany	Only legitimate public interest	Yes, absolute	Only legitimate public interest	Only legitimate public interest	Only legitimate public interest
India	Yes, by analogy	Yes	Yes, by analogy	Yes	Yes, by analogy
Japan	Only legitimate public interest	Only legitimate public interest	Probably not	Only legitimate public interest	Probably not

*Statutory privilege is to be extended under the government's defamation reforms

Table 9.9 *Reporting privilege (2) – Qualified unless otherwise stated*

Applicable law	Public meetings	Press conferences	Official notices	Police statements	Professional bodies
United States	Yes, in some states	Yes, in some states	Yes	Generally subject to constitutional fault standards	Not applicable
Australia	Yes, in some states (e.g. South Australia, Northern Territory)	No, but see Chapter 2 for reporting proceedings of royal commissions and other official bodies	No	No	No
Canada	Yes, in most provinces	No, unless public meeting	Yes	Yes – documents and notices only	Yes
England and Wales	Yes*	No	Yes*	Yes*	Yes*
France	Only legitimate public interest	Only legitimate public interest	Only legitimate public interest	Only legitimate public interest	Only legitimate public interest
Germany	Only legitimate public interest	Only legitimate public interest	Only legitimate public interest	Only legitimate public interest	Only legitimate public interest
India	Yes	Yes	Yes	Yes	Yes
Japan	Public interest	Public interest	Public interest	Public interest	Public interest

*Subject to a right of explanation or contradiction

Table 9.10 *Other restrictions*

Applicable law	Privacy	Contempt of court/restrictions on prejudicial reports	Protection for sources
United States	Yes	No	Yes, but generally not absolute
Australia	No	Yes	Yes, limited
Canada	Yes, in some provinces	Yes	Yes, limited
England and Wales	No	Yes (strict liability)	Yes, limited
France	Yes	No	Yes, limited
Germany	Yes	No, but some restrictions upon reports of ongoing court proceedings	Yes, but not pictures and photos
India	Yes	Yes	Yes, limited
Japan	Yes	No	Yes, limited

10

Risk management

Journalists are entitled to constructive legal advice that goes beyond dull 'spiking' of defamatory content, and that involves managing risk.

Risk management in libel involves two main elements. The first, covered in the preceding comparative chapter, involves evaluating where the story has its centre of gravity in legal terms – that is, the country where a potential plaintiff is most likely to sue – and the benchmark legal rules applicable to that publication. Second, safety in libel rests at least as much upon writing to avoid risk as upon technical defences, for mechanical application of benchmark rules can be a blunt instrument, stifling inquiry. Journalists and lawyers also need to know the defamation culture and risks in the countries where the story will be published.

The purpose of this chapter is to offer some practical guidance for reducing risk. Admittedly, logically consistent rules for international publication are still a long way off, given the radical incongruities in the structure and application of the different laws. Even publication within just one country involves weighing a complex matrix of libel risks. These include the range of possible meanings to be drawn from a story, whether it is technically defensible, the litigiousness – and means – of the subject, and the vagaries of litigation. Introduce an international element, and the picture muddies still further.

Nevertheless, certain basic principles do straddle the laws of different countries. In order that editorial decisions can be made upon a more rational and informed basis, it is worthwhile to attempt an outline here of those principles. Fortunately, many overlap with sound journalistic practice. For example, seeking comment from the subject of an attack is usually legally, journalistically and ethically desirable, unless there is a risk of prior restraint. Similarly, assembling legal evidence has much in common with the discipline of journalistic fact-checking. Even where no technical libel defence can ultimately be sustained, writers and journalists can often avoid the heavier sanctions by applying basic precautions.

This chapter deals initially with writing to reduce risk. It goes on to deal with recurrent tricky situations and fallacies. Finally, some fictitious examples are included to illustrate the interaction of legal analysis and risk management.

Risk reduction

Basic rules for risk reduction include:

- getting the meanings right;
- getting the evidence right;
- getting comment or denial;
- minimizing exposure to sanctions.

Each may be more or less important in a given story.

Meaning

Meaning operates at different levels simultaneously – the literal and implicit meanings of parts of an article and of the whole jostle for precedence. Different aspects will strike journalists, subeditors, producers, lawyers, readers, viewers, judge and any jury as significant or damaging. It is only when the meanings have been identified that you can begin to assess either what evidence you have to support it, or which defences, other than truth, are available. Lawyers can be particularly helpful here as it is their training to scrutinize words or meanings.

For libel purposes, it is important to focus first of all upon the message, not the way it is expressed. Although literal meaning cannot be ignored, it is the drift, the impression created by the story, that counts. A realistic test for defamatory content is the worst meaning that a reasonable person would put on the words complained of.

Think what you are really trying to suggest. If you are trying to get a defamatory meaning across without literally saying it, that purpose will usually be transparent. A court, or worse, a creative plaintiff lawyer, will pore over the words complained of time after time, trying to establish the meaning. Assume that the meaning is what the reader might (not would or should) take away from a third or fourth reading. If, on reviewing your story, you are still worried about a lurking imputation you are not trying to suggest, say so: it may be worth saying 'There is no question of X being involved in any illegal activity'or the like. Of course, the problem is that perhaps you *are* really trying to suggest guilt! So this is no guarantee of safety.

Sometimes all that can justifiably be said is that there are grounds for suspecting wrongdoing. It may then help to phrase the statement as a question, or to say that the allegations merit further investigation. By themselves, however, these devices will be futile if the suggestion is clearly one of guilt.

Headlines

Headlines often steer the meaning of a press story, but they may sometimes be defamatory even in isolation from the remainder. 'X In Insider Dealing Probe' will have a far more incriminating meaning than 'X Denies Link With Insider Scandal'. Such a headline probably means that more space will need to be devoted to counteracting the drift of the allegations. In the broadcast media especially, the general editorial tone and approach are often of great significance in relation to meaning. Thus, in an investigative television programme, the opening and closing remarks may have greater impact than the title of the programme.

Denials and comment

When dealing with breaking stories, the media are often in a quandary about whether and when to go with the story. Fear of libel suits may conflict with fear of losing competitive edge. Denials are the most important way by which news organizations can report defamatory rumours in a relatively risk-free way. For example, a denial in the headline sets the tone for the story and so affects the meaning. By itself, however, it will probably not be enough to establish a non-defamatory meaning for the story as a whole.

It is important to describe your efforts to obtain comment, correctly. For example, if you only called once and failed to get a comment, don't say the subject refused to comment. Depending on your publication and its risk policies, devote at least as much space to a denial as you do to the original allegation, probably more to be on the safe side. Just as importantly, ensure that the denial features prominently in the story and is not buried away in a part of the story a reader might flick past. In newspaper articles, the final paragraphs can have greater subliminal impact than the first few. In agency copy, prominence means inserting the comment at least in the third or fourth paragraph.

Evidence

The first rule – so obvious as hardly to need mention – is that the evidence must cover four-square the defamatory meanings which can be established, including hidden meanings and implications. If insufficient evidence is available, the meanings need to be cut back to harmonize with the evidence.

The best legal evidence is the same as the best journalistic evidence – a first-hand eye-witness account or reliable and admissible documentation. The rules of legal admissibility are esoteric, and it is wise to consult a lawyer if such issues arise, or if you need to rely on other kinds of evidence (e.g. hearsay or fraudulently obtained evidence, to name but two).

Confidential sources

Although naming a source offers no technical protection in most legal systems, the golden rule from a libel perspective is always to do so when you can. This enables your audience to evaluate the source for themselves, in exactly the way that stating the factual basis for an opinion helps the audience to assess its validity.

While there is usually qualified legal protection for the confidentiality of sources, these are of scant practical use in proving truth. Think twice before basing a defamatory story solely upon a confidential source. A good reason for naming sources, where you can, is that the source may then be joined into the litigation, potentially giving you access to the source's evidence and reducing your exposure in damages.

Bringing witnesses to the country where the case is being tried is an expensive business, assuming they are prepared to help. Just as important, try to decide whether the source will stick by you when the heat is on. If you must base a story on testimony where you are doubtful whether the witness will testify, obtain a sworn statement. This may at least be useful in showing that you took reasonable care, and may be used in reducing any fine or damages.

Dishonesty and fraud

Along with insolvency, allegations of financial impropriety, dishonesty and criminal behaviour need to be treated with the utmost care, as normally they will be treated as allegations of fact. It is sometimes helpful to imagine yourself in the role of prosecutor, and to evaluate whether the evidence you have is sufficient to 'convict' the suspect. Lacking such evidence, or identifiable reporting privilege, stick to the known facts. Don't spell out a conclusion, particularly when it relates to a person's state of mind, which is inherently difficult to prove.

So, for example, where you suspect that someone had a guilty motive for a particular act, it is risky without conclusive evidence to jump to that conclusion. It is better to comment that it is surprising that there has been no investigation into the suspect's role in the matter, or to say that the subject has been foolish to lay him or herself open to criticism on that ground. By so doing, you can suggest that there are grounds for suspicion, not actual guilt.

Convictions

Always check out local rules concerning criminal convictions as evidence or proof of wrongdoing. Reporting a conviction as evidence of an offence will usually be safe, but care is needed in drawing wider inferences about a convicted person's character. For example, one offence of shoplifting does not necessarily justify saying that a person is dishonest. Be astute to any irregularity in the conviction or other reason to doubt it.

Pick-ups and rumours

Where you want to 'pick up' a significant breaking story, the temptation is to assume that the original publisher has the evidence it needs to back up the claim. Even if it does (and it may not), it may not be prepared to share the evidence with you. On the other hand, the first publisher is more likely to take the brunt of the plaintiff's wrath, particularly if the style of the pick-up is neutral and unsensational. Making an independent effort to obtain comment can reduce the risk further. Watch out, however, for gold-digging plaintiffs or those trying to squash media speculation, for these may have no scruples about suing anyone who picked up the story.

If a rumour is defamatory, you should obviously check it independently before repeating it. Although republication of a rumour may be punished less severely, the risks may still be significant. Few jurisdictions have a genuine neutral reportage defence, and it is safer to wait until the substance of the story can be evaluated.

Sometimes financial journalists have to report markets moving on particular defamatory rumours. Make it clear, of course, that it is rumour, not fact. Don't say whom the rumour is about, or what it is, except in the vaguest terms, until you have verifiable evidence based on hard sourcing. Normally that would mean checking with the subject of the story. A denial by the subject may dictate further research and fact-checking.

Keeping notebooks

Notes and recordings are evidentially useful for proving admissions, or for proving that particular words were said. In the US, however, keeping records can be a two-edged sword, because the intrusive nature of discovery can throw the imperfections of the journalist's record into sharp relief. You should, theoretically, keep notebooks until the limitation period for claims in the relevant country has expired. In England and Wales, the limitation period is three years. France has a three-month time limit. Libel plaintiffs sometimes lose a degree of credibility if they wait too long to issue proceedings, and two years is probably a good safe period beyond which complaint is unlikely. There may, however, be many circumstances in which a plaintiff will be able to explain even great delay to the satisfaction of the tribunal.

Tapes should ideally be stored in the same way, but this is often impractical. Nevertheless, bear in mind the evidential potency of a tape recording, provided it has been legally obtained. Check local laws for restrictions on unauthorized tape recording.

Under US law since *Sullivan*, it is important for journalists to keep all documents if they wish to show that reasonable care was taken. Civil law systems such as France, Germany and Japan also place great emphasis upon a journalist's duty of care. Relevant documents should be kept when you wish to show that this duty has been discharged.

Seek comment

Seeking comment from the subject has several advantages:

- In countries where freedom from liability depends upon following proper journalistic practice, the court will generally expect the journalist to have obtained a comment, or at least to have made strenuous efforts in good faith to contact the subject.
- Seeking comment will, usually at least, mitigate the punishment or level of damages. It may also reduce the chances of being sued or prosecuted. Plaintiffs are bound to feel less affronted and less able at trial to portray themselves as injured parties.
- It may affect the overall meaning of the story if due weight is given to the comment.
- If the journalist has made a mistake, contacting the subject may hasten realization of the error.

It is important to describe attempts to contact someone accurately. If the subject cannot be contacted, say in the story that he or she was unavailable for comment. Agency journalists might want to do a follow-up story when they have successfully made contact, giving the subject's side of the story.

Journalists sometimes fight shy of seeking comment for fear of attracting an application to court to restrain publication. Most countries have rules against prior restraint, and this factor should not influence your decision.

A subject who refuses to comment or issue a denial may be sending deliberately ambiguous signals to the media. Even if silence suggests guilt, you still need reliable independent evidence. Equally, a canny plaintiff may realize that issuing a denial will help a damaging story to be published safely, and so resist the temptation to comment. It is generally best to infer nothing from silence.

Minimizing exposure

Safety in numbers?

It is often a mistake to try to hide the identity of the subject in a group. Sometimes every member of the group might be able to sue. For example, if you said that a prominent cabinet minister had Aids, a government cabinet is probably small enough for each member to claim to be identified.

Privilege as an anchor

One way of getting a contentious story out is to use some form of reporting privilege, such as a statement in the legislature, which will often be protected. In this way the kernel of the story can be placed in the public domain. Once the rest of the media have started to report the story, there is an element of 'safety in numbers'.

Fact and comment

Definitions of comment and opinion, and levels of protection, vary around the world. Although in many countries expressions of opinion are constitutionally protected, it is safer to follow the harsher rules in England and other Commonwealth countries. Legal advice can be helpful in the tricky exercise of identifying what is comment and what is not.

Portray comment as comment, for example, saying, 'In my view ...'. Set out clearly and distinctly the factual basis for an opinion, and be in a position to prove the facts true. If you are reporting a third party's comment the same applies, but make sure that the maker is able and prepared to give evidence of honest belief at trial.

Tunnel vision

Don't get so absorbed in an obvious libel risk that you forget the seemingly insignificant detail or a potential plaintiff. Television programmers regularly get sued for juxtaposing clips of perfectly innocent plaintiffs with stories about wrongdoing, from which the viewer may draw an unintended but defamatory conclusion.

Disasters

If two ships collide, say so, not that one ship hit the other. If a plane crashes, it may be premature to suggest straight afterwards that a particular piece of machinery failed, for aeroplane manufacturers, like pharmaceutical companies, are often litigious. Eye-witness accounts should be restricted to what visibly and provably occurred, and not speculate on possible causes.

Jumping to conclusions

Where you have facts you can back up or which make you think that a certain conclusion is reasonable, be wary of stating the conclusion overtly. It is usually safer to state the known facts and let your audience make up their own minds. If suggesting a conclusion is essential, try phrasing it as a question, or a quandary such as 'Readers must draw their own conclusions'. This can be risky, however, and it is important in such cases still to stand back from the story and re-evaluate the meaning.

Care with names

People with the same name as the real or fictional subject of a story can, and do, sue for libel. It is safer to say in non-fictional writing that a name has been disguised (e.g. 'not her real name'). In fictional work a disclaimer of the type seen in the titles to motion pictures is advisable.

Danger spots

Risky plaintiffs

Some plaintiffs elicit habitual caution because of their reputation for litigiousness. Corporations and public figures (even in the United States), be they politicians, showbiz personalities or prominent business or sportspeople, are more likely to sue. Lawyers and journalists will often know in their own familiar environment, even if only subliminally, whom it is risky to attack. One of the hazards of international publication, on the other hand, is the difficulty of obtaining this vital information from foreign countries. Deadlines rarely allow proper enquiries to this end.

Especially dangerous are plaintiffs sophisticated and wealthy enough to indulge in 'forum shopping' – choosing a forum in which to sue, based on anticipated prospects of success. It requires a modicum of opportunism for individual plaintiffs to sue in foreign countries when their own denies them a remedy. Conversely, a multinational corporation may do just that to protect its reputation and market share in a given country. Fear of being labelled cynical is not likely to be at the top of its list of concerns, for that is what most shareholders will expect.

Arrests and charges

Arrest and the commencement of proceedings are a flashpoint for libel litigation. Best practice varies from country to country. The most restrictive laws, if logically applied, would prevent any reporting of a person's arrest, as that would suggest probable guilt. This explains the trite incantation 'A man is helping the police with their inquiries', designed to avoid a libel suit from those subsequently released without arrest or charge. An arrested plaintiff's litigation arsenal, temporarily diverted by the arrest, may revive upon the charges being dropped.

Assume that there are grounds for suspicion only when a suspect has been formally charged. It is then usually safe to report charges, provided this is done fairly and accurately. If possible, mention whether the suspect denies the charges and write the story so that no-one could claim there is an imputation of guilt. It is safer to say that someone has been arrested 'in connection with the police investigation into the murder of ...' than 'on suspicion of the murder'. Don't call a person a suspect unless you have evidence that he or she is guilty or are sure that there are real grounds for suspicion.

Remember the risk of contempt of court in many Commonwealth countries: restrictions on reporting frequently operate when proceedings are pending, imminent or 'active'. In such cases, avoid all seriously prejudicial material such as information about previous convictions, eccentric lifestyles, identifying photographs (where identification might be in issue at trial) or prejudgements about the case. Otherwise, seek legal advice locally.

Reporting court proceedings

Again, this is highly country-specific, and there is no substitute for knowing local laws. Few national or state laws provide any real protection for reports of foreign courts, unless these are of compelling interest to the domestic audience. Certain commonsense principles nevertheless apply, which will reduce risk.

Proceedings in open court

Reports of proceedings in open court will normally be safe, except in some civil systems, such as (on occasion) Germany. Be alert to any reporting restrictions which the court may have imposed, or which apply automatically in certain classes of proceedings. Danger areas include:

- children (as defendants and witnesses);
- family proceedings;
- sexual assaults and rape.

In civil cases, it is often unsafe to report allegations contained in the pleadings. These are essentially private documents, and while the parties may be free of libel risk in mutual service of such documents, the press is usually not. Once read out in court, press reports of the contents of the documents will usually be privileged, subject to considerations of fairness, accuracy, identification and delay in reporting.

Fairness

A slanted headline can give an impression of unfairness, as can a misleading excerpt. For example, reporting in the headline a controversial prosecution allegation without adding, '…, says prosecutor …' could be unfair, as it does not make clear that it is an unproven allegation. Likewise, make this clear when reporting the prosecution's opening speech in the body of the story, as otherwise you may create a lingering impression of guilt.

Stay in court for as much of the proceedings as you can. It can be argued that a denial of the charges should be carried in each successive report of the prosecution, together with the magic words, 'The case continues' or something similar. Reporting privilege may, in theory, be lost if you only turn up for the lurid opening allegations. At the end of the case, report any statement that a party intends to appeal.

Accuracy

Don't be tempted to simplify the charges – always report the precise charges, especially where there are several defendants. Some simplification of court-room proceedings is inevitable, but try to do it in a balanced way, giving equal weight if possible to both sides of the argument.

Identity

In court reporting, it is standard newspaper practice to report an accused's age, full name (including any second names) and address. This would obviously be impractical in broadcast and agency reporting, but some identifying tag, such as occupation, can usually be included to narrow the risk of unintentionally identifying innocent parties. Beware, however, of local data protection and other personality right restrictions in Germany. These sometimes pro-hibit identification of the accused by the media, in spite of the risk of misidentification.

Time

A contemporaneous report is optimal, but latitude will be extended to the normal deadlines of the publication concerned. Books, which are almost by definition not contemporaneous, may not be able to take advantage of the various privileges extended to the press.

Civil proceedings

It is sometimes unsafe to report the commencement of civil proceedings, espe-cially where the allegations are explosive, unless, of course, there is a specific local privilege to do so. That a person has issued a writ for libel does not give a blank cheque to repeat its allegations. Much depends upon the overall meaning conveyed.

Corporate collapses

Like 'helping the police with their inquiries', the word 'troubled' applied to struggling companies seems to have found a veneer of journalistic respectability, but, like other euphemisms, it can suggest insolvency. The precise meaning of the words used to describe the stages and types of insol-vency vary subtly from country to country.

Breaking stories

There comes an indefinable moment in any breaking story carrying defamatory allegations where it is probably safe to publish. This applies particularly to official aspects of such stories, such as the announcement of a criminal investigation into a rock star's relationship with children.

Public denials can betoken an implicit acceptance that a story is effectively in the public domain. For example, before Woody Allen denied that he had been involved in child abuse, although official investigations were under way, it was hard to report the story safely. By the time Allen issued a denial, the international media could probably rely on safety in numbers.

Caught in the middle

Journalists sometimes get caught in defamatory crossfire between warring parties, for example in boardroom battles, or in cases such as the row between Opel and Volkswagen over alleged industrial espionage. In some countries there may be a right for victims of a defamatory attack to defend themselves. However, reporting the exchanges can be risky for the publisher and tricky to evaluate. Probably the safest course is to try to manage the risk by adopting a neutral editorial line – at risk of anodyne coverage – and rigorously giving equal emphasis and space to the competing claims. Make sure the story is deadpan and lends credence to neither side.

Public meetings and press conferences

Reports of public meetings are sometimes privileged, depending upon local law. Press conferences may not amount to public meetings in the technical sense, and should be treated with great caution. After all, anyone can call a press conference at any time, and plaintiffs may be keener to sue the 'deep pocket' of the media than the original speaker, especially those intent upon throttling all media comment.

Police and other official notices

Usually there is little real risk in reporting official announcements of criminal investigations, as long as nothing is done to suggest guilt prematurely. Of course, many countries protect reports of such announcements, but most public companies and many individuals would not in any event sue in these cases, particularly if they had been given a chance to comment.

Police announcements should attract a higher level of caution. Rely only on announcements by higher-ranking officers, and source the report to the named officer where possible.

Identification

It is often difficult to escape liability by not naming a subject. You may end up libelling the whole group unless it is large (perhaps fifty or more). Similarly, identifying circumstances known only to a restricted group of people may result in an unintended reference. At the same time, disguising identity effectively can be a complete protection against liability.

When naming a company, always give its full name at least once at the beginning of the story. Make sure that, where appropriate, other group companies with similar names are not confused. For example, in the early stages of BCCI's collapse it might have been dangerous to refer to the wrong subsidiary or holding company.

Pictures and film

Juxtaposition of pictures and text may make material defamatory when otherwise it would not have been, or identify individuals as libel subjects quite unwittingly. The danger is acute with the illustrative use of library material or 'wallpaper shots' in television programmes. Here tight production schedules can lead producers to overlook clear but unintended defamatory imputations.

Live programmes

Broadcasters face particular difficulties in screening out deranged or malevolent callers to phone-in programmes, or unpredictable allegations by panellists and interviewees. Although, strictly speaking, the broadcaster may be liable, call-in hosts and interviewers require skill in defusing such defamatory statements succinctly. If done effectively, this may distance the broadcaster from the allegation as far as possible and reduce any potential liability to a manageable level.

Fallacies

'It's been published before'

In most countries, the libel clock starts ticking anew with each fresh publication. The fact that a plaintiff has chosen not to sue on previous occasions does not guarantee that publication will be risk-free this time. It is, however, a fact to be borne in mind in assessing risk.

'Everyone knows it's true'

Knowing is not the same as proving. Journalists should assume that they will have to stand a story up by admissible evidence. What is admissible usually depends upon the country where the action is brought. As a rule of thumb, first-hand testimony of the facts alleged and/or convincing and verifiable documentary evidence will normally be admissible. In the United States, the burden may be much lower, especially in relation to lawsuits brought by public figures and public officials. Under French law, if the matter in question relates to a person's 'private life', proof of truth is inadmissible. Stick rigidly to facts you know you can prove.

'But I said "allegedly" '

Use of 'allegedly' is no defence, but it can be a useful adjunct in trying to show that the article does not support the accusations the plaintiff claims. It is particularly helpful in court reporting.

'Everyone knows he's a crook'

General bad character on the part of the plaintiff will rarely be relevant. But if it relates directly to the allegations made, it may put the journalist in a better light so far as damages or punishment are concerned.

'But I didn't name her'

Plaintiffs have only to show that people understood the article as referring to them, not that they were named. A journalist deciding not to name a subject should always be asking, 'Could anyone, even only someone with inside knowledge, know or guess who I am referring to?' Disguising identity can, carefully handled, be a useful means of avoiding liability, but can be dangerous because of the risk of identifying wider groups instead.

Worked examples

In the following examples, no reference is intended to any living or dead person.

Example 1

You are the producer on a New York-based network's flagship news programme, distributed primarily in the United States, but also in Canada, the United Kingdom and continental Europe. The network has a subsidiary in the United Kingdom and bureaux in Paris and Bonn. On a quiet night for news, a leading wire service carries a flash – while you are on air – that the Canadian women's 100 metres gold medal winner in the last Olympics has been tested positive for steroids. The story is sourced to unnamed but authoritative sources. You do not have time to contact the subject for comment. What do you do?

The story is, of course, defamatory by any standards, as it damages the athlete in her profession. The most natural forum for her to sue in would be New York, because the network is based there and because of the high awards and availability of contingency fee litigation. Under the US rules, however, the athlete would almost certainly be an 'all-purpose public figure', and so would need to prove 'actual malice' by the publisher to succeed in a libel action. This would be extremely difficult for the plaintiff. Even without this, many US courts would probably hold that republication from a reliable wire service is defensible, in the absence of any reason to doubt its accuracy.

The athlete is wealthy, and known to be litigious, so can you assume that she will not sue outside the United States? In theory she can bring proceedings in any country where publication took place, and the obvious places are Canada and the United Kingdom. Both countries have strict libel laws, but the United Kingdom seems a more likely venue because the broadcaster has substantial assets there and awards seem to be higher. If it is safe to publish in the United Kingdom, it is probably safe to publish anywhere.

If the story is untrue, under English law even a public figure plaintiff – as here – is almost certain to succeed in her libel action. In this case you have no way of knowing what kind of evidence you will be able to muster to establish a plea of justification. In particular, the source is confidential so there is no practical prospect of persuading him or her to give evidence. Therefore, a determined plaintiff might well be able to extract damages for this type of story.

Just when you were about to shelve the story, you hear that a rival USA network is carrying it as its lead. You feel under commercial pressure to publish, despite warnings from your lawyers. The safer course, if you intend to publish, would be to lead on a denial by the subject but, as a denial is currently unavailable, you should immediately make – and continue to make – strenuous efforts to contact her. Say that the subject is not immediately available for comment, and make it clear that the allegation is only an allegation. You may not receive a writ, but, if you do, you may be able to force a settlement relatively easily and cheaply in the English courts.

Example 2

A leading German national newspaper's Tokyo correspondent wishes to report on independent drug tests from Japan. Initial laboratory tests suggest that a new anti-arthritis drug from a multinational Italian-based pharmaceutical giant may be carcinogenic, and the correspondent wishes to suggest that the company knew this and tried to cover it up. The drug was approved by the US Food and Drugs Administration three months ago, but has not yet been approved in any other country. There are indications that questions will be raised in the German parliament tomorrow. The newspaper sells 300 000 copies in Germany, 4000 in England, 1000 in France and 6000 in Canada, but it has no offices or assets except in Germany.

The most obvious place for the drug company to sue is Germany, because of the extent of publication and the fact that the newspaper is based there. It is possible under German law that the newspaper could show that publication of the results of the laboratory tests is in the public interest, but the same may not apply to the allegation of a 'cover-up'. This is a serious allegation, and a great deal more cogent evidence will be needed if legitimate public interest or truth are to be established. Similar public interest defences may apply in France and Japan, and if the Italian company wants damages it may wish to sue in England or Canada.

Canada has a relatively broad qualified privilege defence in cases where protection of public health requires publication in the media, and so will be less attractive a forum than England. On the other hand, relatively few copies of the newspaper are sold in England, nor is the company established there, and substantial damages may not be recoverable, so that England may not be a sensible forum for the plaintiff. More importantly, if that is the company's aim, it will be very difficult to achieve prior restraint of publication. It may therefore be worth assuming that the company would sue in Germany and nowhere else.

It will almost certainly not help to try to disguise the identity of the company. To avoid unjustifiable risk, no reference should be made to the alleged cover-up, while the disturbing laboratory results can perhaps be reported if a comment is obtained from the company and the article does nothing at this stage to suggest that the story has real substance.

Example 3

An international wire service is based in London, but has assets in many juris-dictions around the world, including Australia, and numbers most media organizations among its subscribers. Allegations surface in Switzerland from a former Israeli spy that a retired Australian diplomat has links with the arms industry and has received 'kickbacks' for sanctioning arms deals. He issues a statement through his lawyers threatening to sue anyone who repeats the alle-gations.

If the story is published, the plaintiff may have difficulty suing in Australia because of the emergent 'public official' defence introduced by the *Theophanous* case. The agency will have to show that it was unaware of any falsity, that the material was not published recklessly, and that publication was reasonable in the circumstances. In practice, it may be tricky for the agency to discharge this burden because of the dubious sourcing of the story. An addi-tional uncertainty is whether the diplomat is still a public official – he has no official duties but is chairman of a large charity.

It would be easier for the diplomat to sue in England than Australia because of the lack of any public interest or public official defence. How then could the story be made safe for international publication? There is no easy answer. Certainly there would have been no obvious defence under English law, even if the diplomat had been British. The risk can, however, probably be brought within acceptable limits.

First, it is arguable that the diplomat has consented to publication of at least an outline of the allegations by issuing what amounts to a press release, although he plainly does not consent to stories lending credence to the allegations. Second, if the story is structured around his denial, including the denial in the headline and within the first three paragraphs of the story, and provided there is nothing in the story which tries to suggest that the allegations are true, the story may be held not to have a defamatory meaning. Even if it does, the level of damages available may not be high and the case may be disposed of by a carefully judged payment into court to force settlement.

Example 4

A Paris-based European-wide cable TV operator hears that the British Prime Minister has sired several illegitimate children, some of whom are allegedly being maintained at the taxpayer's expense. The editor publishes the story on a hunch that it is true, and the station is sued for civil damages by the Prime Minister. Four weeks later he obtains hard evidence that the allegations are true.

The Prime Minister may be able to sue to restrain publication of the story in France. The reason is not so much because it is a breach of his privacy – there is at least a genuine public interest element – but because the defence of truth may be unavailable since he may not be able to muster the evidence within the requisite ten-day period.

However, the story is syndicated to the United States, Australia, Canada and the United Kingdom In none of these countries can the story be suppressed because, unlike the position in France, the evidence will be admissible.

Checklist

In writing the article:

1   Check the headline and both the literal and implicit meanings;
2   Make sure any party attacked gets the chance to comment on or deny the allegations;
3   Place any comment or denial in a prominent position in the story;
4   Ensure that no extraneous material, such as photographs or background film clips, skews the meaning;
5   Check for subsidiary libels which you may not have noticed;
6   Stand back from the story to evaluate the overall impression;
7   Check for other torts (breach of copyright, confidence or privacy) or contempt of court (in some Commonwealth countries);
8   Consider whether to call in a lawyer, especially in cases of doubt over meaning or admissibility of evidence. Always use a lawyer to evaluate whether truth can be established and the evidence needed to do so.

Together with the lawyer:

1   Try to decide whether the subject is likely to be litigious, or has the means to sue;
2   Try to identify the country where you are most likely to be sued or prosecuted for libel. Bear in mind:

- where the subject has a substantial reputation
- where the media organization is based
- where the material will be published
- where the subject has the most to gain by suing
- whether it would occur to the plaintiff to sue in a foreign country

and take into account the laws of the country or countries where you think you might be sued;

3   Identify and evaluate the available defences;
4   If the defences cannot be 'stood up', rewrite to reduce risk or take out the defamatory content.

Select bibliography

United States

Lewis, (1991). *Make No Law*. Random House.
Libel Defense Resource Center. *50-State Libel Survey* (published annually).
Sack, and Baron (1994). *Libel, Slander and Related Problems* (2nd edn.) Practising Law Institute.
Sanford, B. (1994). *Libel and Privacy* (2nd edn.). Prentice-Hall.
Smolla, R. (1992). *Free Speech In An Open Society*. Knopf.

Australia

Arnold-Moore, T. (1984). 'Legal pitfalls in cyberspace: defamation on computer networks', *Journal of Law and Information Science*, **5** (2) 165.
Armstrong, Blakeney, and Watterson, (1990). *Media Law in Australia – a Manual*. OUP.
Burke, Cooper, Donald, and Smith, (1989). *Defamation and Media Law*. BLEC.
Fleming, J. G. (1992). *The Law of Torts* (8th edn.). Law Book Company.
Hunt, D., Nicholas, H., Sackar, J. H. et al. (1990). *Aspects of the Law of Defamation in New South Wales*.
Tobin, T. K. and Sexton, M. G. (1991). *Australian Defamation Law and Practice*. Butterworths.

Canada

Baudouin J-L. (1994). *La Responsabilité Civile* (4th edn.) paragraph 415. Les Editions Yvon Blais.
Brown, R. E. (1987). *The Law of Defamation in Canada* (2nd edn.). Carswell.
Porter, J. and Potts, D. A. (1986). *Canadian Libel Practice*. Butterworths.
Williams, J. S. (1988). *The Law of Libel and Slander in Canada* (2nd edn.). Butterworths.

England and Wales

Carter-Ruck, P. F. and Walker, R. (1992). *Carter-Ruck on Libel and Slander* (3rd edn.). Butterworths.

Crone, T. (1991). *Law and the Media* (2nd edn.). Butterworth-Heinemann.

Duncan, C. and Neill, B. (1983). *Defamation* (2nd edn.). Butterworths.

Greenwood, W. and Welsh, T (1995). *McNae's Essential Law for Journalists* (12th edn.).

Lewis, P. (ed.) (1981). *Gatley on Libel and Slander* (8th edn.). Sweet & Maxwell.

Robertson, G. and Nichol, A. (1992). *Media Law* (3rd edn.). Penguin.

France

Blin, H., Boinet, J., Chavanne, A. and Drago, R. (1993). *Droit de la Presse*. Litec.

Germany

Fuhr, E. W., Rudolph, W. and Wasserburg, K. (ed.) (1989). *Recht der neuen Medien*. C. F. Müller.

Löffler, M. and Ricker, R. (1994). *Handbuch des Presserechts* (3rd edn.). C. H. Beck.

Palandt, O. (1995). *Bürgerliches Gesetzbuch* (54th edn.). C. H. Neck.

Schönke, A. and Schröder, H. (1991). *Strafgesetzbuch – Kommentar* (24th edn.). C. H. Beck.

Wenzel, E. (1994). *Das Recht der Wort- und Bildberichterstattung* (4th edn.). Otto Schmidt.

India

Dr Durga Das Basu, *The Law of Torts* (10th edn.), Chapter IX.

Ramaswamy, Iyer, *The Law of Torts* (8th edn.), Chapter VII.

Ratanlal, and Dhirajlal, *Law of Crimes* (23rd edn.), Vol II, Chapter XXI.

Ratanlal, and Dhirajlal, *Law of Torts* (22nd edn.), Chapter XII.

Japan

Bender, M., *Doing business in Japan*.

Martindale-Hubbell Law Dictionary.

Yuhikaku Soshyo (newspaper reports and reputation/privacy). Yuhikaku.

Index

Throughout the index the following abbreviations have been used:
Aus (Australia); Can (Canada); Eng (England and Wales); Fr (France); Ger (Germany), Ind (India); Jap (Japan); USA (United States of America)

Absolute privilege, *see* Privilege
Abuse:
    all country comparison, 199–200
    England and Wales (Eng), 91
    France, 121
Accuracy, in court reporting, 230
'Actual injury' proof (USA), 21
'Actual malice':
    applicable to public figures/officials (USA), 10, 11–13
    and circumstantial evidence (USA), 13
    and damages (USA), 21
    from distortion of facts (USA), 14
    and *New York Times* v *Sullivan*, 2, 4
    for private figure plaintiffs (USA), 14–16
    and reliance on unreliable sources (USA), 13–14
Allegation (Fr), 120
'Allegedly', use of, 233
Allusion (Fr), 120
Apologies:
    Australia, 52
    Canada, 76
    Japan, 175
Arrests, reporting, 228–9
Associations, as suing entities (Fr), 125
Australia:
    abuse or insult, 199
    Broadcasting Services Act, 35
    Capital Territory, 34, 43, 48, 50, 54
    Code States, 33–4
    common law defences, 41–51
    common law jurisdiction, 32–3
    constitutional protection, 40
    contempt of court, 56
    costs, 56, 203
    criminal defamation, 53–4
    damages, 51–2, 209
    defamation, 31–2, 33, 184
    defences, 200
    defendant's task, 40–51
    falsity, 190, 211
    fault, proof of, 192
    financial loss by plaintiff, 210
    free speech protection, 209
    humour, parody and satire, 186
    identification, 186, 187
    inaccuracy, 206–7
    injunctive relief, 52–3
    injurious falsehood, 53
    journalistic privilege, 55
    New South Wales, 31, 32, 33, 35, 42–3, 48, 50, 51, 52, 54, 56
    Northern Territory, 34, 49, 54
    opinion statements, 196
    Parliamentary Privileges Act (1987), 48
    plaintiff's task, 35–40
    privacy, 57, 205
    Privacy Act (1988), 57
    privilege/immunity reporting, 45–51, 197
    proof of falsity/defence of truth, 195
    public figures, 200
    public interest as a defence, 44, 194, 215
    publication/republication, 188, 210
    Queensland, 32, 33, 43, 48, 49, 54
    remedies, 51–3
    sources, protection of, 201
    South Australia, 32, 43, 49, 54
    sue, who can?, 35, 213
    sued, who can be?, 35, 214
    Tasmania, 32, 33, 42, 48, 49, 54
    time limitation, 216
    truth, as a defence, 33, 42–3, 53–4, 190, 211, 215
    Victoria, 32, 48, 49, 54
    Western Australia, 32, 48, 49, 54

'Backpacker murders' (Aus), 56
Bad character, relevance of, 233
Bad faith (Fr), 123–4, 140
Bankrupts, suing (Eng), 88